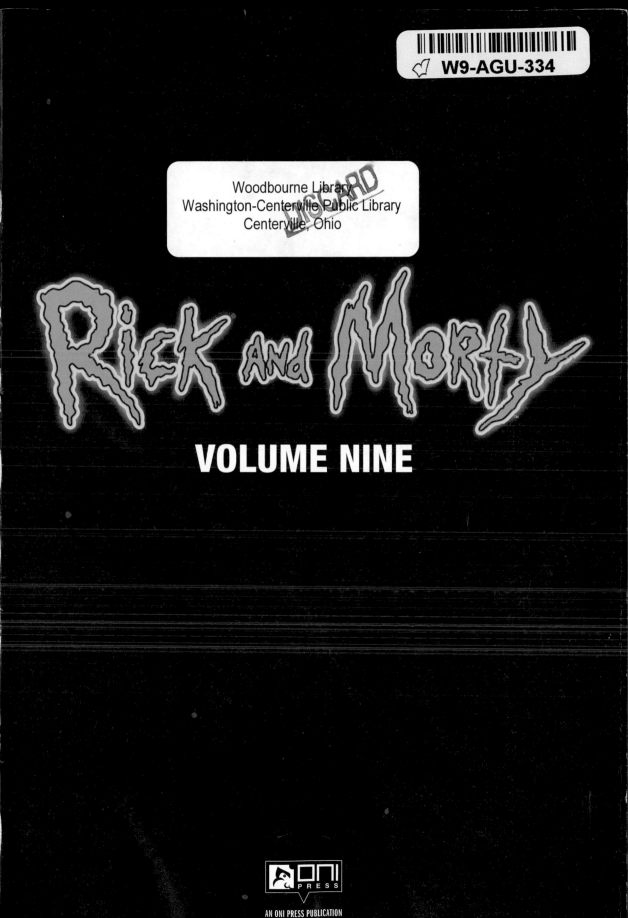

RICK AND MORTY

VOLUME NINE

ONI
PRESS

AN ONI PRESS PUBLICATION

VOLUME NINE

RICK AND MORTY™ CREATED BY **DAN HARMON** AND **JUSTIN ROILAND**

RETAIL COVER BY
MARC ELLERBY AND **SARAH STERN**

ONI EXCLUSIVE COVER BY
JULIETA COLÁS

EDITED BY
ARI YARWOOD WITH **SARAH GAYDOS**

DESIGNED BY
ANGIE KNOWLES

ONI
PRESS

[adult swim]™

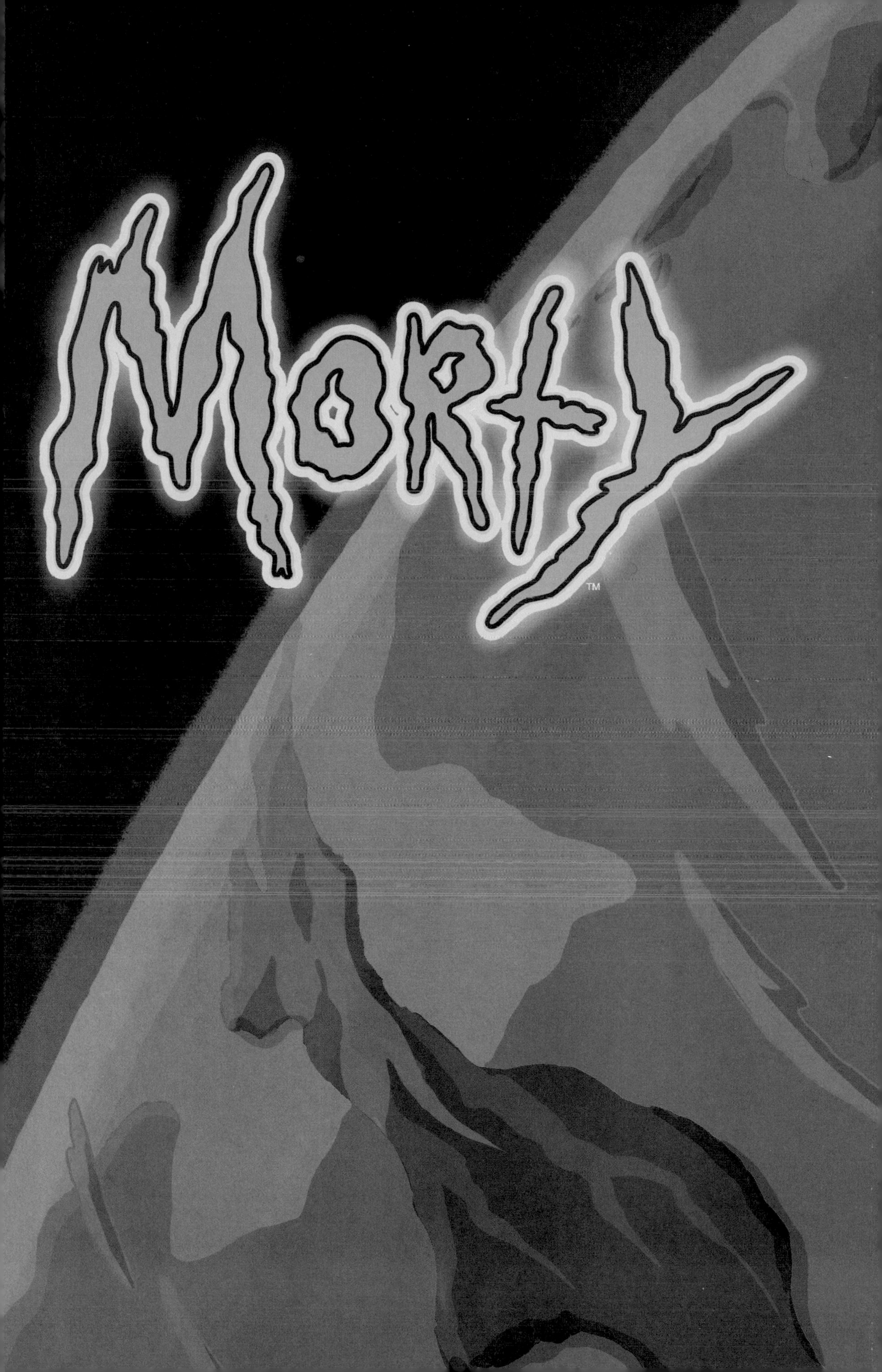
Morty™

PUBLISHED BY ONI PRESS, INC.

JOE NOZEMACK FOUNDER & CHIEF FINANCIAL OFFICER

JAMES LUCAS JONES PUBLISHER

SARAH GAYDOS EDITOR IN CHIEF

CHARLIE CHU V.P. OF CREATIVE & BUSINESS DEVELOPMENT

BRAD ROOKS DIRECTOR OF OPERATIONS

MELISSA MESZAROS DIRECTOR OF PUBLICITY

MARGOT WOOD DIRECTOR OF SALES

SANDY TANAKA MARKETING DESIGN MANAGER

AMBER O'NEILL SPECIAL PROJECTS MANAGER

TROY LOOK DIRECTOR OF DESIGN & PRODUCTION

KATE Z. STONE SENIOR GRAPHIC DESIGNER

SONJA SYNAK GRAPHIC DESIGNER

ANGIE KNOWLES DIGITAL PREPRESS LEAD

ARI YARWOOD SENIOR EDITOR

ROBIN HERRERA SENIOR EDITOR

DESIREE WILSON ASSOCIATE EDITOR

KATE LIGHT EDITORIAL ASSISTANT

MICHELLE NGUYEN EXECUTIVE ASSISTANT

JUNG LEE LOGISTICS COORDINATOR

[adult swim]

ONIPRESS.COM
FACEBOOK.COM/ONIPRESS
TWITTER.COM/ONIPRESS
INSTAGRAM.COM/ONIPRESS
ADULTSWIM.COM
TWITTER.COM/RICKANDMORTY
FACEBOOK.COM/RICKANDMORTY

THIS VOLUME COLLECTS ISSUES #41-45
OF THE ONI PRESS SERIES RICK AND MORTY™.

FIRST EDITION: JUNE 2019

ISBN 978-1-62010-641-9
EISBN 978-1-62010-643-3
ONI EXCLUSIVE ISBN 978-1-62010-642-6

PRINTED IN USA.

LIBRARY OF CONGRESS CONTROL NUMBER: 2018963598

1 2 3 4 5 6 7 8 9 10

SPECIAL THANKS TO JUSTIN ROILAND, DAN HARMON, MARISA MARIONAKIS, ELYSE SALAZAR, MIKE MENDEL, JANET NO, AND MEAGAN BIRNEY.

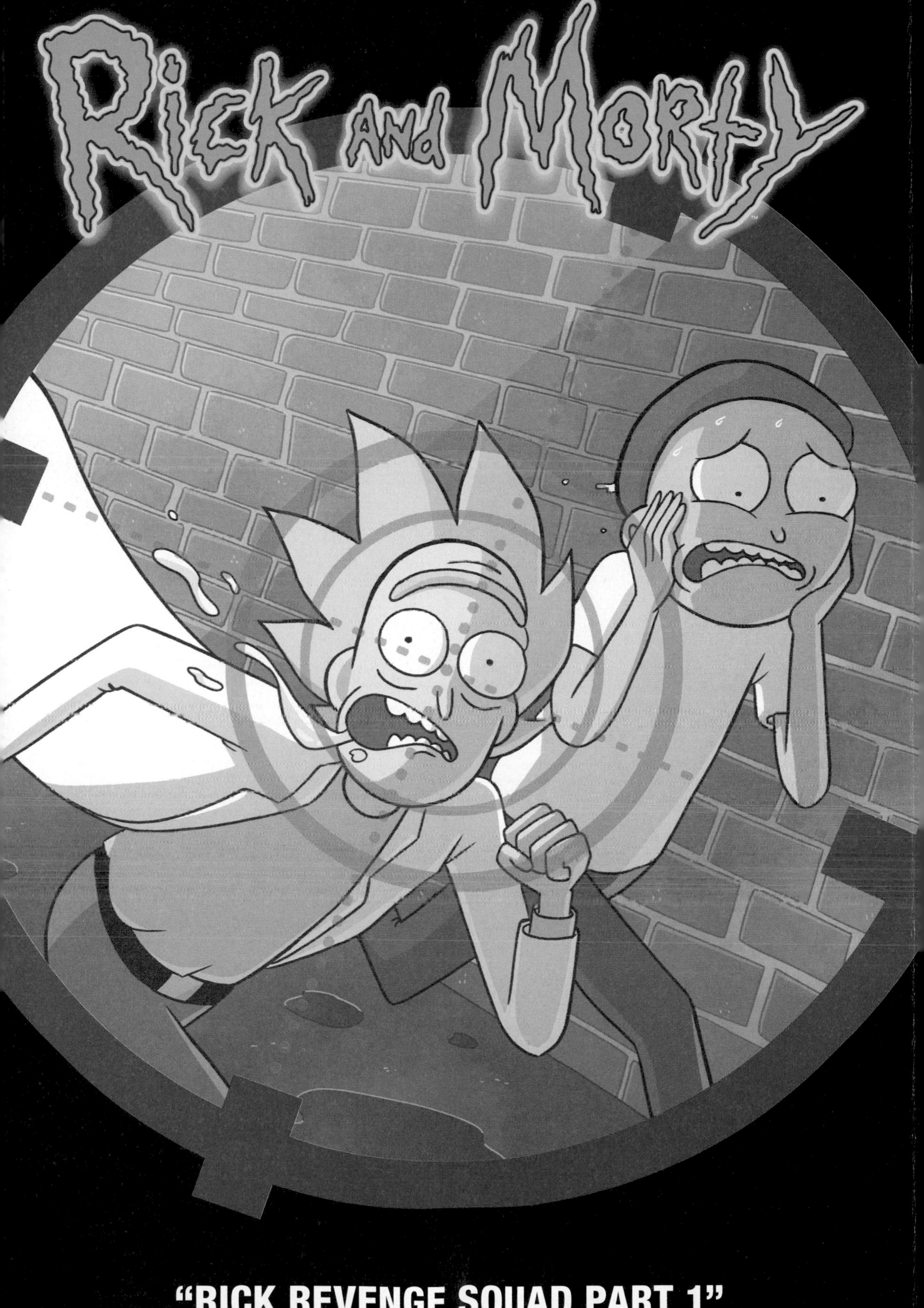
Rick and Morty

"RICK REVENGE SQUAD PART 1"

WRITTEN BY **KYLE STARKS** ILLUSTRATED BY **MARC ELLERBY** COLORED BY **SARAH STERN** LETTERED BY **CRANK!**

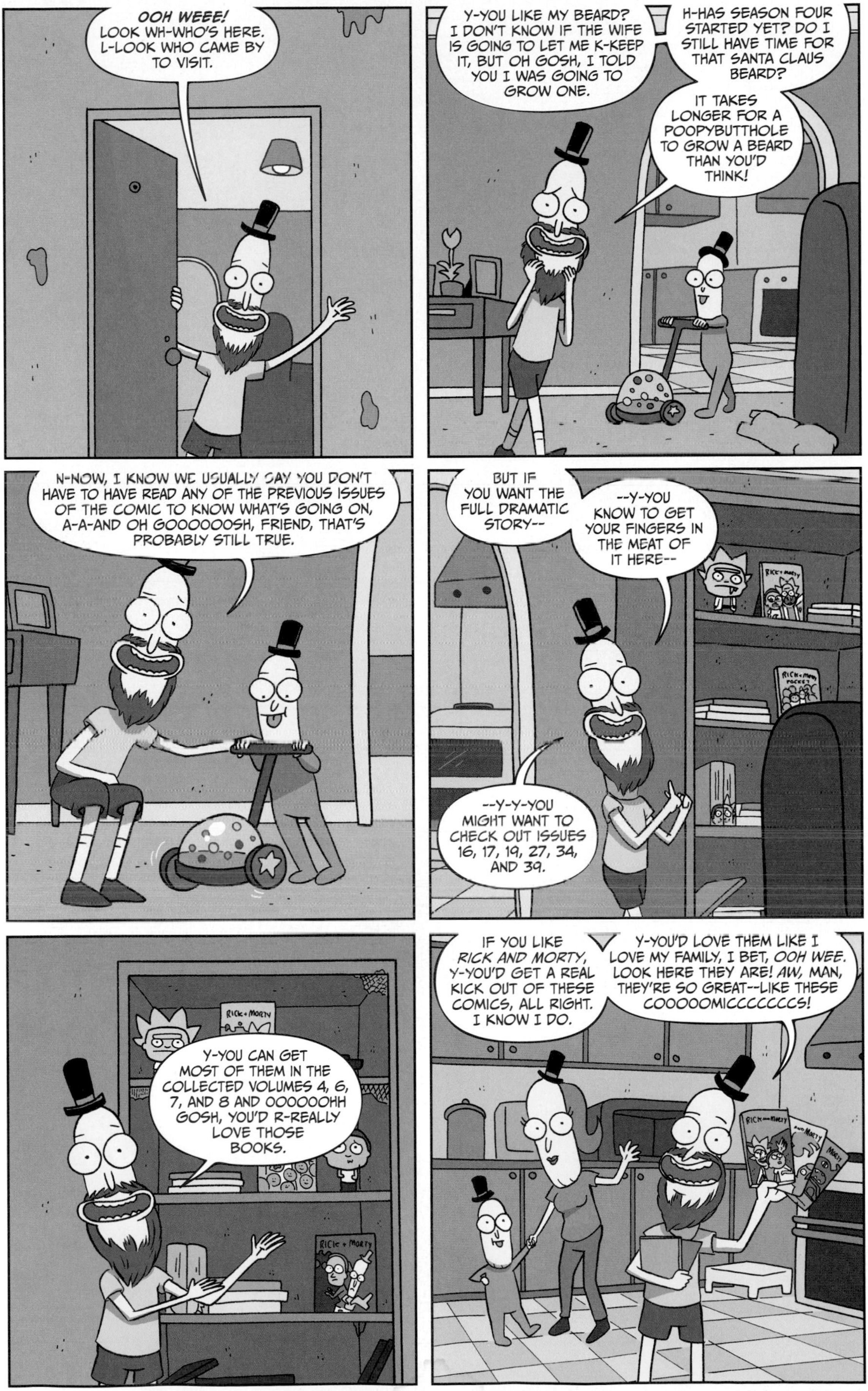
OOH WEEE! LOOK WH-WHO'S HERE. L-LOOK WHO CAME BY TO VISIT.
Y-YOU LIKE MY BEARD? I DON'T KNOW IF THE WIFE IS GOING TO LET ME K-KEEP IT, BUT OH GOSH, I TOLD YOU I WAS GOING TO GROW ONE.
H-HAS SEASON FOUR STARTED YET? DO I STILL HAVE TIME FOR THAT SANTA CLAUS BEARD?
IT TAKES LONGER FOR A POOPYBUTTHOLE TO GROW A BEARD THAN YOU'D THINK!
N-NOW, I KNOW WE USUALLY SAY YOU DON'T HAVE TO HAVE READ ANY OF THE PREVIOUS ISSUES OF THE COMIC TO KNOW WHAT'S GOING ON, A-A-AND OH GOOOOOOSH, FRIEND, THAT'S PROBABLY STILL TRUE.
BUT IF YOU WANT THE FULL DRAMATIC STORY--
--Y-YOU KNOW TO GET YOUR FINGERS IN THE MEAT OF IT HERE--
--Y-Y-YOU MIGHT WANT TO CHECK OUT ISSUES 16, 17, 19, 27, 34, AND 39.
Y-YOU CAN GET MOST OF THEM IN THE COLLECTED VOLUMES 4, 6, 7, AND 8 AND OOOOOOHH GOSH, YOU'D R-REALLY LOVE THOSE BOOKS.
IF YOU LIKE *RICK AND MORTY*, Y-YOU'D GET A REAL KICK OUT OF THESE COMICS, ALL RIGHT. I KNOW I DO.
Y-YOU'D LOVE THEM LIKE I LOVE MY FAMILY, I BET, *OOH WEE.* LOOK HERE THEY ARE! *AW,* MAN, THEY'RE SO GREAT--LIKE THESE COOOOOMICCCCCCCS!

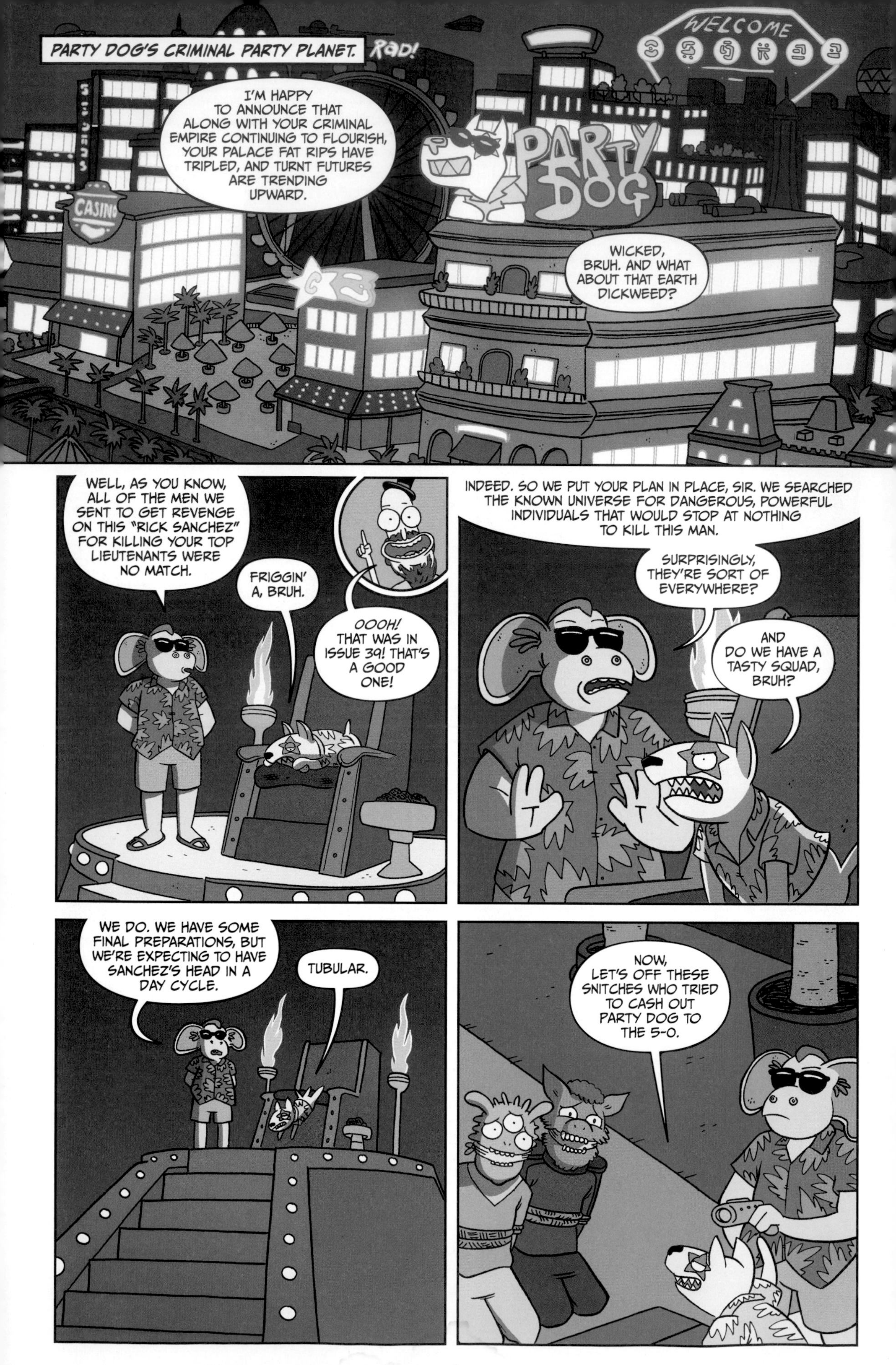
PARTY DOG'S CRIMINAL PARTY PLANET.
RAD!
WELCOME
CASINO
PARTY DOG
I'M HAPPY TO ANNOUNCE THAT ALONG WITH YOUR CRIMINAL EMPIRE CONTINUING TO FLOURISH, YOUR PALACE FAT RIPS HAVE TRIPLED, AND TURNT FUTURES ARE TRENDING UPWARD.
WICKED, BRUH. AND WHAT ABOUT THAT EARTH DICKWEED?
WELL, AS YOU KNOW, ALL OF THE MEN WE SENT TO GET REVENGE ON THIS "RICK SANCHEZ" FOR KILLING YOUR TOP LIEUTENANTS WERE NO MATCH.
FRIGGIN' A, BRUH.
OOOH! THAT WAS IN ISSUE 39! THAT'S A GOOD ONE!
INDEED. SO WE PUT YOUR PLAN IN PLACE, SIR. WE SEARCHED THE KNOWN UNIVERSE FOR DANGEROUS, POWERFUL INDIVIDUALS THAT WOULD STOP AT NOTHING TO KILL THIS MAN.
SURPRISINGLY, THEY'RE SORT OF EVERYWHERE?
AND DO WE HAVE A TASTY SQUAD, BRUH?
WE DO. WE HAVE SOME FINAL PREPARATIONS, BUT WE'RE EXPECTING TO HAVE SANCHEZ'S HEAD IN A DAY CYCLE.
TUBULAR.
NOW, LET'S OFF THESE SNITCHES WHO TRIED TO CASH OUT PARTY DOG TO THE 5-O.

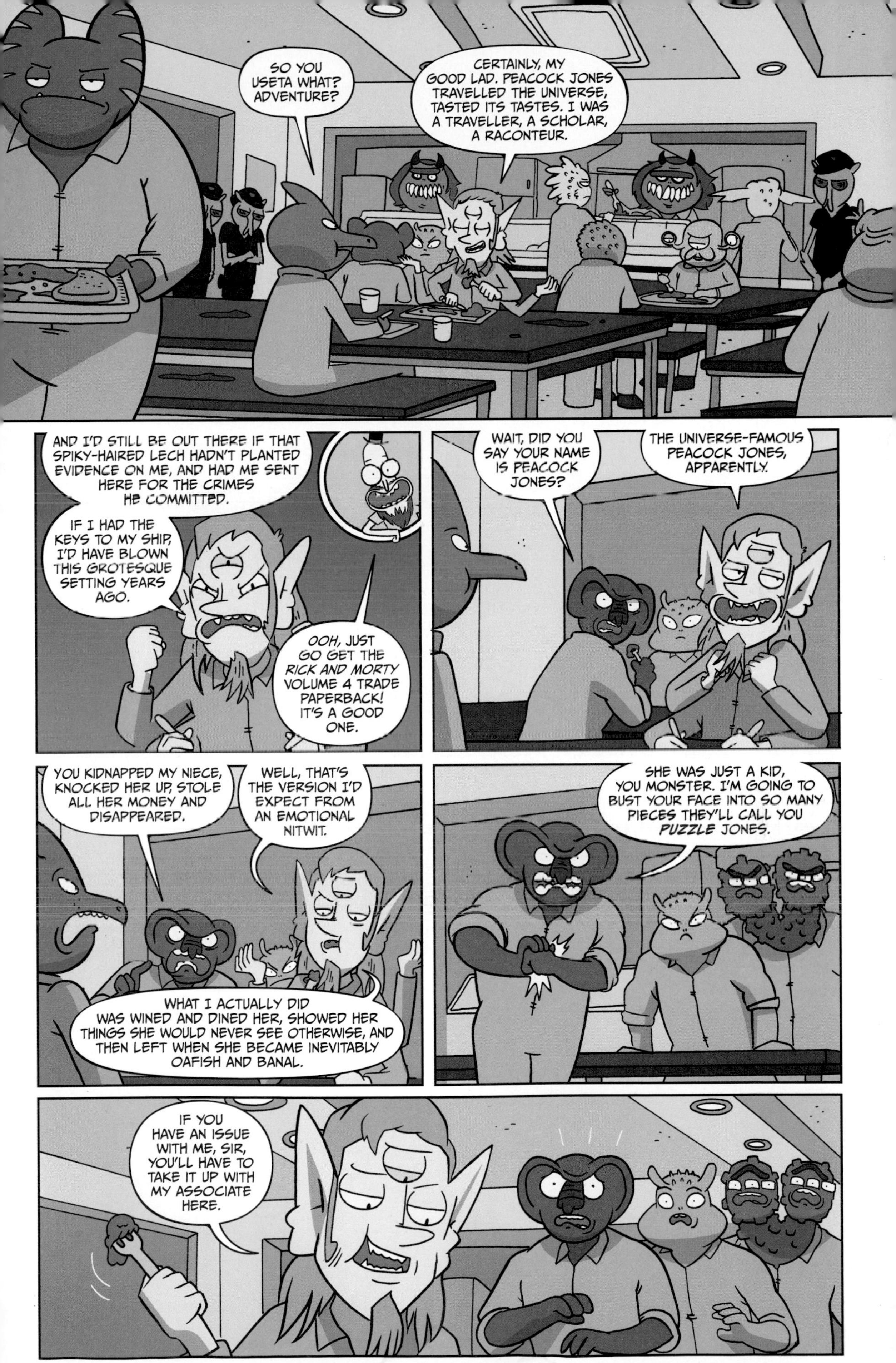

SO YOU USETA WHAT? ADVENTURE?
CERTAINLY, MY GOOD LAD. PEACOCK JONES TRAVELLED THE UNIVERSE, TASTED ITS TASTES. I WAS A TRAVELLER, A SCHOLAR, A RACONTEUR.
AND I'D STILL BE OUT THERE IF THAT SPIKY-HAIRED LECH HADN'T PLANTED EVIDENCE ON ME, AND HAD ME SENT HERE FOR THE CRIMES HE COMMITTED.
IF I HAD THE KEYS TO MY SHIP, I'D HAVE BLOWN THIS GROTESQUE SETTING YEARS AGO.
OOH, JUST GO GET THE RICK AND MORTY VOLUME 4 TRADE PAPERBACK! IT'S A GOOD ONE.
WAIT, DID YOU SAY YOUR NAME IS PEACOCK JONES?
THE UNIVERSE-FAMOUS PEACOCK JONES, APPARENTLY.
YOU KIDNAPPED MY NIECE, KNOCKED HER UP, STOLE ALL HER MONEY AND DISAPPEARED.
WELL, THAT'S THE VERSION I'D EXPECT FROM AN EMOTIONAL NITWIT.
WHAT I ACTUALLY DID WAS WINED AND DINED HER, SHOWED HER THINGS SHE WOULD NEVER SEE OTHERWISE, AND THEN LEFT WHEN SHE BECAME INEVITABLY OAFISH AND BANAL.
SHE WAS JUST A KID, YOU MONSTER. I'M GOING TO BUST YOUR FACE INTO SO MANY PIECES THEY'LL CALL YOU PUZZLE JONES.
IF YOU HAVE AN ISSUE WITH ME, SIR, YOU'LL HAVE TO TAKE IT UP WITH MY ASSOCIATE HERE.

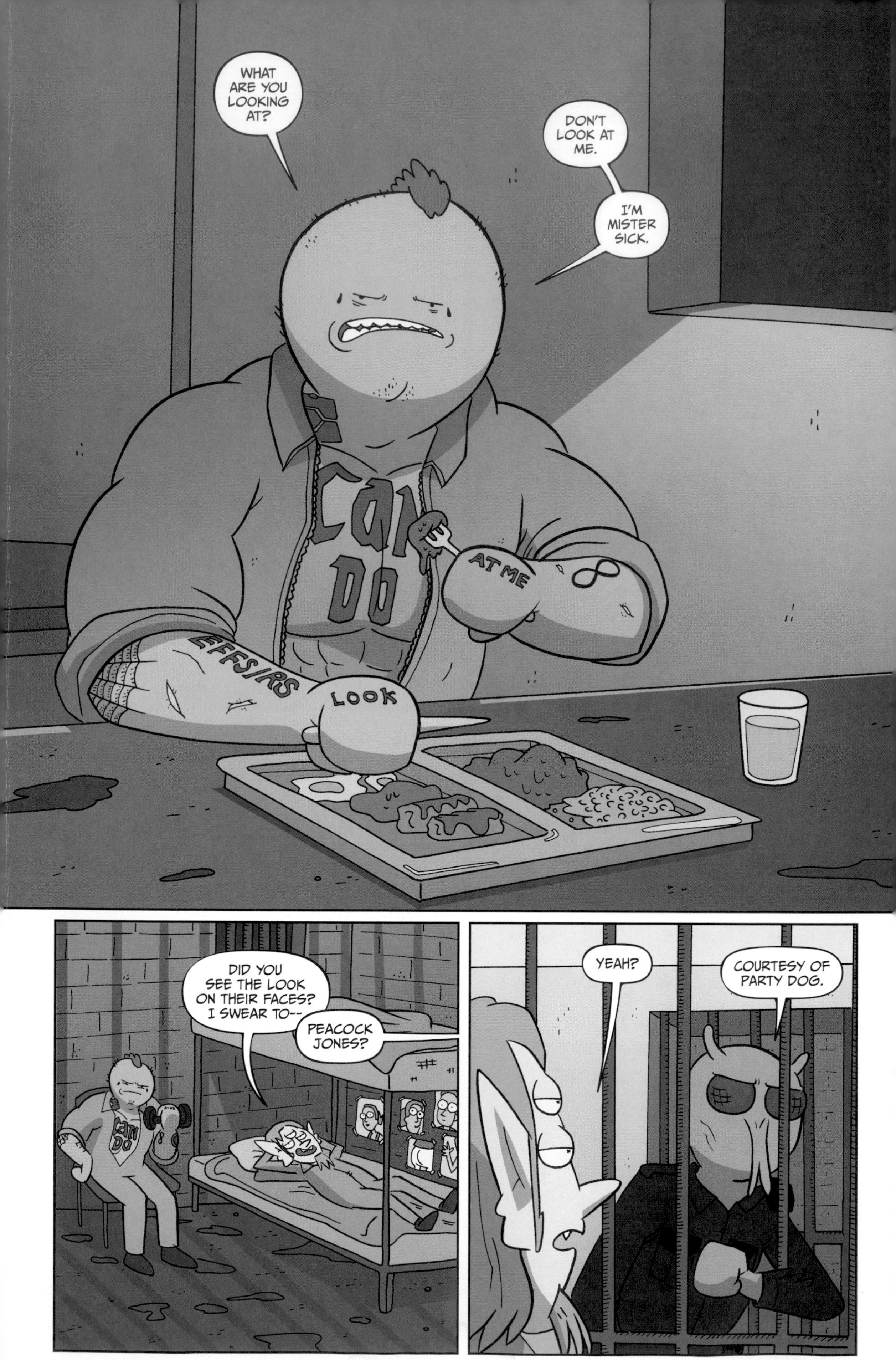
WHAT ARE YOU LOOKING AT?
DON'T LOOK AT ME.
I'M MISTER SICK.
AT ME
LOOK
DID YOU SEE THE LOOK ON THEIR FACES? I SWEAR TO--
PEACOCK JONES?
YEAH?
COURTESY OF PARTY DOG.

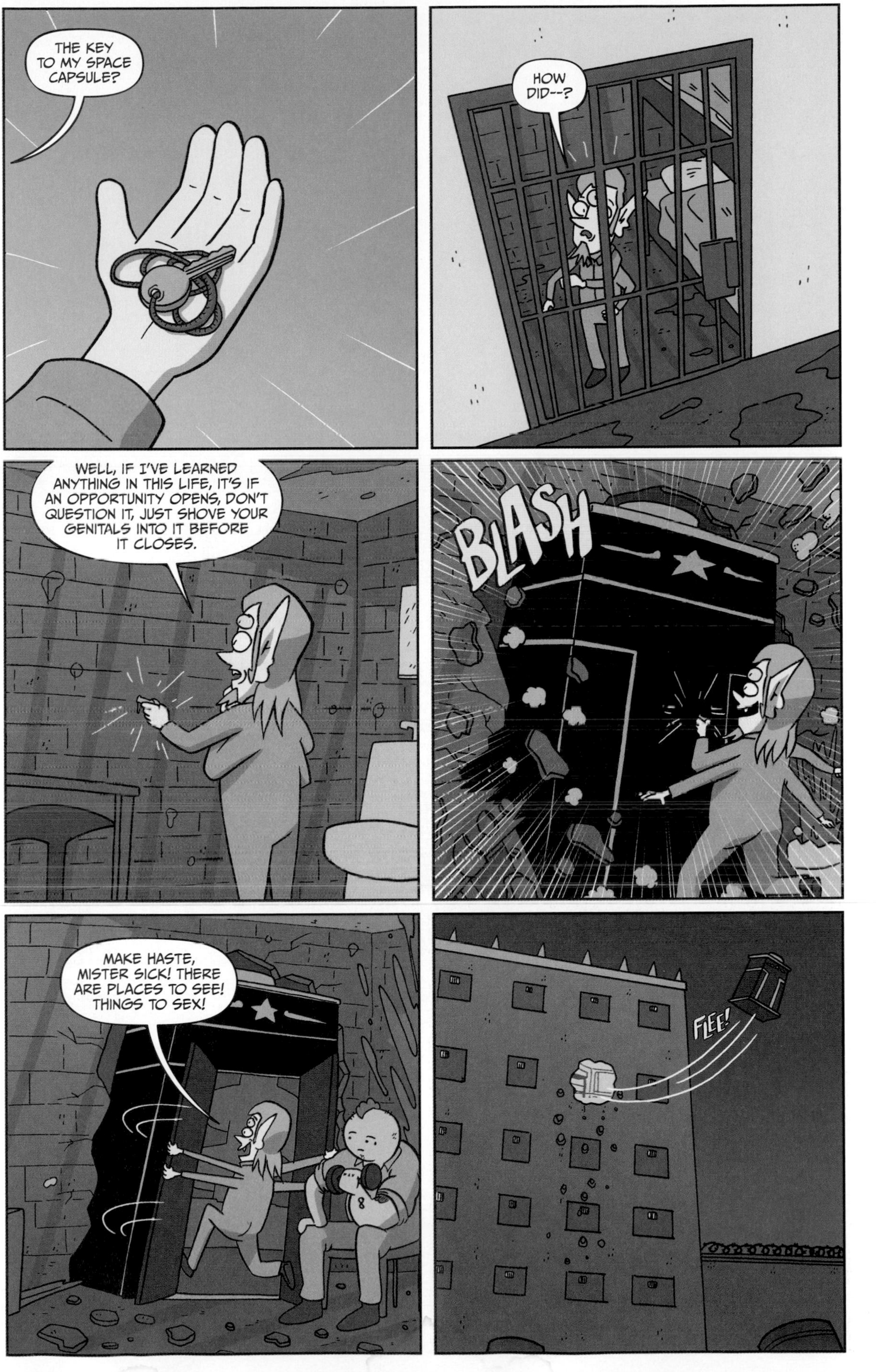
THE KEY TO MY SPACE CAPSULE?
HOW DID--?
WELL, IF I'VE LEARNED ANYTHING IN THIS LIFE, IT'S IF AN OPPORTUNITY OPENS, DON'T QUESTION IT, JUST SHOVE YOUR GENITALS INTO IT BEFORE IT CLOSES.
BLASH
MAKE HASTE, MISTER SICK! THERE ARE PLACES TO SEE! THINGS TO SEX!
FLEE!

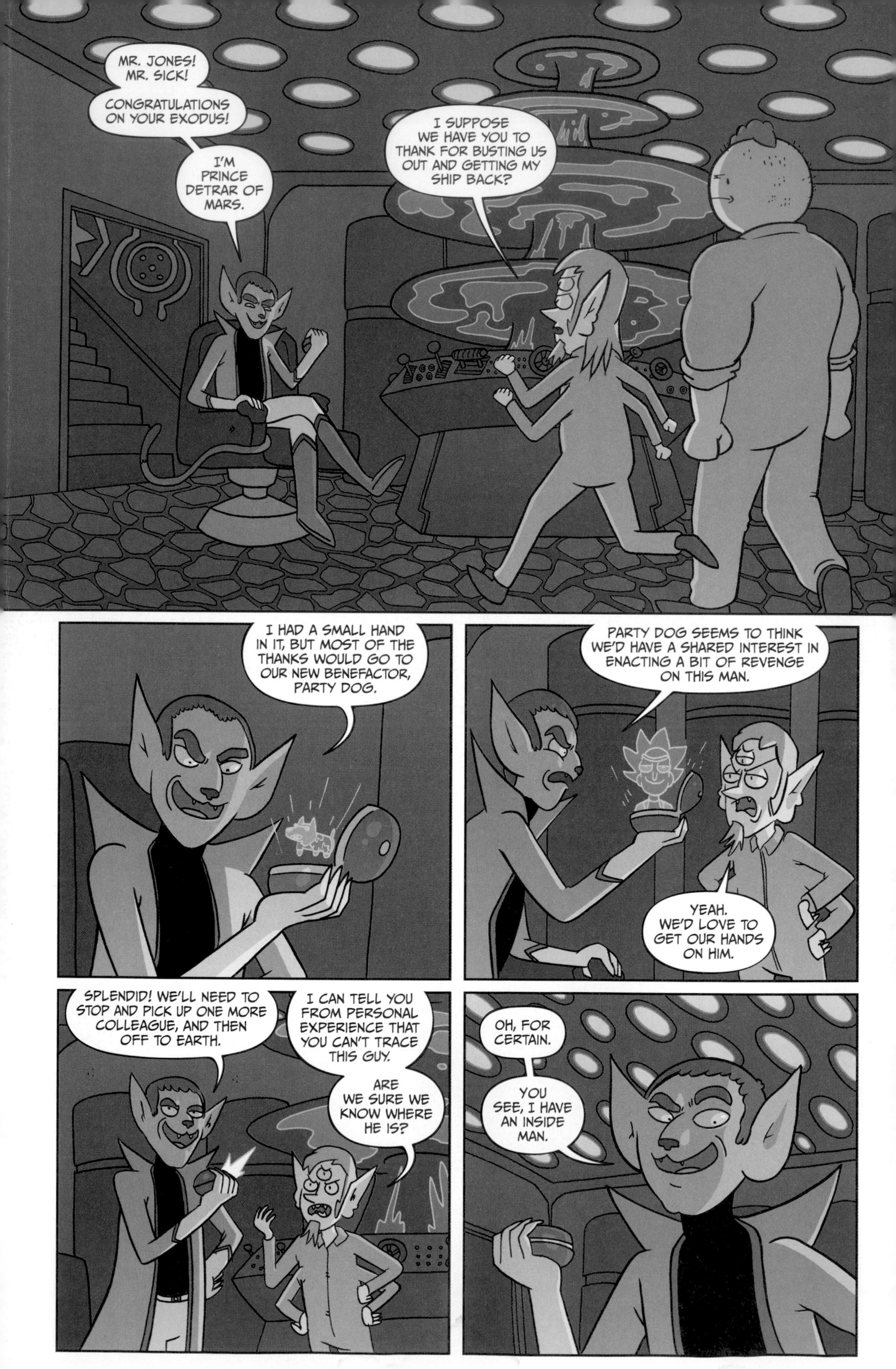
MR. JONES! MR. SICK!
CONGRATULATIONS ON YOUR EXODUS!
I'M PRINCE DETRAR OF MARS.
I SUPPOSE WE HAVE YOU TO THANK FOR BUSTING US OUT AND GETTING MY SHIP BACK?
I HAD A SMALL HAND IN IT, BUT MOST OF THE THANKS WOULD GO TO OUR NEW BENEFACTOR, PARTY DOG.
PARTY DOG SEEMS TO THINK WE'D HAVE A SHARED INTEREST IN ENACTING A BIT OF REVENGE ON THIS MAN.
YEAH. WE'D LOVE TO GET OUR HANDS ON HIM.
SPLENDID! WE'LL NEED TO STOP AND PICK UP ONE MORE COLLEAGUE, AND THEN OFF TO EARTH.
I CAN TELL YOU FROM PERSONAL EXPERIENCE THAT YOU CAN'T TRACE THIS GUY.
ARE WE SURE WE KNOW WHERE HE IS?
OH, FOR CERTAIN.
YOU SEE, I HAVE AN INSIDE MAN.

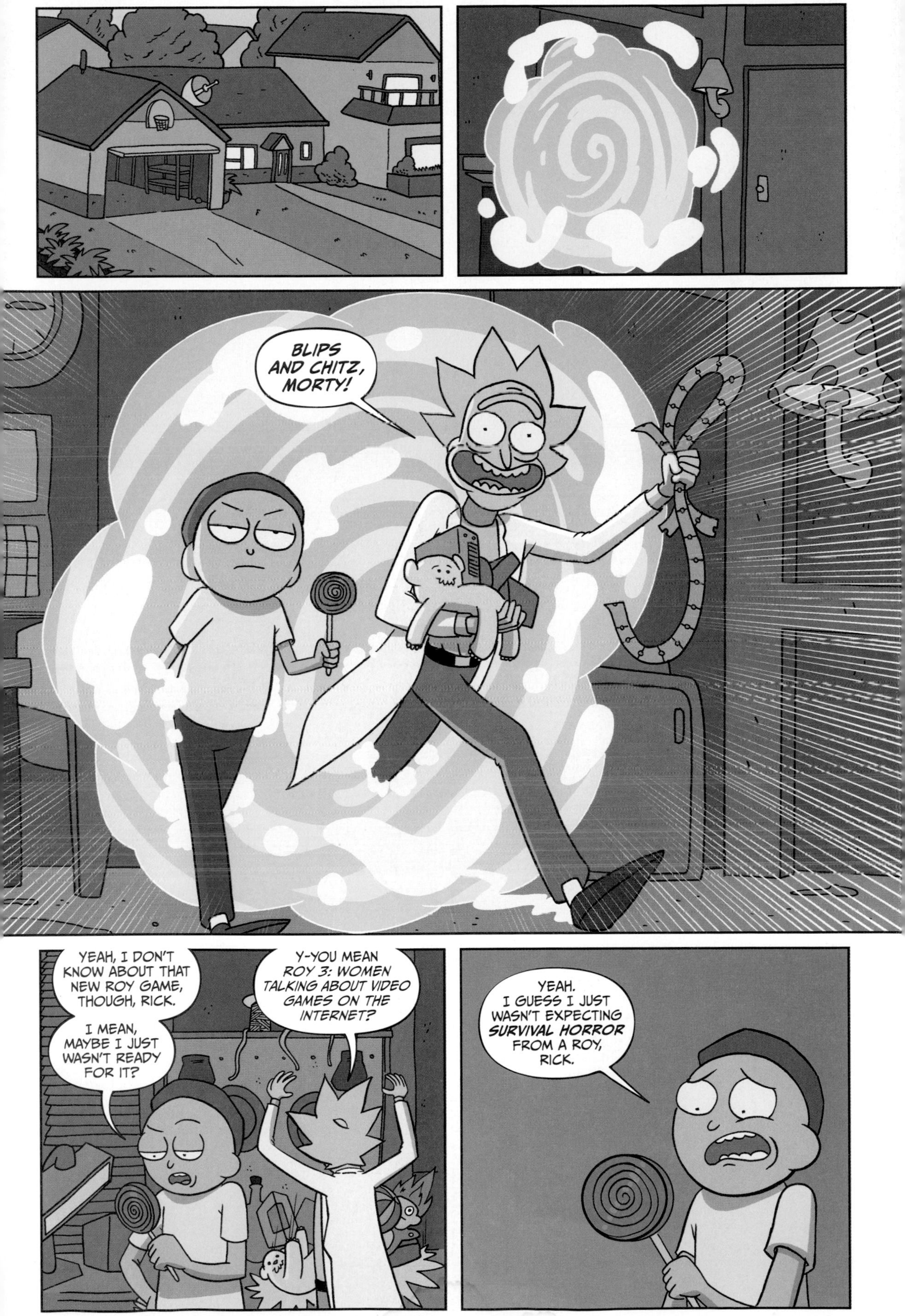
BLIPS AND CHITZ, MORTY!
YEAH, I DON'T KNOW ABOUT THAT NEW ROY GAME, THOUGH, RICK.
I MEAN, MAYBE I JUST WASN'T READY FOR IT?
Y-YOU MEAN *ROY 3: WOMEN TALKING ABOUT VIDEO GAMES ON THE INTERNET?*
YEAH. I GUESS I JUST WASN'T EXPECTING ***SURVIVAL HORROR*** FROM A ROY, RICK.

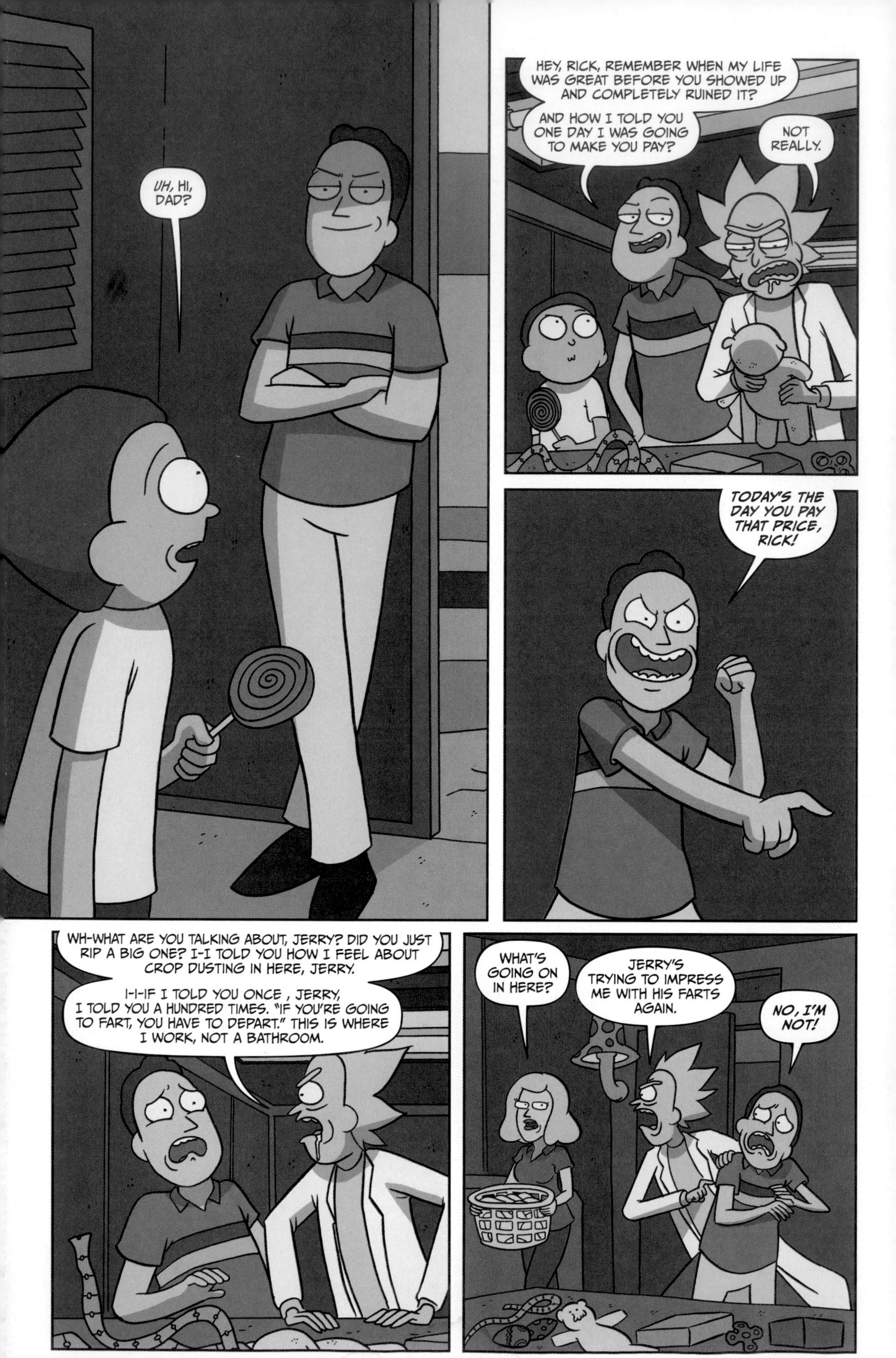
UH, HI, DAD?
HEY, RICK, REMEMBER WHEN MY LIFE WAS GREAT BEFORE YOU SHOWED UP AND COMPLETELY RUINED IT?
AND HOW I TOLD YOU ONE DAY I WAS GOING TO MAKE YOU PAY?
NOT REALLY.
TODAY'S THE DAY YOU PAY THAT PRICE, RICK!
WH-WHAT ARE YOU TALKING ABOUT, JERRY? DID YOU JUST RIP A BIG ONE? I-I TOLD YOU HOW I FEEL ABOUT CROP DUSTING IN HERE, JERRY.
I-I-IF I TOLD YOU ONCE , JERRY, I TOLD YOU A HUNDRED TIMES. "IF YOU'RE GOING TO FART, YOU HAVE TO DEPART." THIS IS WHERE I WORK, NOT A BATHROOM.
WHAT'S GOING ON IN HERE?
JERRY'S TRYING TO IMPRESS ME WITH HIS FARTS AGAIN.
NO, I'M NOT!

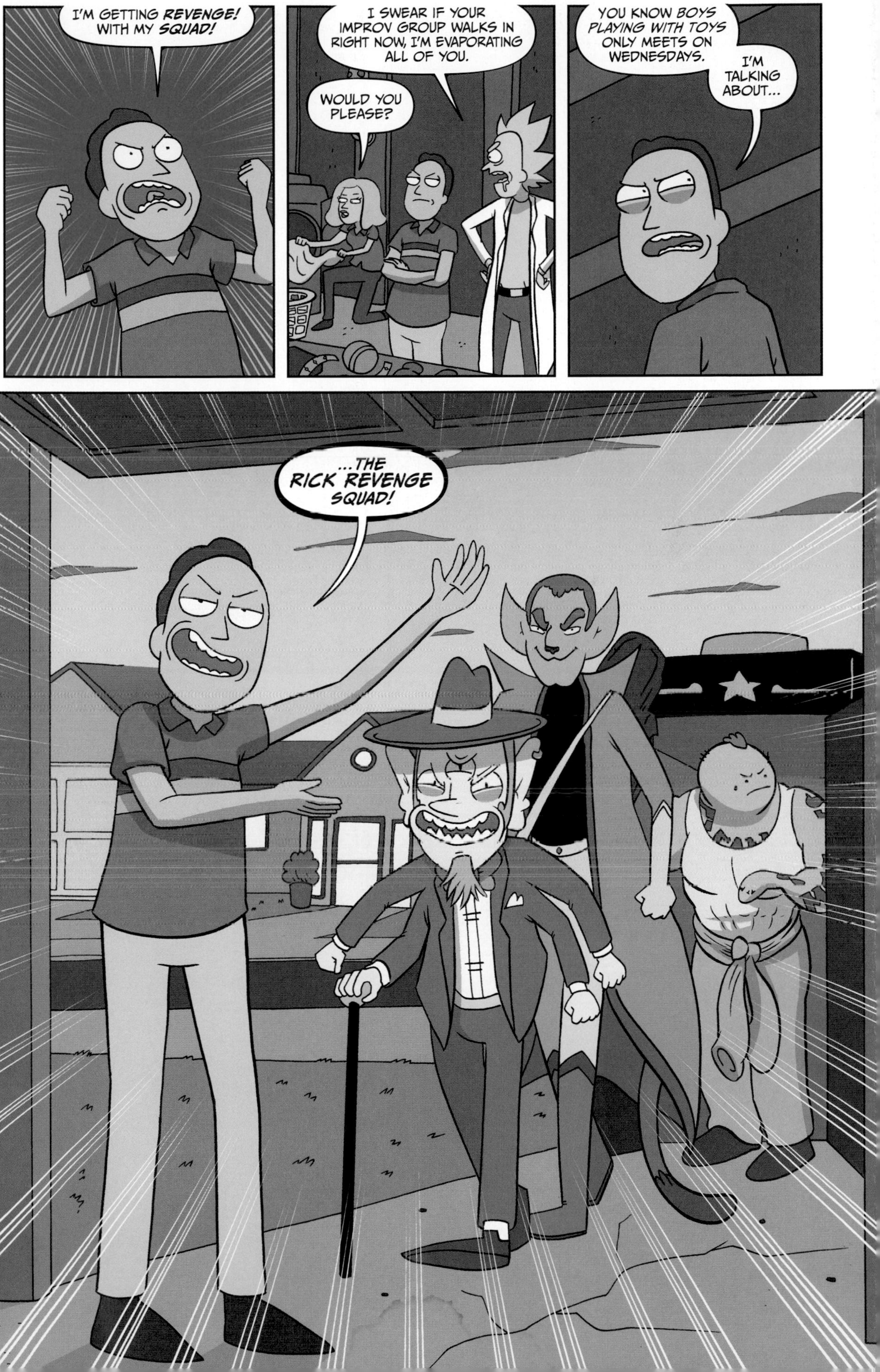
I'M GETTING REVENGE! WITH MY SQUAD!
I SWEAR IF YOUR IMPROV GROUP WALKS IN RIGHT NOW, I'M EVAPORATING ALL OF YOU.
WOULD YOU PLEASE?
YOU KNOW BOYS PLAYING WITH TOYS ONLY MEETS ON WEDNESDAYS.
I'M TALKING ABOUT...
...THE RICK REVENGE SQUAD!

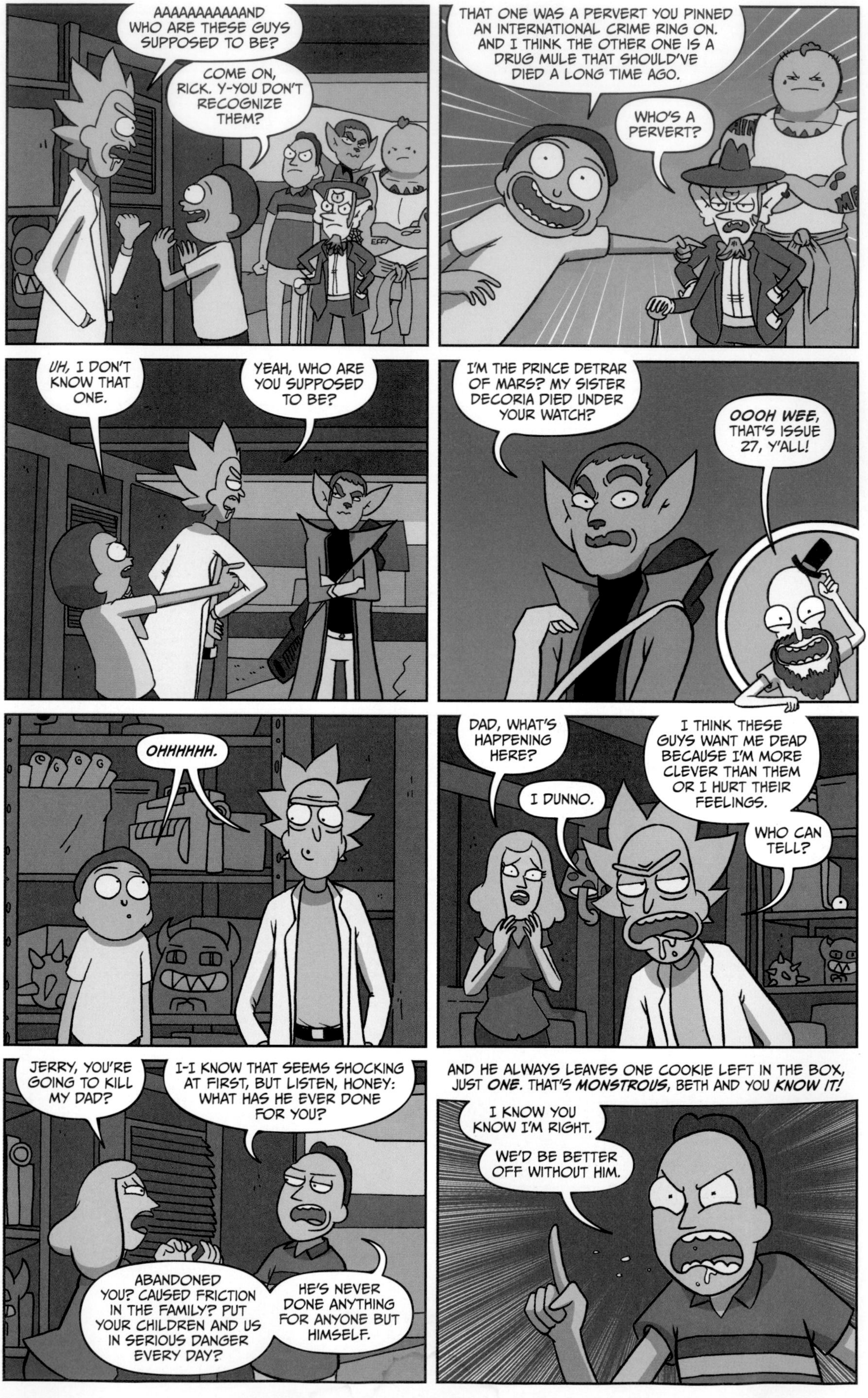
AAAAAAAAAAAAND WHO ARE THESE GUYS SUPPOSED TO BE?
COME ON, RICK. Y-YOU DON'T RECOGNIZE THEM?
THAT ONE WAS A PERVERT YOU PINNED AN INTERNATIONAL CRIME RING ON. AND I THINK THE OTHER ONE IS A DRUG MULE THAT SHOULD'VE DIED A LONG TIME AGO.
WHO'S A PERVERT?
UH, I DON'T KNOW THAT ONE.
YEAH, WHO ARE YOU SUPPOSED TO BE?
I'M THE PRINCE DETRAR OF MARS? MY SISTER DECORIA DIED UNDER YOUR WATCH?
OOOH WEE, THAT'S ISSUE 27, Y'ALL!
OHHHHHH.
DAD, WHAT'S HAPPENING HERE?
I DUNNO.
I THINK THESE GUYS WANT ME DEAD BECAUSE I'M MORE CLEVER THAN THEM OR I HURT THEIR FEELINGS.
WHO CAN TELL?
JERRY, YOU'RE GOING TO KILL MY DAD?
I-I KNOW THAT SEEMS SHOCKING AT FIRST, BUT LISTEN, HONEY: WHAT HAS HE EVER DONE FOR YOU?
ABANDONED YOU? CAUSED FRICTION IN THE FAMILY? PUT YOUR CHILDREN AND US IN SERIOUS DANGER EVERY DAY?
HE'S NEVER DONE ANYTHING FOR ANYONE BUT HIMSELF.
AND HE ALWAYS LEAVES ONE COOKIE LEFT IN THE BOX, JUST ONE. THAT'S MONSTROUS, BETH AND YOU KNOW IT!
I KNOW YOU KNOW I'M RIGHT.
WE'D BE BETTER OFF WITHOUT HIM.

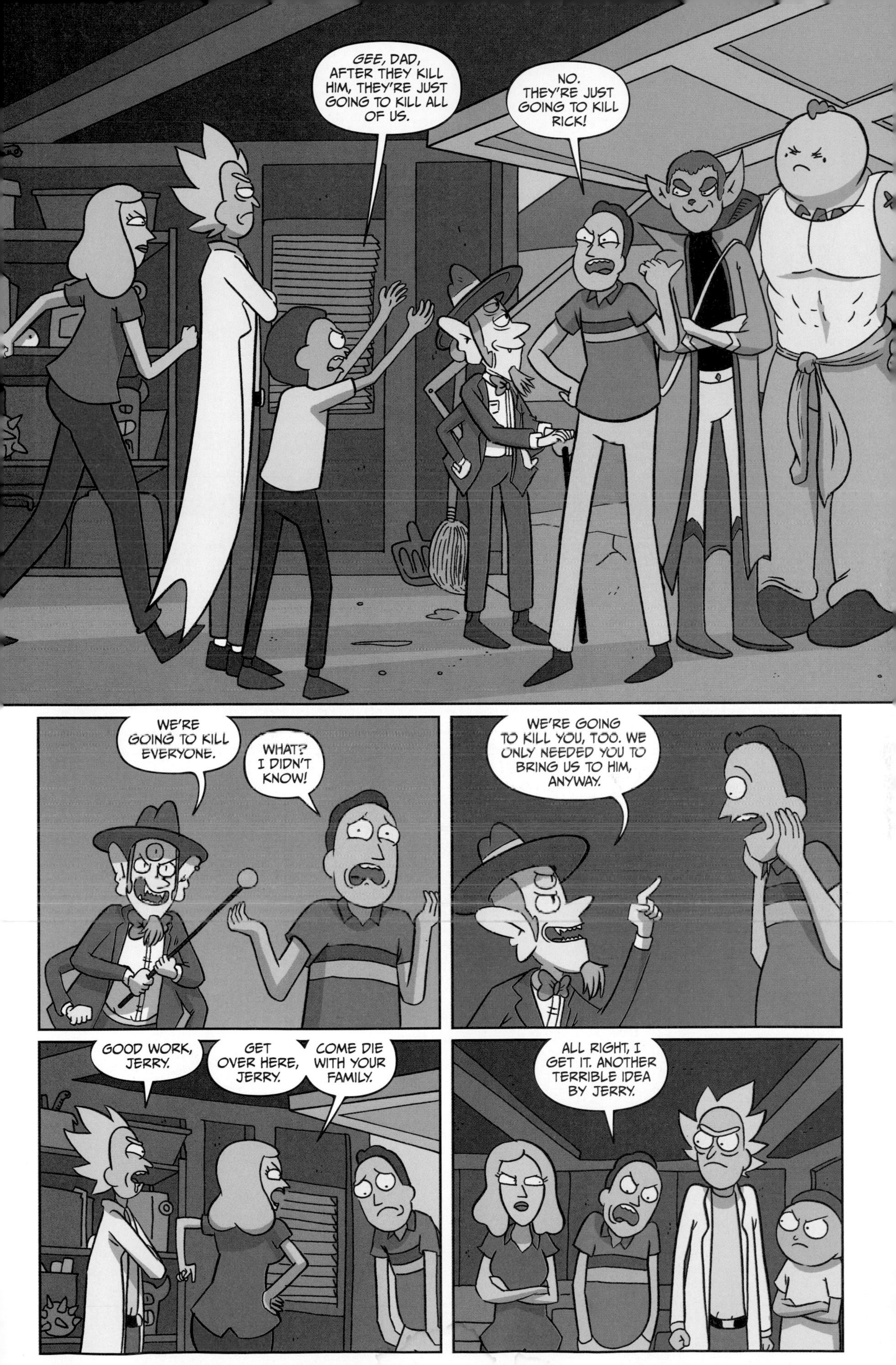
GEE, DAD, AFTER THEY KILL HIM, THEY'RE JUST GOING TO KILL ALL OF US.
NO. THEY'RE JUST GOING TO KILL RICK!
WE'RE GOING TO KILL EVERYONE.
WHAT? I DIDN'T KNOW!
WE'RE GOING TO KILL YOU, TOO. WE ONLY NEEDED YOU TO BRING US TO HIM, ANYWAY.
GOOD WORK, JERRY.
GET OVER HERE, JERRY.
COME DIE WITH YOUR FAMILY.
ALL RIGHT, I GET IT. ANOTHER TERRIBLE IDEA BY JERRY.

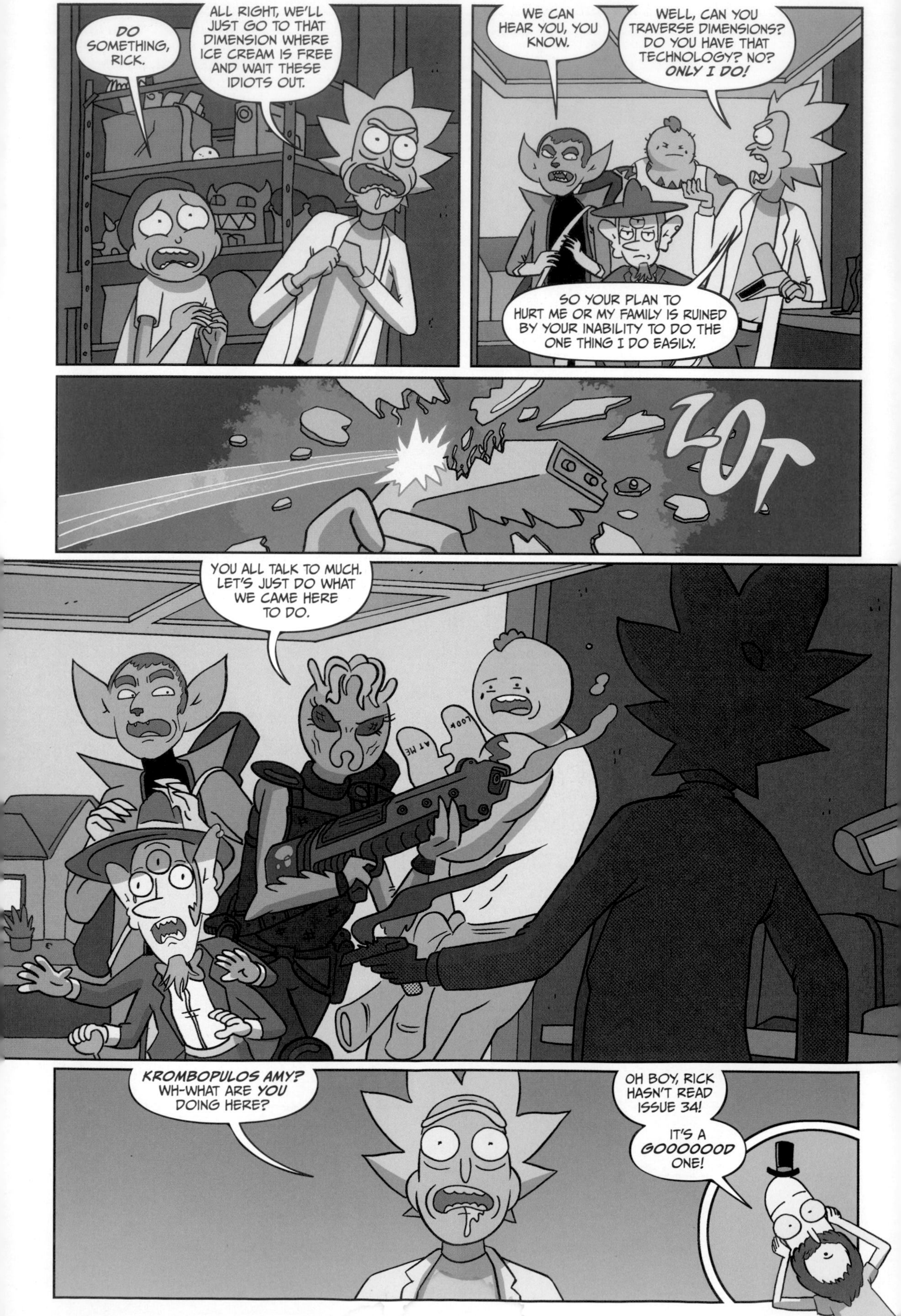

DO SOMETHING, RICK.
ALL RIGHT, WE'LL JUST GO TO THAT DIMENSION WHERE ICE CREAM IS FREE AND WAIT THESE IDIOTS OUT.
WE CAN HEAR YOU, YOU KNOW.
WELL, CAN YOU TRAVERSE DIMENSIONS? DO YOU HAVE THAT TECHNOLOGY? NO? ONLY I DO!
SO YOUR PLAN TO HURT ME OR MY FAMILY IS RUINED BY YOUR INABILITY TO DO THE ONE THING I DO EASILY.
ZOT!
YOU ALL TALK TO MUCH. LET'S JUST DO WHAT WE CAME HERE TO DO.
LOOK
AT ME
KROMBOPULOS AMY? WH-WHAT ARE YOU DOING HERE?
OH BOY, RICK HASN'T READ ISSUE 34!
IT'S A GOOOOOOD ONE!

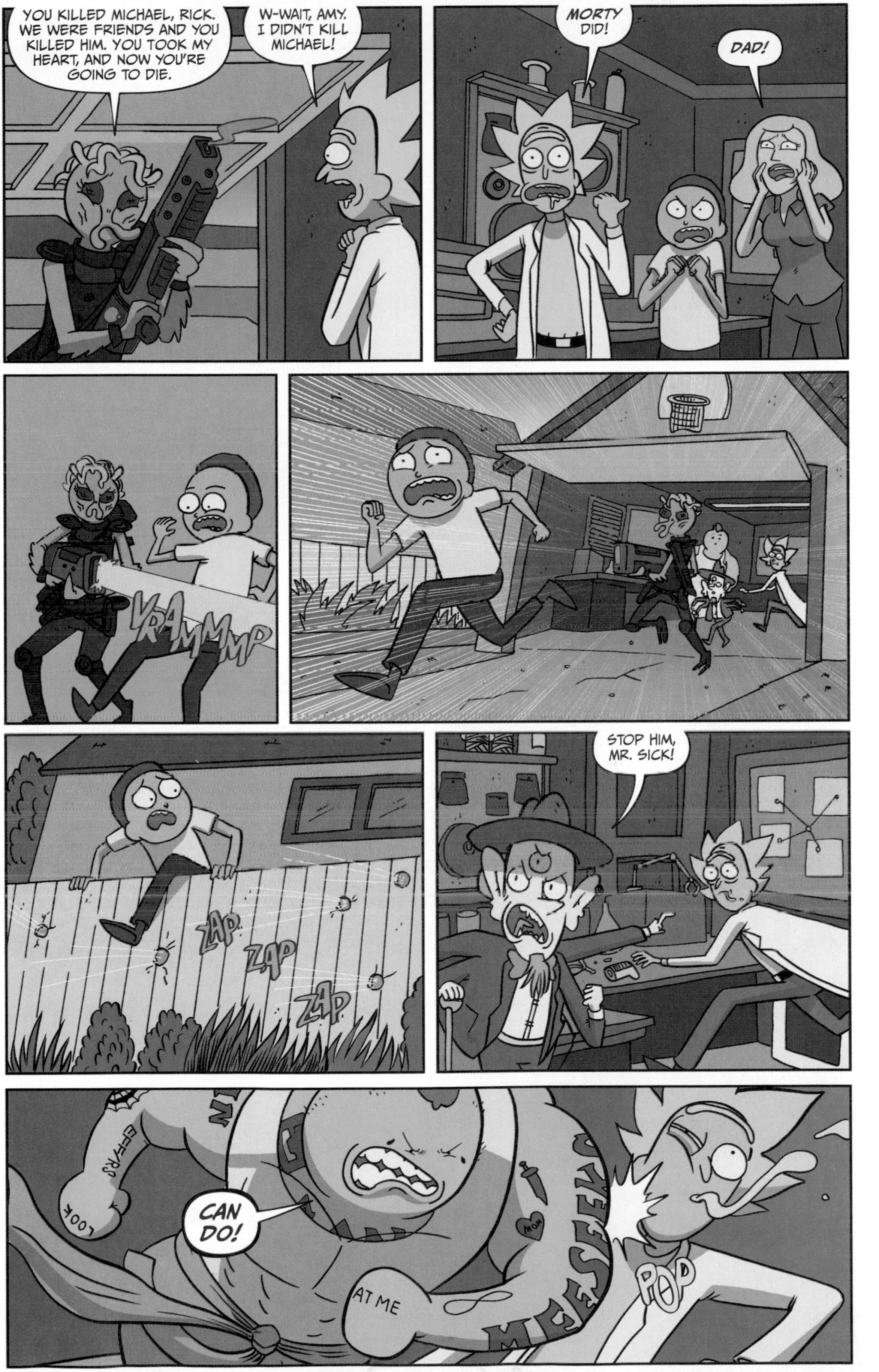
YOU KILLED MICHAEL, RICK. WE WERE FRIENDS AND YOU KILLED HIM. YOU TOOK MY HEART, AND NOW YOU'RE GOING TO DIE.
W-WAIT, AMY. I DIDN'T KILL MICHAEL!
MORTY DID!
DAD!
VRAMMMP
ZAP
ZAP
ZAP
STOP HIM, MR. SICK!
CAN DO!
AT ME
POP

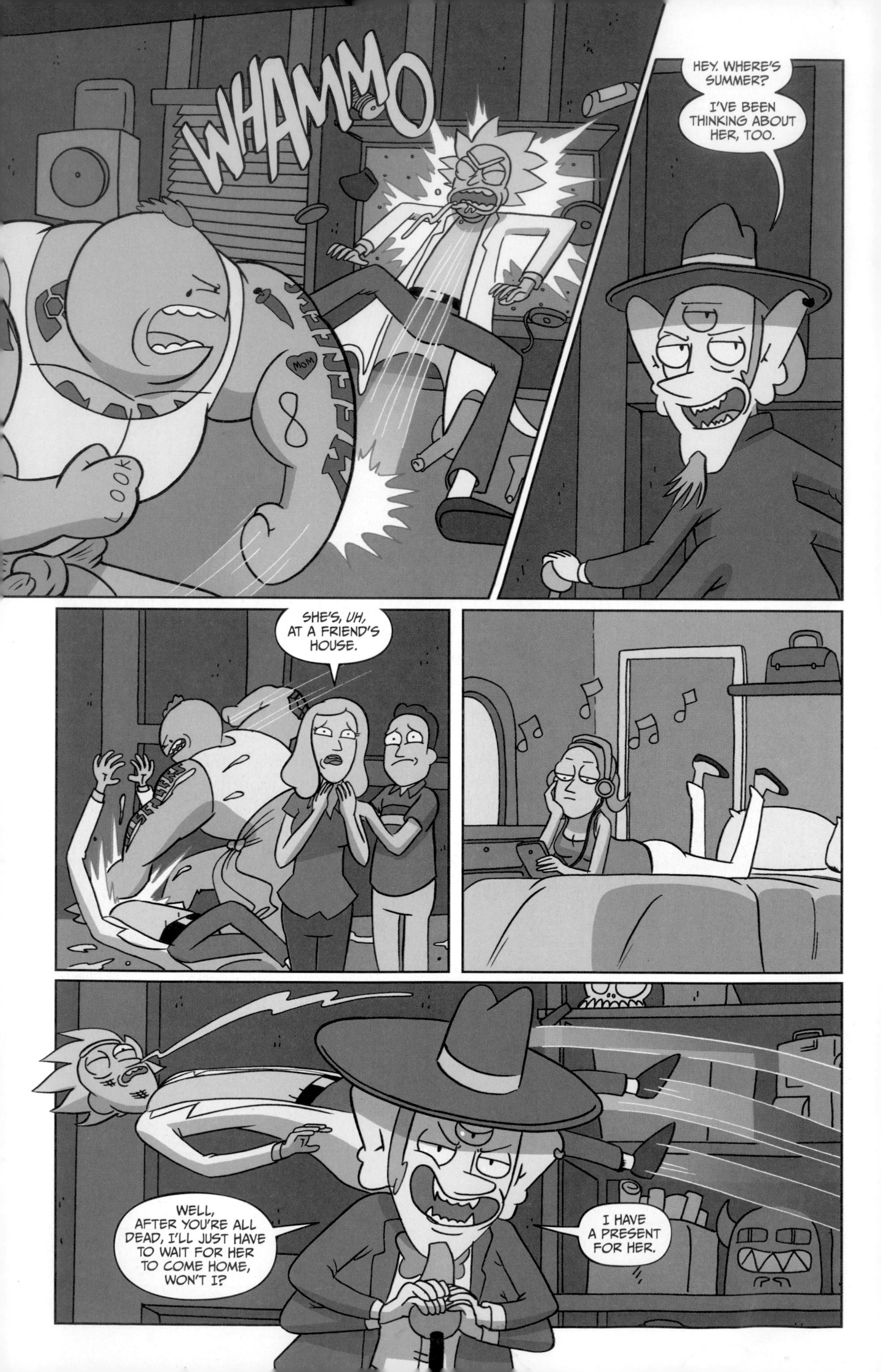
WHAMMO
HEY. WHERE'S SUMMER?
I'VE BEEN THINKING ABOUT HER, TOO.
MOM
LOOK
SHE'S, UH, AT A FRIEND'S HOUSE.
WELL, AFTER YOU'RE ALL DEAD, I'LL JUST HAVE TO WAIT FOR HER TO COME HOME, WON'T I?
I HAVE A PRESENT FOR HER.

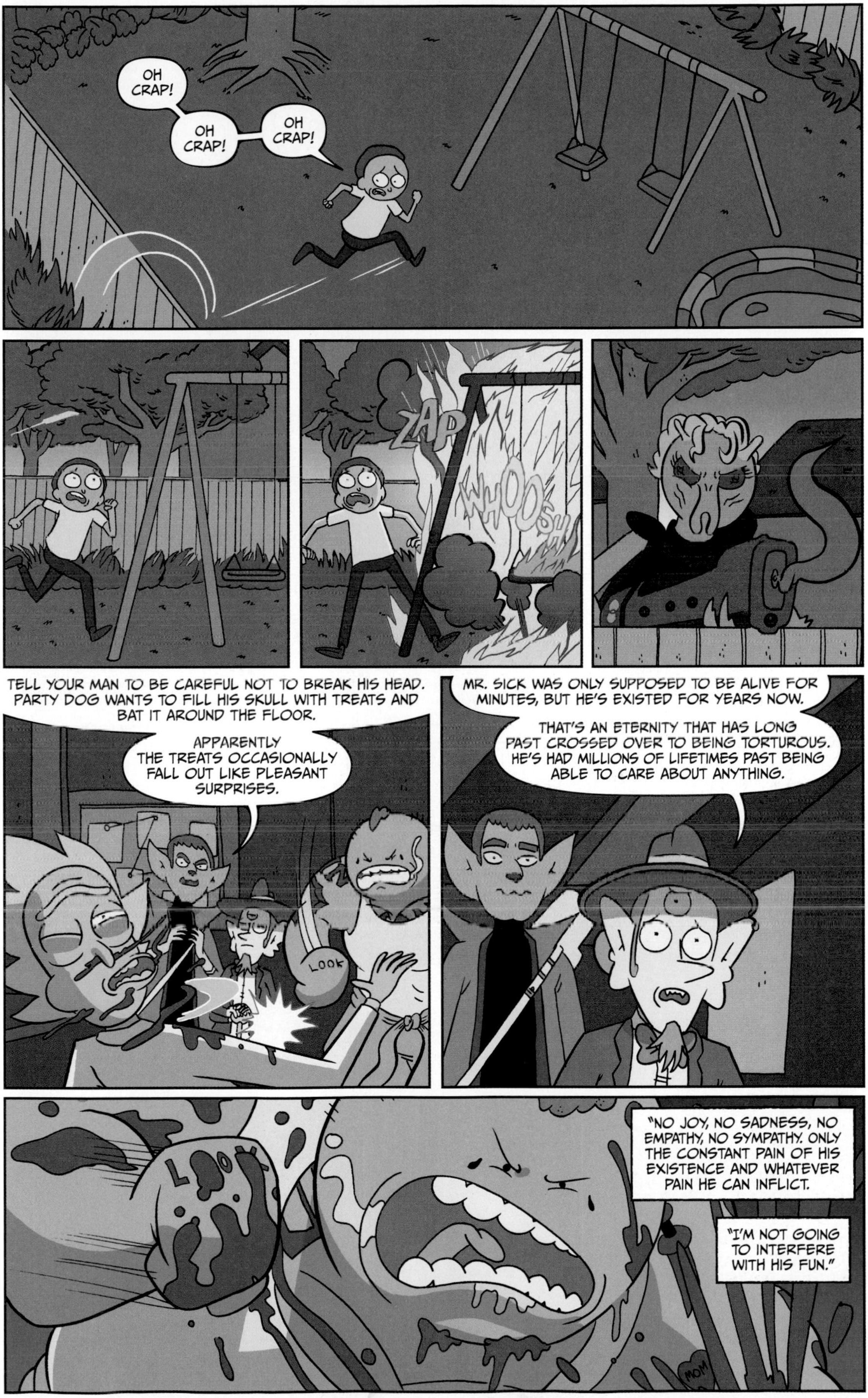
OH CRAP!
OH CRAP!
OH CRAP!
ZAP
WHOOSH
TELL YOUR MAN TO BE CAREFUL NOT TO BREAK HIS HEAD. PARTY DOG WANTS TO FILL HIS SKULL WITH TREATS AND BAT IT AROUND THE FLOOR.
APPARENTLY THE TREATS OCCASIONALLY FALL OUT LIKE PLEASANT SURPRISES.
LOOK
MR. SICK WAS ONLY SUPPOSED TO BE ALIVE FOR MINUTES, BUT HE'S EXISTED FOR YEARS NOW.
THAT'S AN ETERNITY THAT HAS LONG PAST CROSSED OVER TO BEING TORTUROUS. HE'S HAD MILLIONS OF LIFETIMES PAST BEING ABLE TO CARE ABOUT ANYTHING.
"NO JOY, NO SADNESS, NO EMPATHY, NO SYMPATHY. ONLY THE CONSTANT PAIN OF HIS EXISTENCE AND WHATEVER PAIN HE CAN INFLICT.
"I'M NOT GOING TO INTERFERE WITH HIS FUN."
MOM

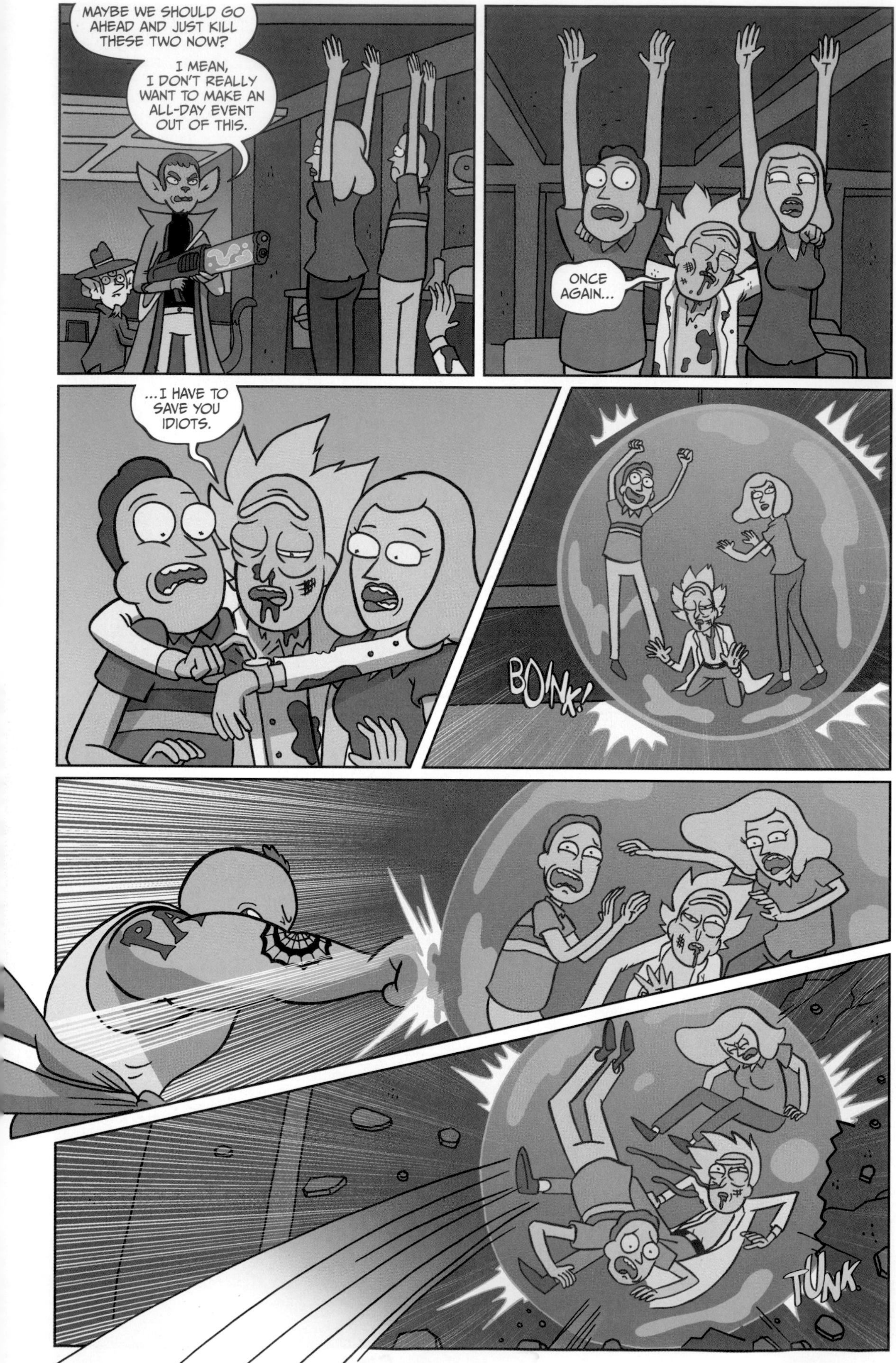
MAYBE WE SHOULD GO AHEAD AND JUST KILL THESE TWO NOW?
I MEAN, I DON'T REALLY WANT TO MAKE AN ALL-DAY EVENT OUT OF THIS.
ONCE AGAIN...
...I HAVE TO SAVE YOU IDIOTS.
BOINK!
TUNK.

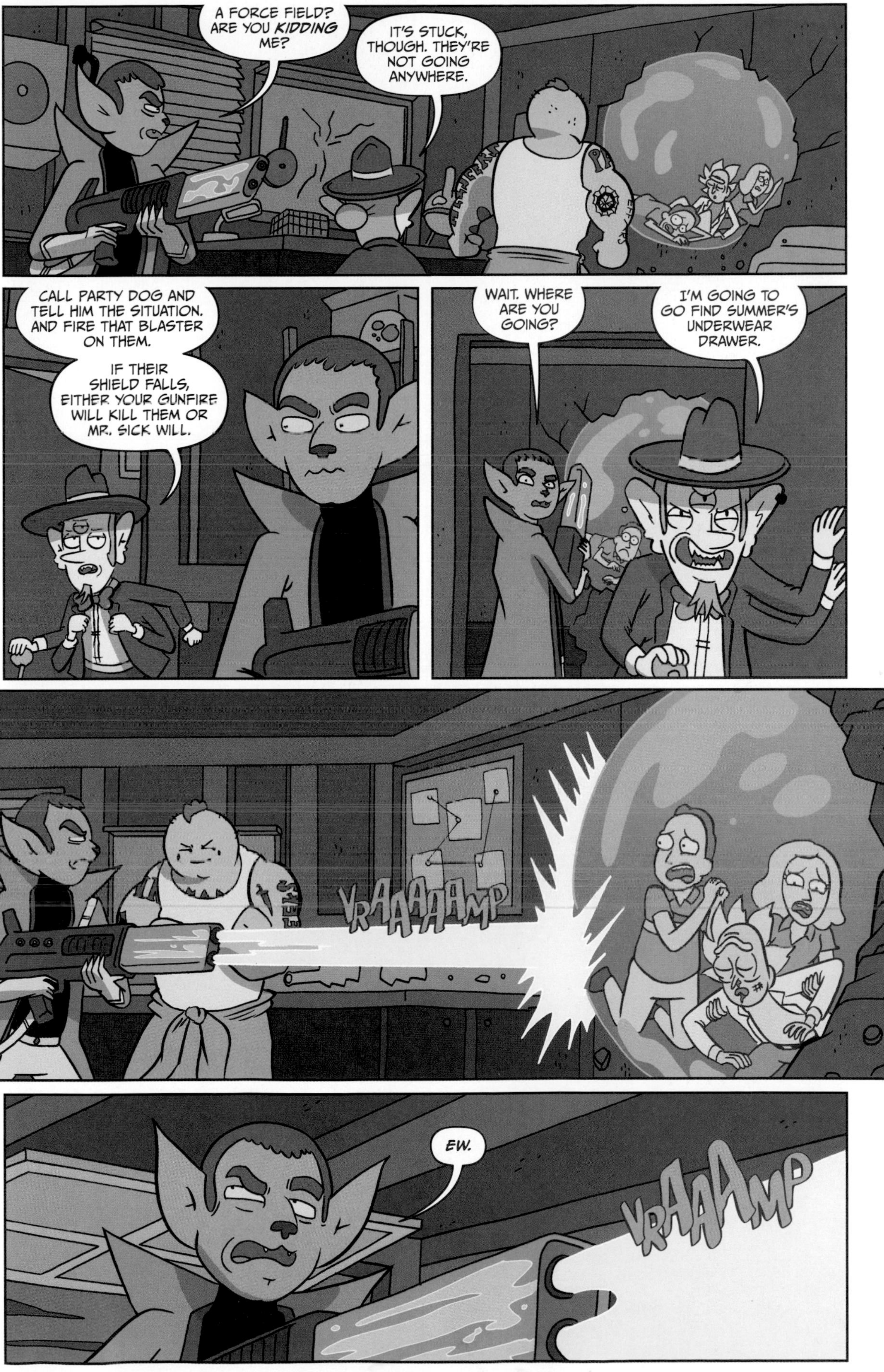
A FORCE FIELD? ARE YOU *KIDDING* ME?
IT'S STUCK, THOUGH. THEY'RE NOT GOING ANYWHERE.
CALL PARTY DOG AND TELL HIM THE SITUATION. AND FIRE THAT BLASTER ON THEM.
IF THEIR SHIELD FALLS, EITHER YOUR GUNFIRE WILL KILL THEM OR MR. SICK WILL.
WAIT. WHERE ARE YOU GOING?
I'M GOING TO GO FIND SUMMER'S UNDERWEAR DRAWER.
VRAAAAAMP
EW.
VRAAAMP

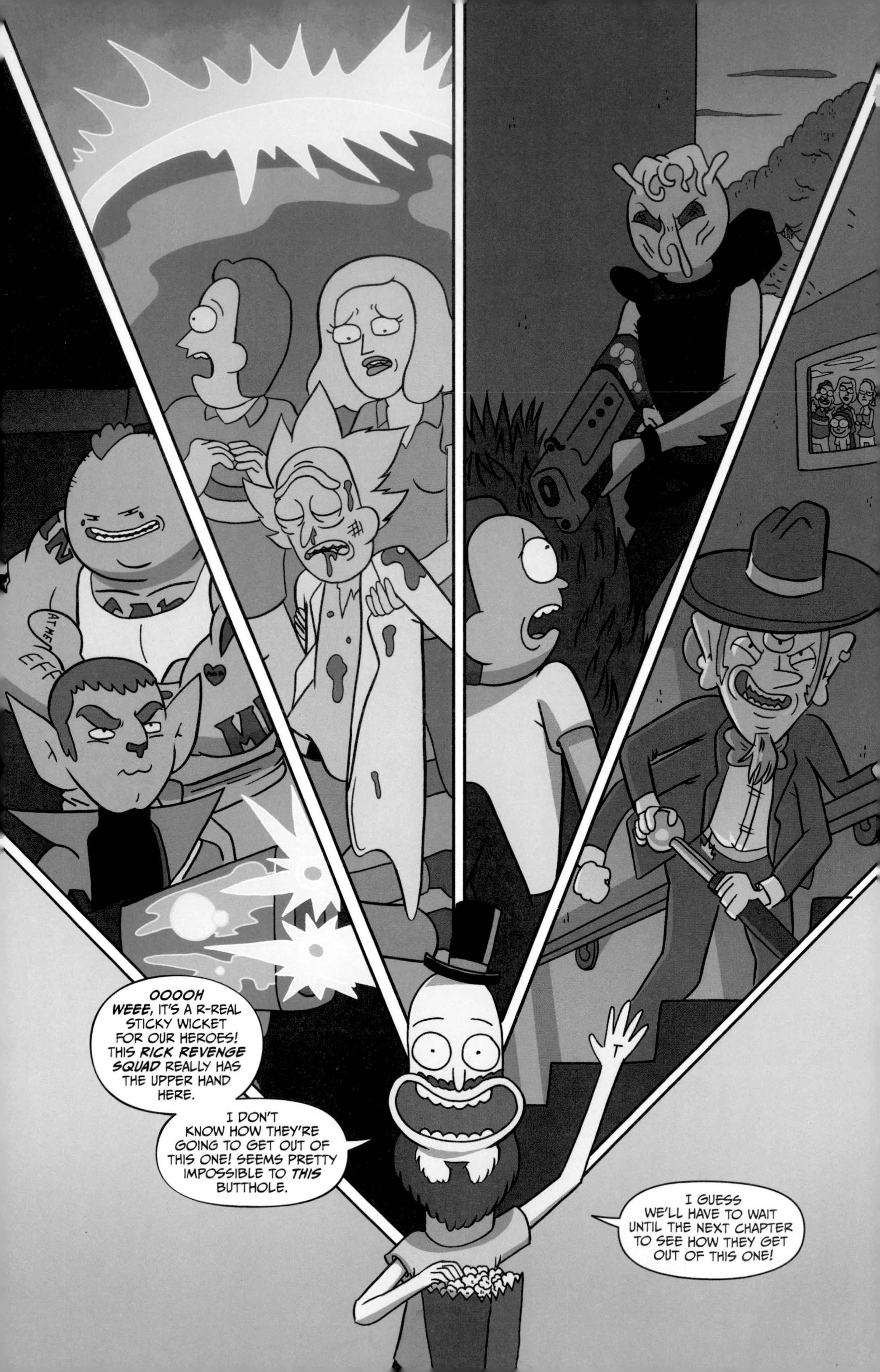
OOOOH WEEE, IT'S A R-REAL STICKY WICKET FOR OUR HEROES! THIS RICK REVENGE SQUAD REALLY HAS THE UPPER HAND HERE.
I DON'T KNOW HOW THEY'RE GOING TO GET OUT OF THIS ONE! SEEMS PRETTY IMPOSSIBLE TO THIS BUTTHOLE.
I GUESS WE'LL HAVE TO WAIT UNTIL THE NEXT CHAPTER TO SEE HOW THEY GET OUT OF THIS ONE!

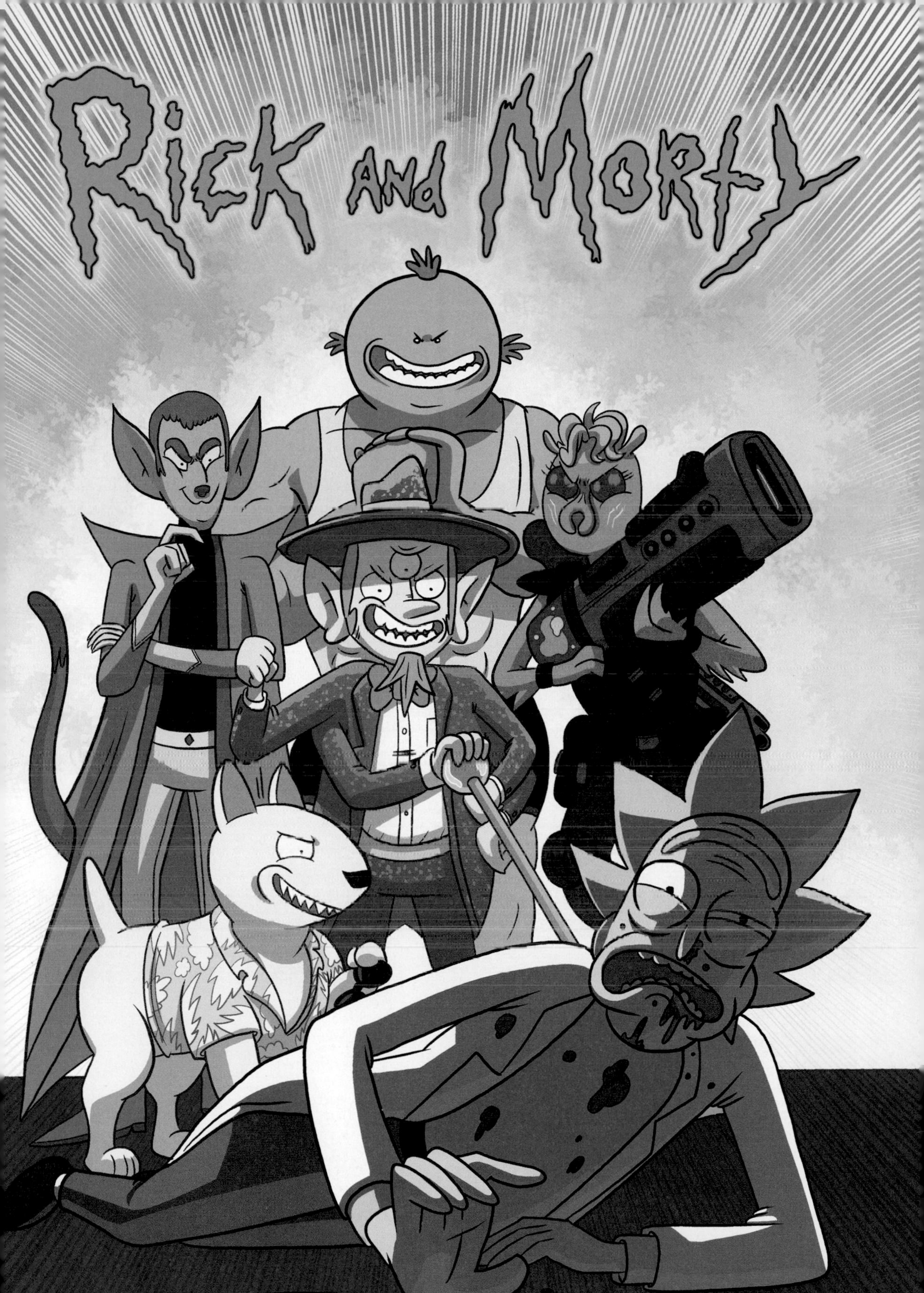
Rick and Morty

"RICK REVENGE SQUAD PART 2"

WRITTEN BY **KYLE STARKS** ILLUSTRATED BY **MARC ELLERBY** COLORED BY **SARAH STERN** LETTERED BY **CRANK!**

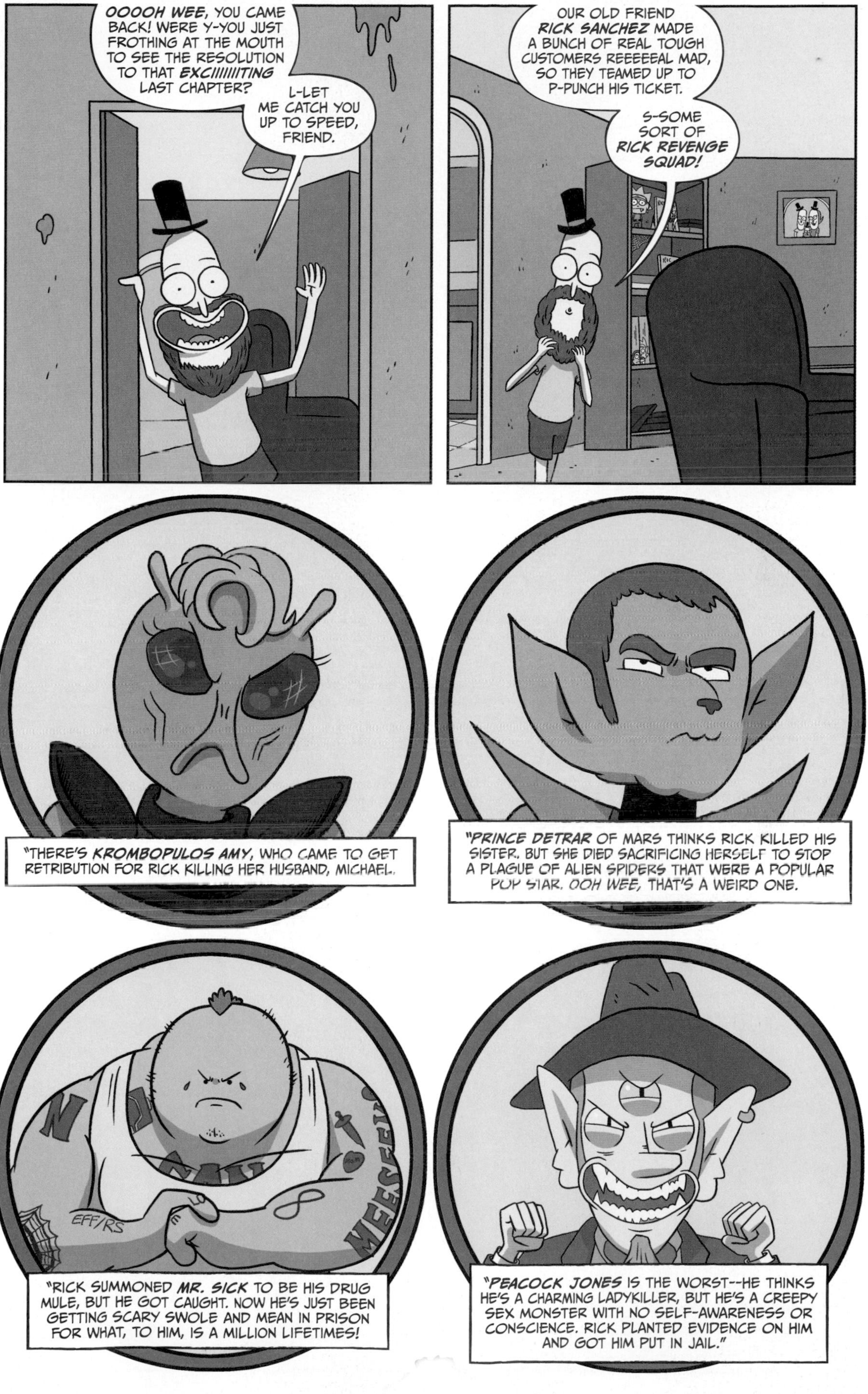
OOOOH WEE, YOU CAME BACK! WERE Y-YOU JUST FROTHING AT THE MOUTH TO SEE THE RESOLUTION TO THAT EXCIIIIIIITING LAST CHAPTER?
L-LET ME CATCH YOU UP TO SPEED, FRIEND.
OUR OLD FRIEND RICK SANCHEZ MADE A BUNCH OF REAL TOUGH CUSTOMERS REEEEEAL MAD, SO THEY TEAMED UP TO P-PUNCH HIS TICKET.
S-SOME SORT OF RICK REVENGE SQUAD!
"THERE'S KROMBOPULOS AMY, WHO CAME TO GET RETRIBUTION FOR RICK KILLING HER HUSBAND, MICHAEL.
"PRINCE DETRAR OF MARS THINKS RICK KILLED HIS SISTER. BUT SHE DIED SACRIFICING HERSELF TO STOP A PLAGUE OF ALIEN SPIDERS THAT WERE A POPULAR POP STAR. OOH WEE, THAT'S A WEIRD ONE.
EFF/RS
"RICK SUMMONED MR. SICK TO BE HIS DRUG MULE, BUT HE GOT CAUGHT. NOW HE'S JUST BEEN GETTING SCARY SWOLE AND MEAN IN PRISON FOR WHAT, TO HIM, IS A MILLION LIFETIMES!
"PEACOCK JONES IS THE WORST--HE THINKS HE'S A CHARMING LADYKILLER, BUT HE'S A CREEPY SEX MONSTER WITH NO SELF-AWARENESS OR CONSCIENCE. RICK PLANTED EVIDENCE ON HIM AND GOT HIM PUT IN JAIL."

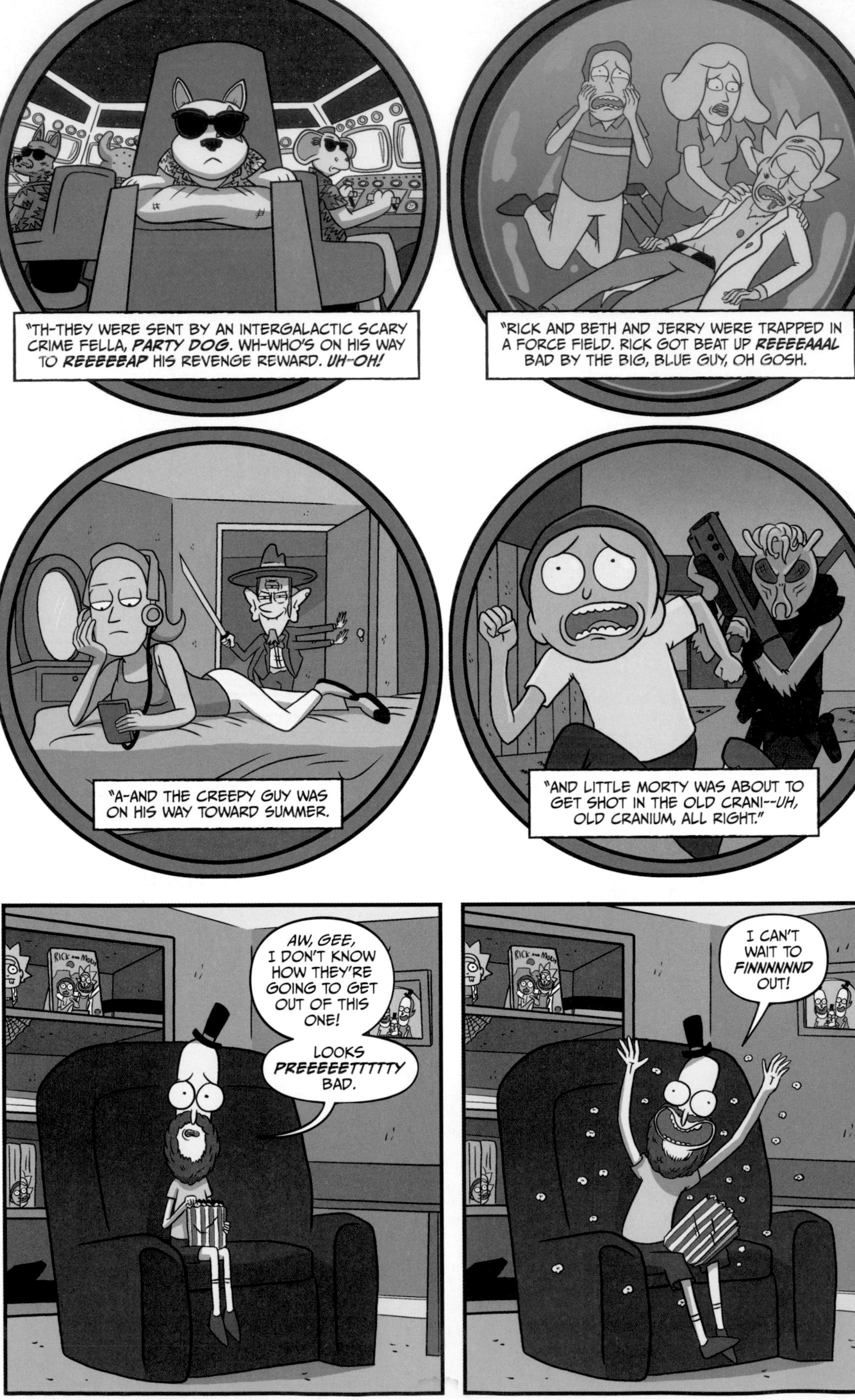

"TH-THEY WERE SENT BY AN INTERGALACTIC SCARY CRIME FELLA, PARTY DOG. WH-WHO'S ON HIS WAY TO REEEEEAP HIS REVENGE REWARD. UH-OH!
"RICK AND BETH AND JERRY WERE TRAPPED IN A FORCE FIELD. RICK GOT BEAT UP REEEEAAAL BAD BY THE BIG, BLUE GUY, OH GOSH.
"A-AND THE CREEPY GUY WAS ON HIS WAY TOWARD SUMMER.
"AND LITTLE MORTY WAS ABOUT TO GET SHOT IN THE OLD CRANI--UH, OLD CRANIUM, ALL RIGHT."
AW, GEE, I DON'T KNOW HOW THEY'RE GOING TO GET OUT OF THIS ONE!
LOOKS PREEEEETTTTTY BAD.
I CAN'T WAIT TO FINNNNNND OUT!

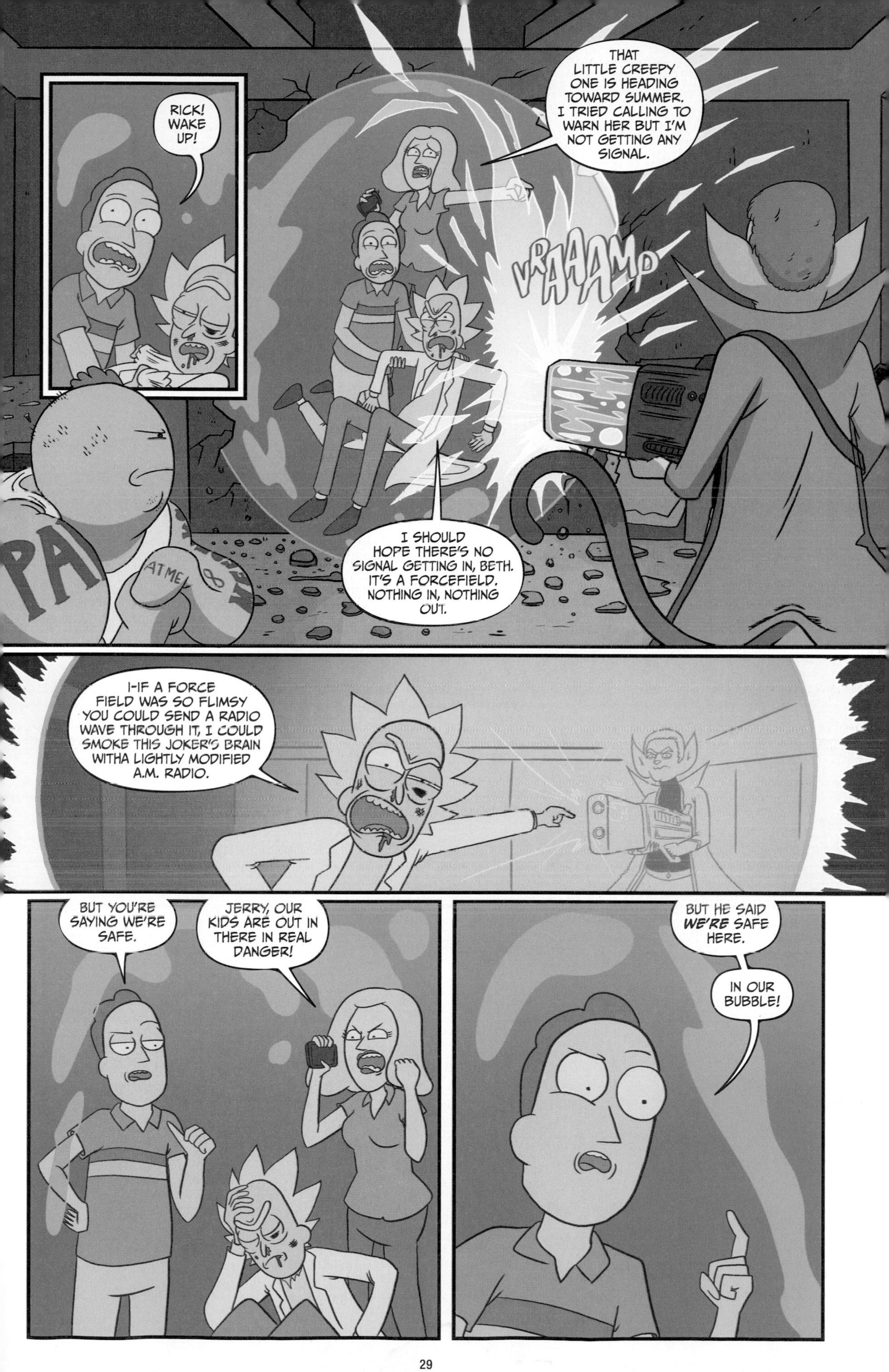
RICK! WAKE UP!
THAT LITTLE CREEPY ONE IS HEADING TOWARD SUMMER. I TRIED CALLING TO WARN HER BUT I'M NOT GETTING ANY SIGNAL.
VRAAAMP
I SHOULD HOPE THERE'S NO SIGNAL GETTING IN, BETH. IT'S A FORCEFIELD. NOTHING IN, NOTHING OUT.
I-IF A FORCE FIELD WAS SO FLIMSY YOU COULD SEND A RADIO WAVE THROUGH IT, I COULD SMOKE THIS JOKER'S BRAIN WITHA LIGHTLY MODIFIED A.M. RADIO.
BUT YOU'RE SAYING WE'RE SAFE.
JERRY, OUR KIDS ARE OUT IN THERE IN REAL DANGER!
BUT HE SAID *WE'RE* SAFE HERE.
IN OUR BUBBLE!

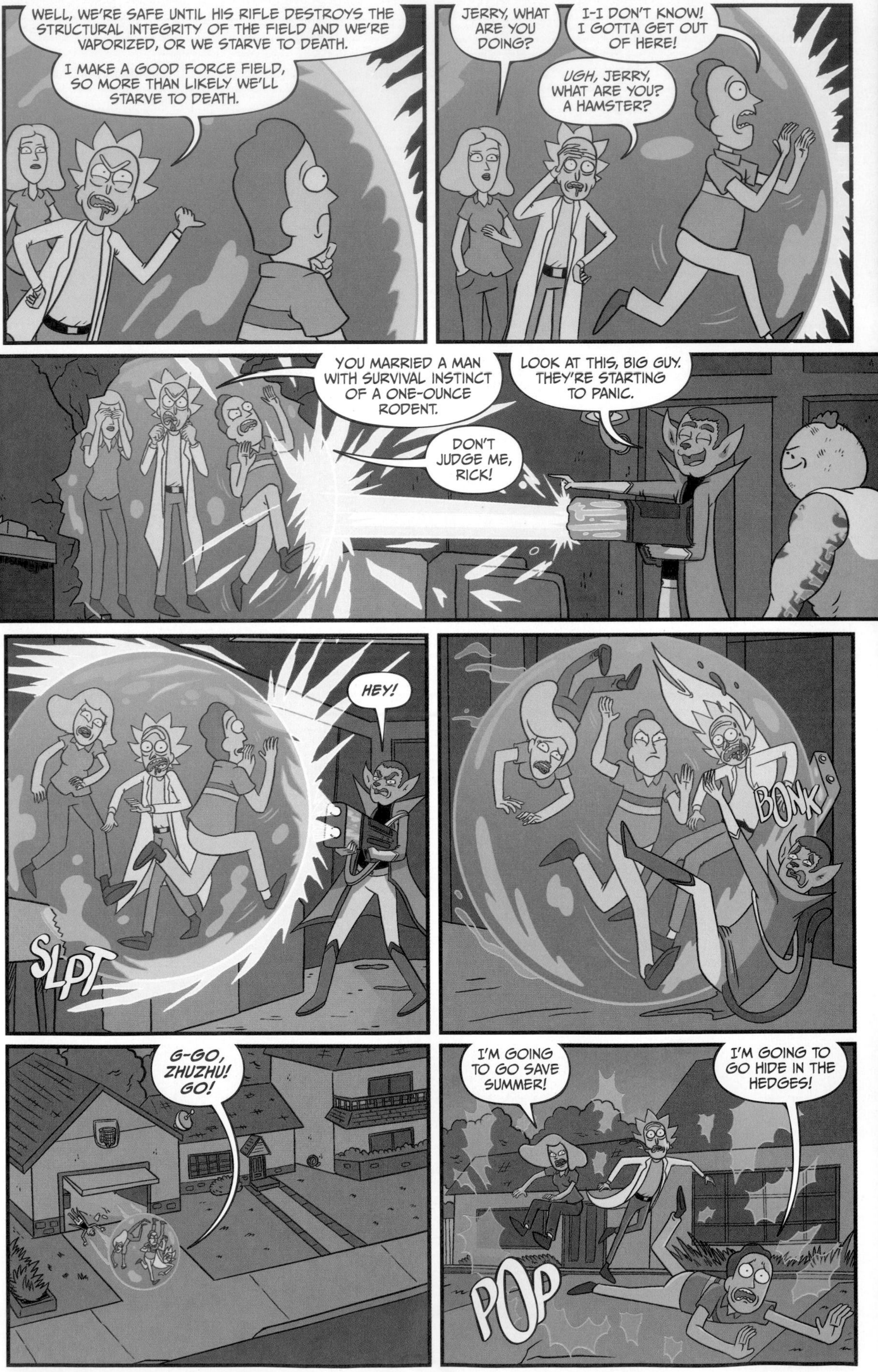
WELL, WE'RE SAFE UNTIL HIS RIFLE DESTROYS THE STRUCTURAL INTEGRITY OF THE FIELD AND WE'RE VAPORIZED, OR WE STARVE TO DEATH.
I MAKE A GOOD FORCE FIELD, SO MORE THAN LIKELY WE'LL STARVE TO DEATH.
JERRY, WHAT ARE YOU DOING?
I-I DON'T KNOW! I GOTTA GET OUT OF HERE!
UGH, JERRY, WHAT ARE YOU? A HAMSTER?
YOU MARRIED A MAN WITH SURVIVAL INSTINCT OF A ONE-OUNCE RODENT.
DON'T JUDGE ME, RICK!
LOOK AT THIS, BIG GUY. THEY'RE STARTING TO PANIC.
HEY!
SLPT
BONK
G-GO, ZHUZHU! GO!
I'M GOING TO GO SAVE SUMMER!
I'M GOING TO GO HIDE IN THE HEDGES!
POP

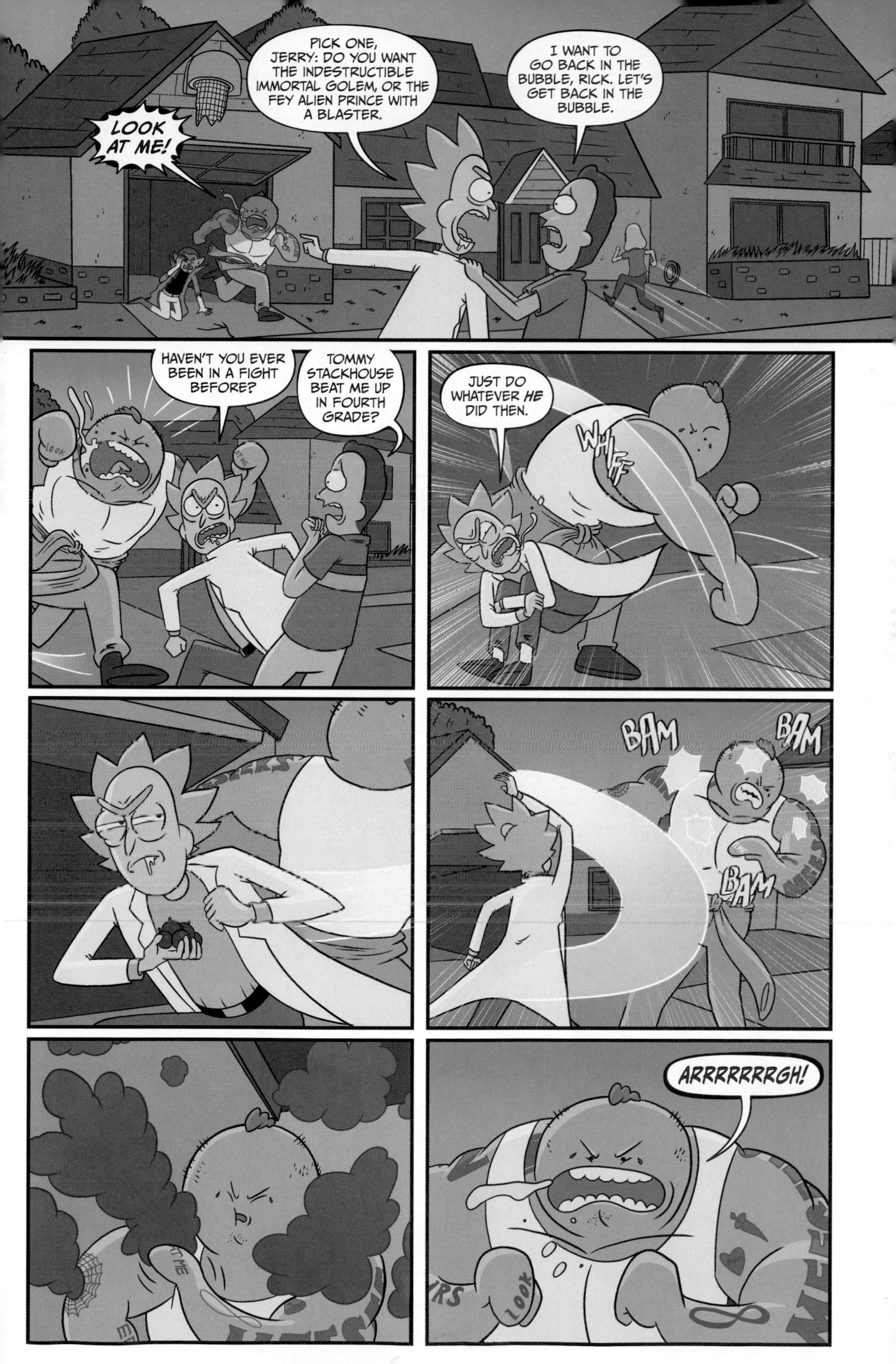
LOOK AT ME!
PICK ONE, JERRY: DO YOU WANT THE INDESTRUCTIBLE IMMORTAL GOLEM, OR THE FEY ALIEN PRINCE WITH A BLASTER.
I WANT TO GO BACK IN THE BUBBLE, RICK. LET'S GET BACK IN THE BUBBLE.
HAVEN'T YOU EVER BEEN IN A FIGHT BEFORE?
TOMMY STACKHOUSE BEAT ME UP IN FOURTH GRADE?
JUST DO WHATEVER *HE* DID THEN.
WHIFF
BAM
BAM
BAM
ARRRRRRRGH!

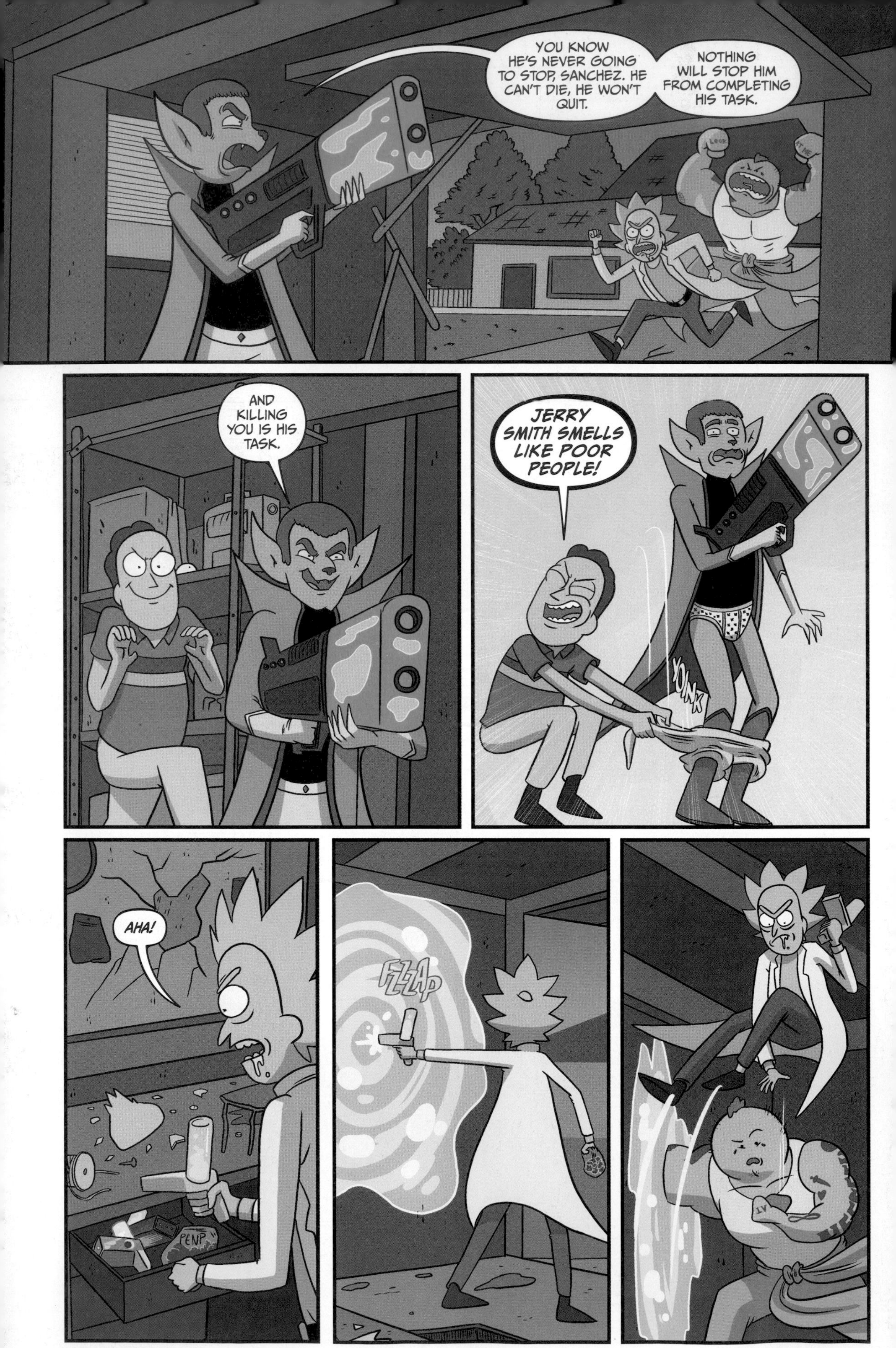
YOU KNOW HE'S NEVER GOING TO STOP, SANCHEZ. HE CAN'T DIE, HE WON'T QUIT.
NOTHING WILL STOP HIM FROM COMPLETING HIS TASK.
AND KILLING YOU IS HIS TASK.
JERRY SMITH SMELLS LIKE POOR PEOPLE!
YOINK
AHA!
FZZZAP

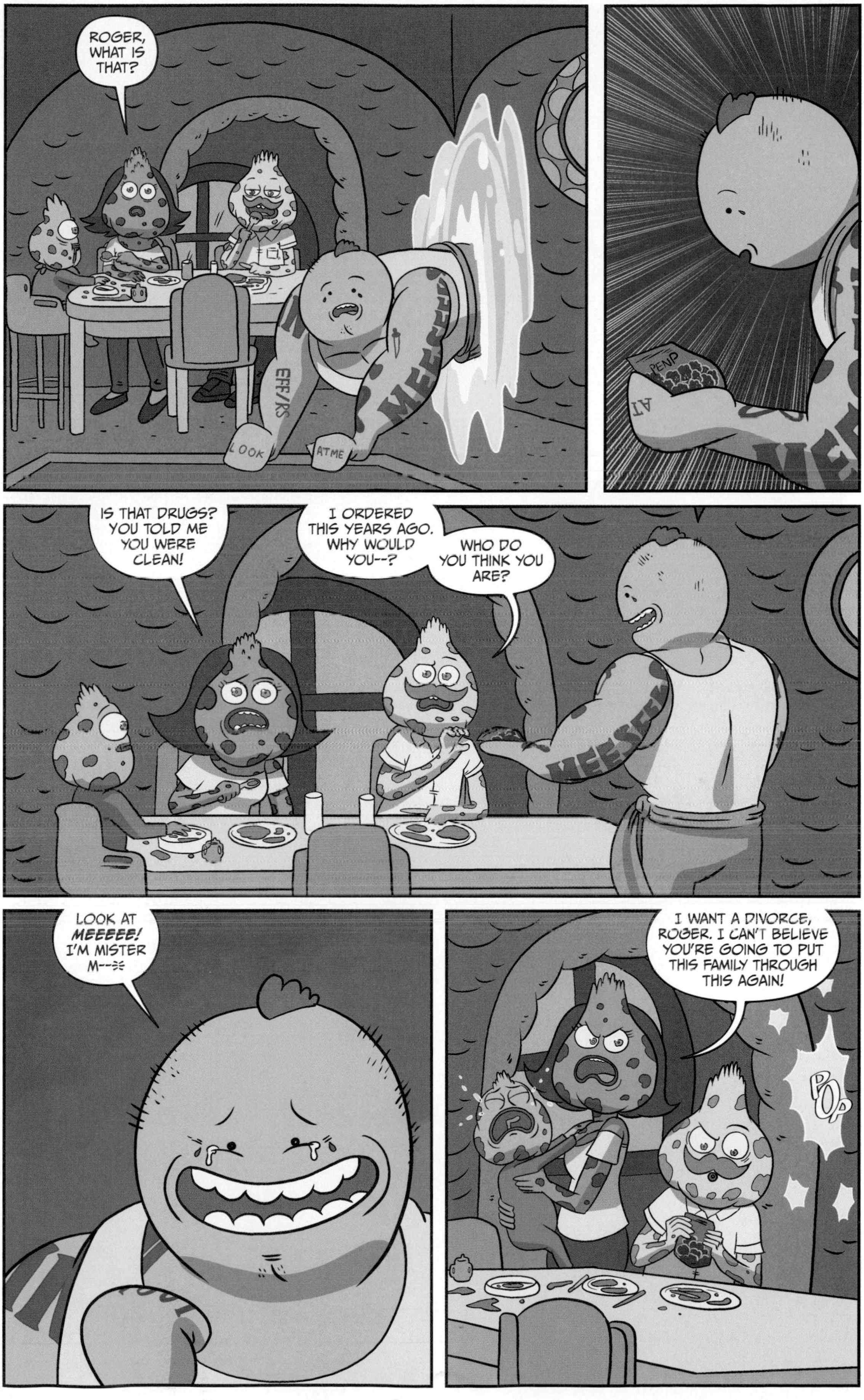

ROGER, WHAT IS THAT?
IS THAT DRUGS? YOU TOLD ME YOU WERE CLEAN!
I ORDERED THIS YEARS AGO. WHY WOULD YOU--?
WHO DO YOU THINK YOU ARE?
LOOK AT MEEEEE! I'M MISTER M--
I WANT A DIVORCE, ROGER. I CAN'T BELIEVE YOU'RE GOING TO PUT THIS FAMILY THROUGH THIS AGAIN!
POP

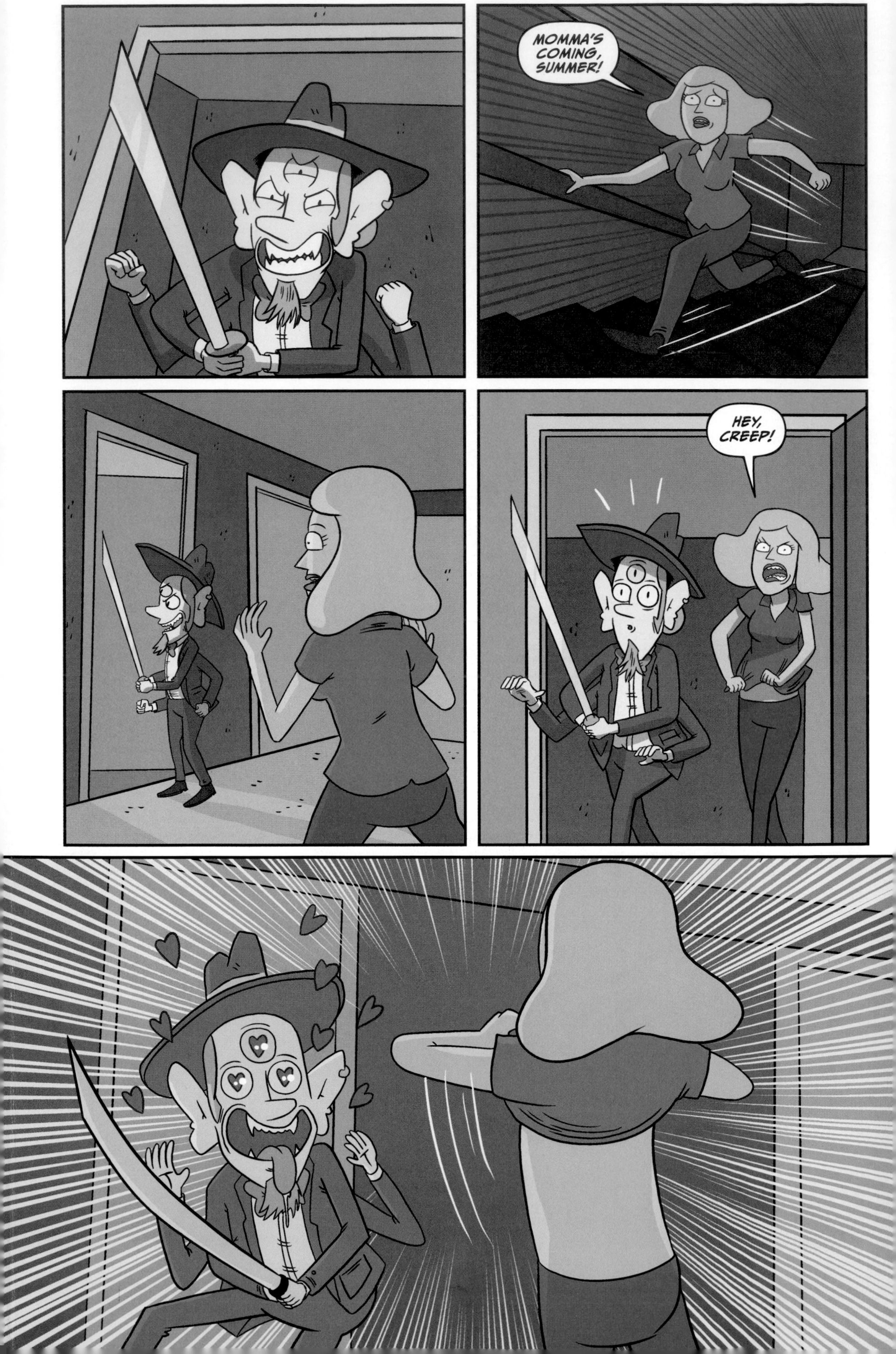
MOMMA'S COMING, SUMMER!
HEY, CREEP!

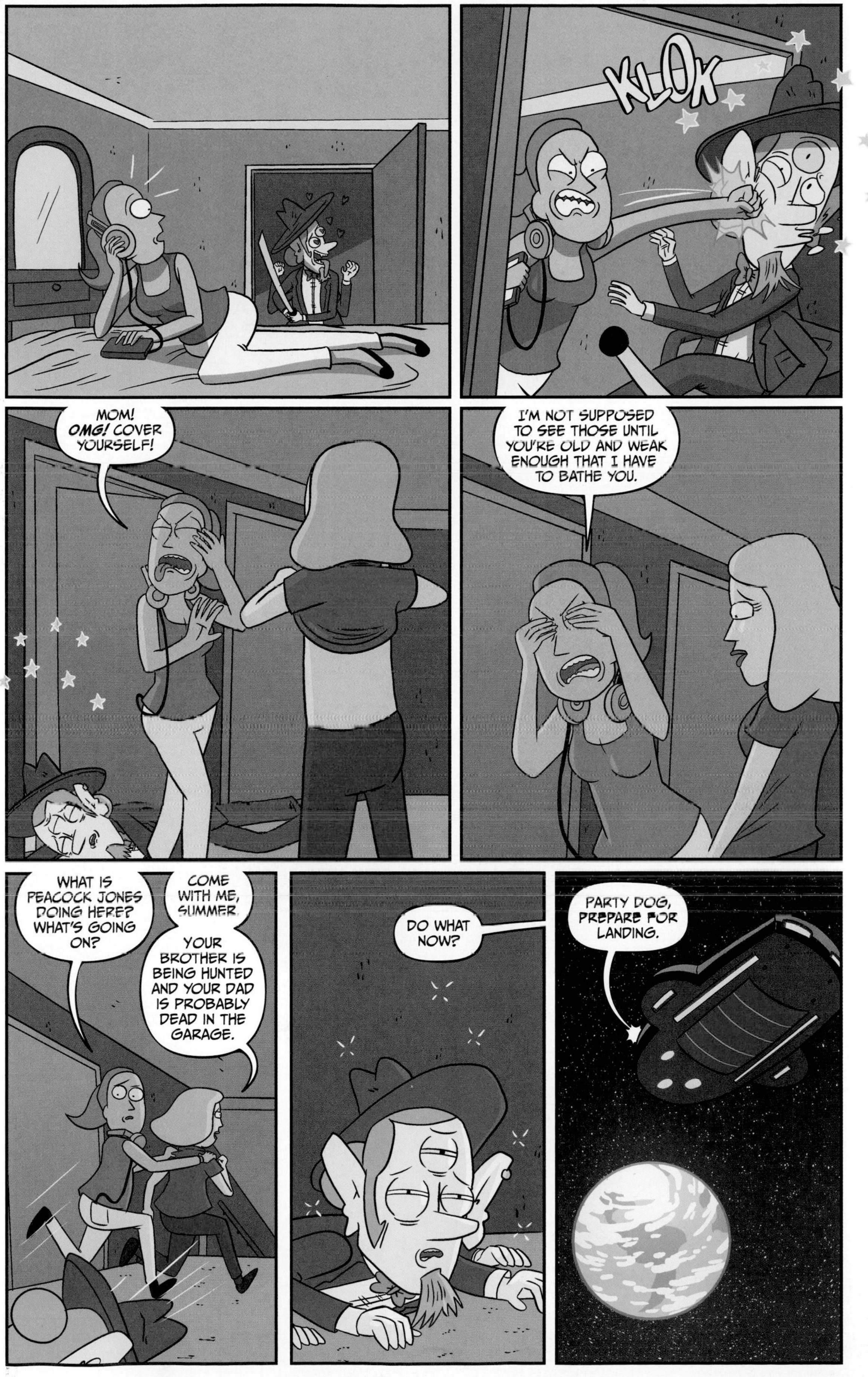
KLOK
MOM! OMG! COVER YOURSELF!
I'M NOT SUPPOSED TO SEE THOSE UNTIL YOU'RE OLD AND WEAK ENOUGH THAT I HAVE TO BATHE YOU.
WHAT IS PEACOCK JONES DOING HERE? WHAT'S GOING ON?
COME WITH ME, SUMMER.
YOUR BROTHER IS BEING HUNTED AND YOUR DAD IS PROBABLY DEAD IN THE GARAGE.
DO WHAT NOW?
PARTY DOG, PREPARE FOR LANDING.

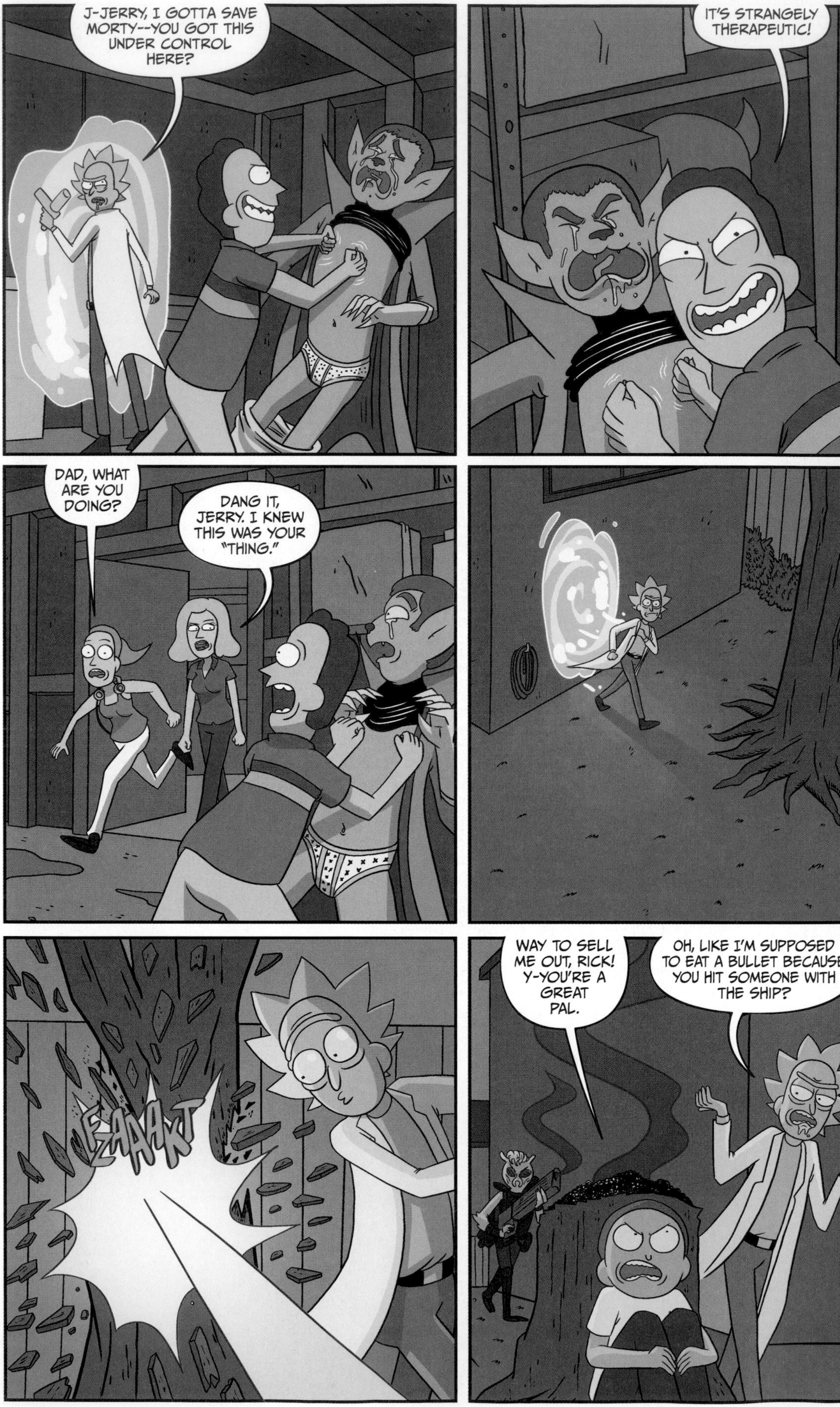
J-JERRY, I GOTTA SAVE MORTY--YOU GOT THIS UNDER CONTROL HERE?
IT'S STRANGELY THERAPEUTIC!
DAD, WHAT ARE YOU DOING?
DANG IT, JERRY. I KNEW THIS WAS YOUR "THING."
FZAAAKT
WAY TO SELL ME OUT, RICK! Y-YOU'RE A GREAT PAL.
OH, LIKE I'M SUPPOSED TO EAT A BULLET BECAUSE YOU HIT SOMEONE WITH THE SHIP?

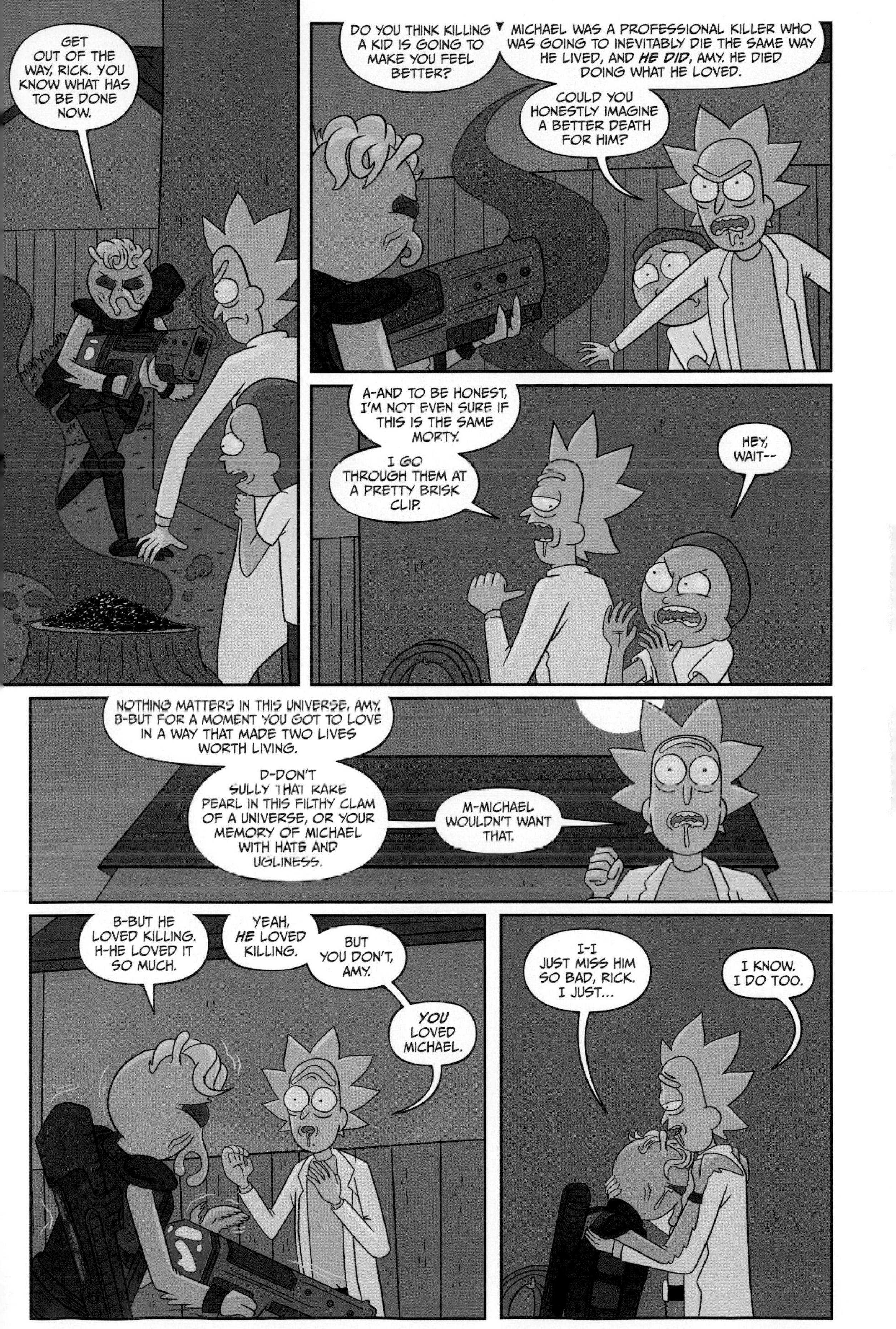
GET OUT OF THE WAY, RICK. YOU KNOW WHAT HAS TO BE DONE NOW.
DO YOU THINK KILLING A KID IS GOING TO MAKE YOU FEEL BETTER?
MICHAEL WAS A PROFESSIONAL KILLER WHO WAS GOING TO INEVITABLY DIE THE SAME WAY HE LIVED, AND HE DID, AMY. HE DIED DOING WHAT HE LOVED.
COULD YOU HONESTLY IMAGINE A BETTER DEATH FOR HIM?
A-AND TO BE HONEST, I'M NOT EVEN SURE IF THIS IS THE SAME MORTY.
I GO THROUGH THEM AT A PRETTY BRISK CLIP.
HEY, WAIT--
NOTHING MATTERS IN THIS UNIVERSE, AMY. B-BUT FOR A MOMENT YOU GOT TO LOVE IN A WAY THAT MADE TWO LIVES WORTH LIVING.
D-DON'T SULLY THAT RARE PEARL IN THIS FILTHY CLAM OF A UNIVERSE, OR YOUR MEMORY OF MICHAEL WITH HATE AND UGLINESS.
M-MICHAEL WOULDN'T WANT THAT.
B-BUT HE LOVED KILLING. H-HE LOVED IT SO MUCH.
YEAH, HE LOVED KILLING.
BUT YOU DON'T, AMY.
YOU LOVED MICHAEL.
I-I JUST MISS HIM SO BAD, RICK. I JUST...
I KNOW. I DO TOO.

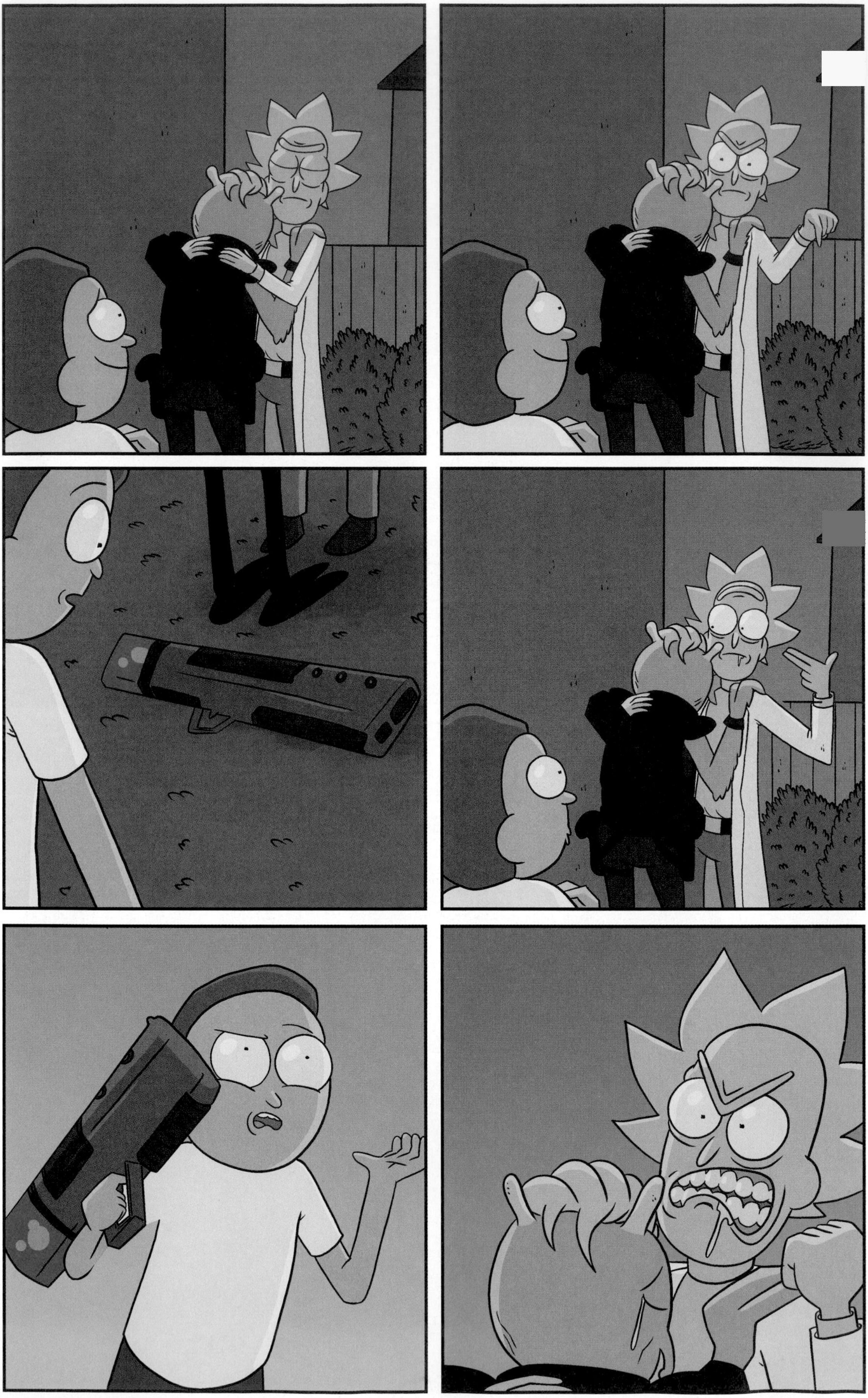

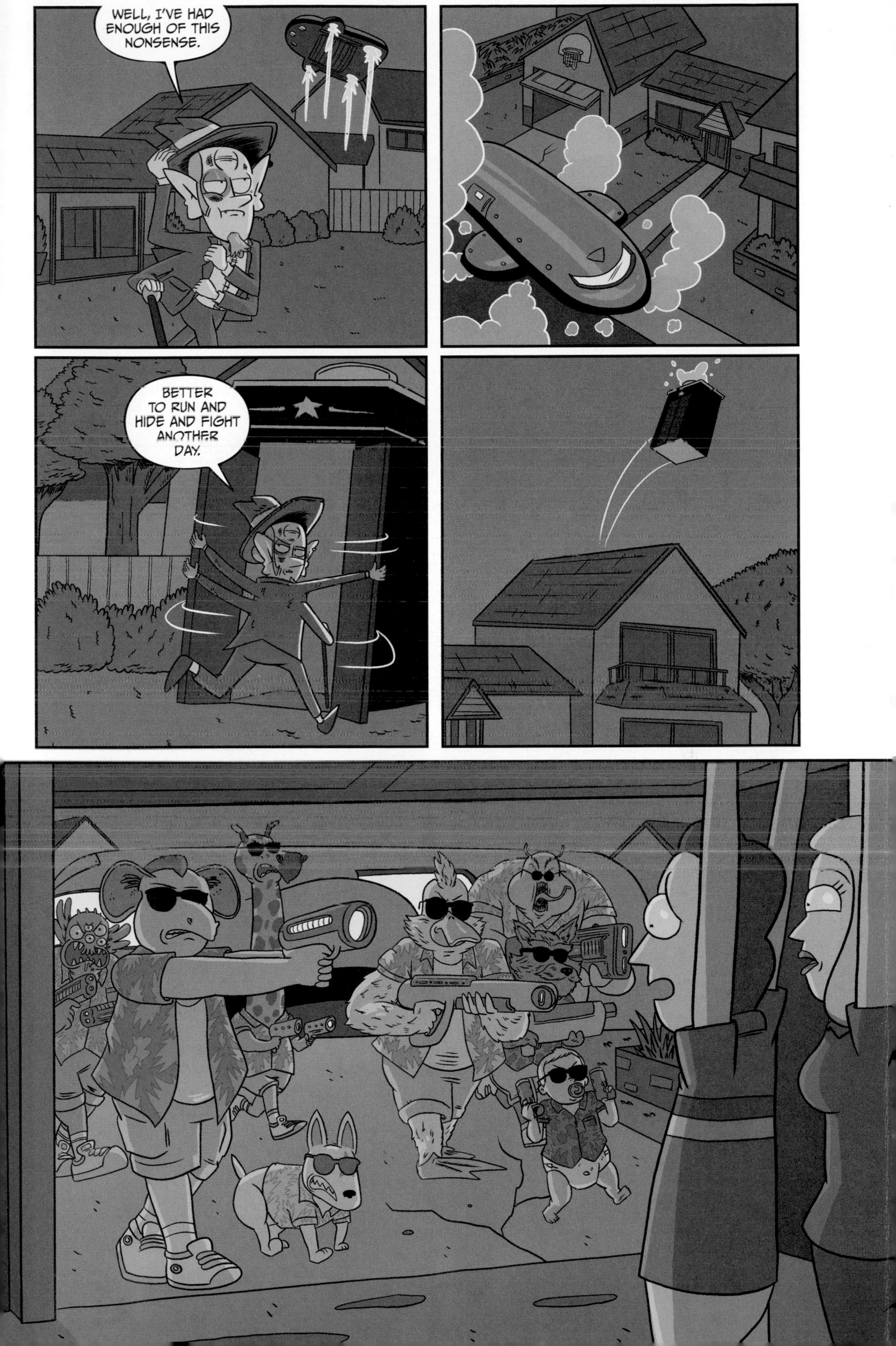
WELL, I'VE HAD ENOUGH OF THIS NONSENSE.
BETTER TO RUN AND HIDE AND FIGHT ANOTHER DAY.

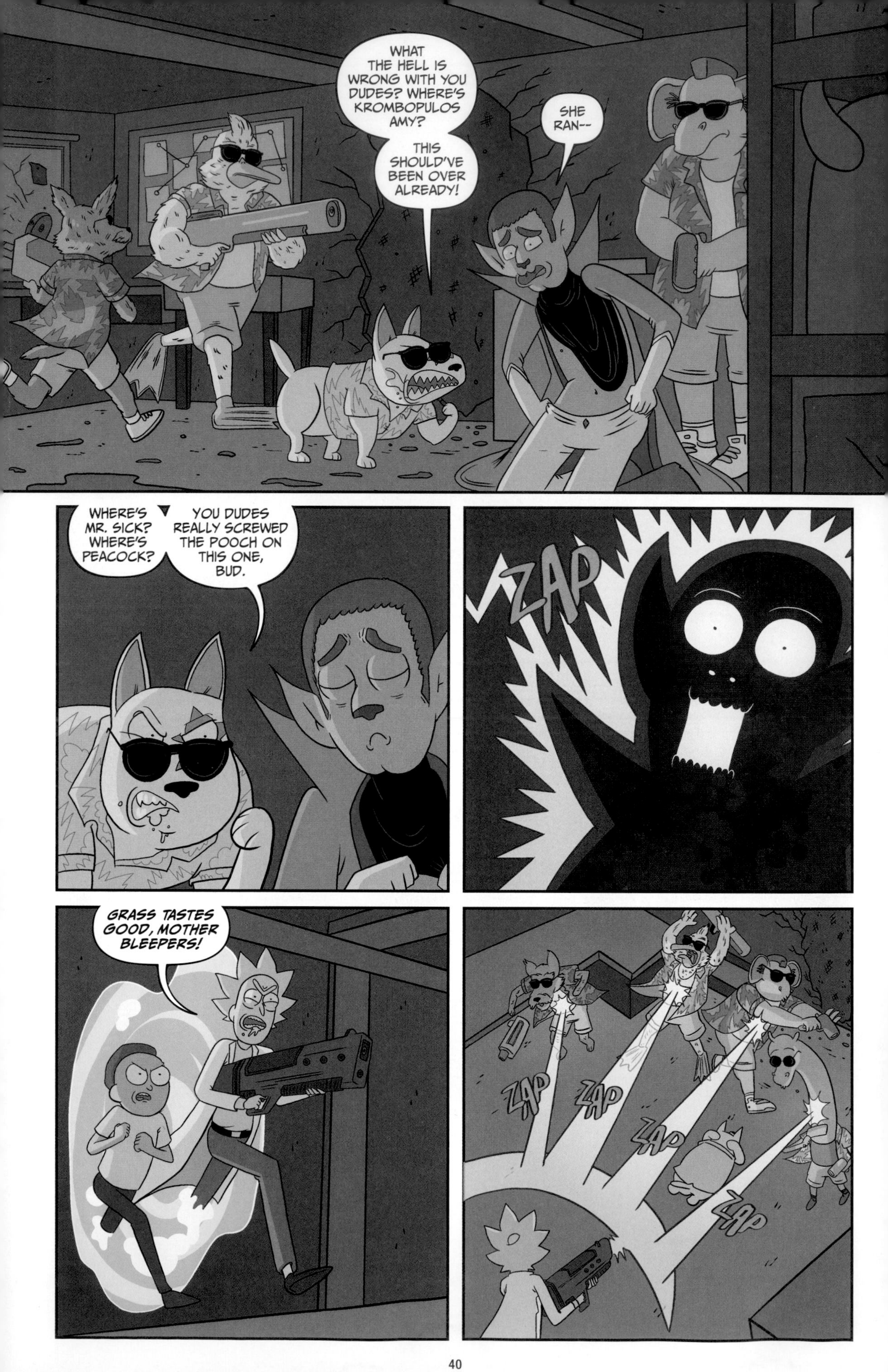
WHAT THE HELL IS WRONG WITH YOU DUDES? WHERE'S KROMBOPULOS AMY?
THIS SHOULD'VE BEEN OVER ALREADY!
SHE RAN--
WHERE'S MR. SICK? WHERE'S PEACOCK?
YOU DUDES REALLY SCREWED THE POOCH ON THIS ONE, BUD.
ZAP
GRASS TASTES GOOD, MOTHER BLEEPERS!
ZAP
ZAP
ZAP
ZAP

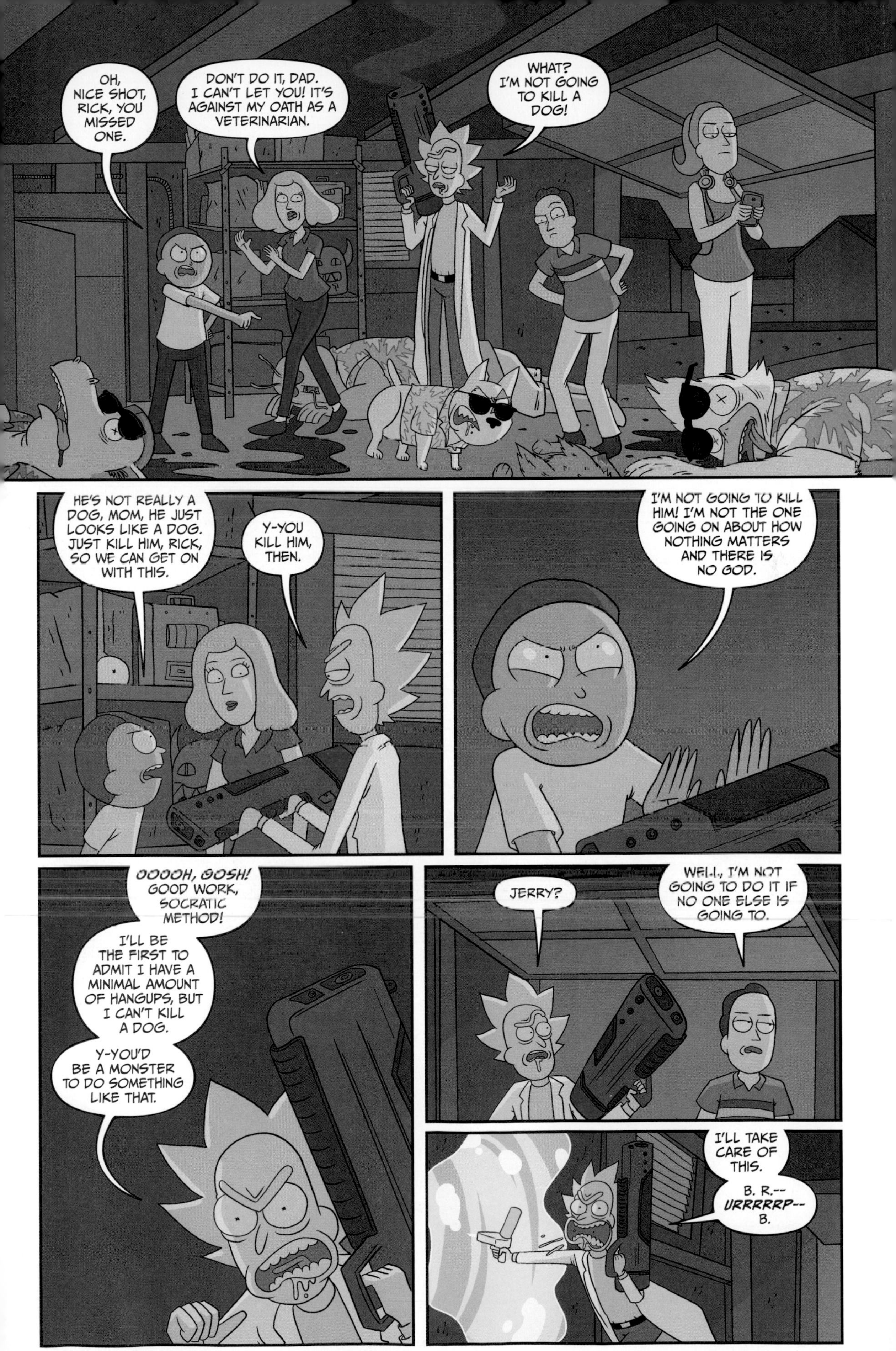

OH, NICE SHOT, RICK, YOU MISSED ONE.
DON'T DO IT, DAD. I CAN'T LET YOU! IT'S AGAINST MY OATH AS A VETERINARIAN.
WHAT? I'M NOT GOING TO KILL A DOG!
HE'S NOT REALLY A DOG, MOM, HE JUST LOOKS LIKE A DOG. JUST KILL HIM, RICK, SO WE CAN GET ON WITH THIS.
Y-YOU KILL HIM, THEN.
I'M NOT GOING TO KILL HIM! I'M NOT THE ONE GOING ON ABOUT HOW NOTHING MATTERS AND THERE IS NO GOD.
OOOOH, GOSH! GOOD WORK, SOCRATIC METHOD!
I'LL BE THE FIRST TO ADMIT I HAVE A MINIMAL AMOUNT OF HANGUPS, BUT I CAN'T KILL A DOG.
Y-YOU'D BE A MONSTER TO DO SOMETHING LIKE THAT.
JERRY?
WELL, I'M NOT GOING TO DO IT IF NO ONE ELSE IS GOING TO.
I'LL TAKE CARE OF THIS.
B. R.-- URRRRRP-- B.

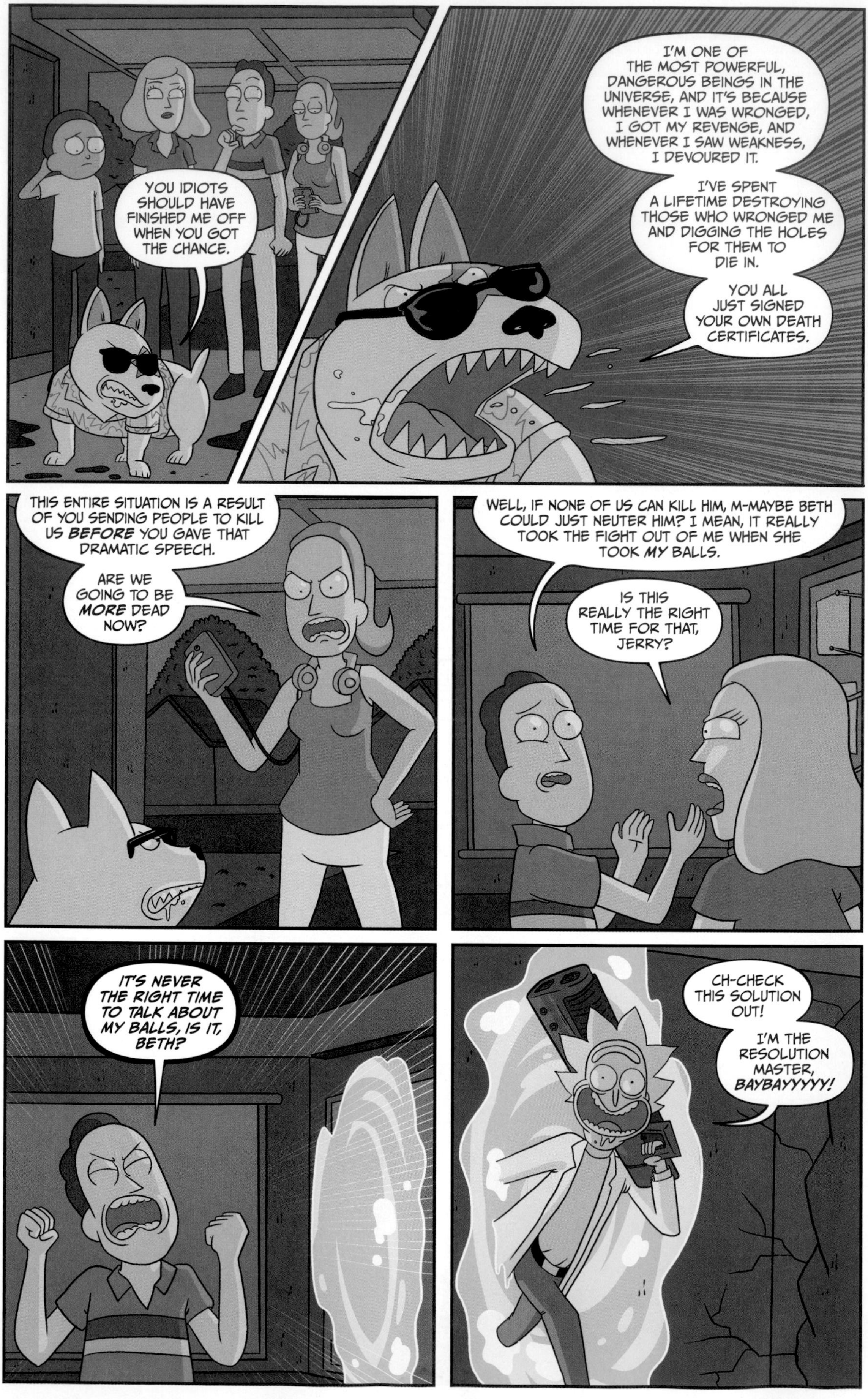
YOU IDIOTS SHOULD HAVE FINISHED ME OFF WHEN YOU GOT THE CHANCE.
I'M ONE OF THE MOST POWERFUL, DANGEROUS BEINGS IN THE UNIVERSE, AND IT'S BECAUSE WHENEVER I WAS WRONGED, I GOT MY REVENGE, AND WHENEVER I SAW WEAKNESS, I DEVOURED IT.
I'VE SPENT A LIFETIME DESTROYING THOSE WHO WRONGED ME AND DIGGING THE HOLES FOR THEM TO DIE IN.
YOU ALL JUST SIGNED YOUR OWN DEATH CERTIFICATES.
THIS ENTIRE SITUATION IS A RESULT OF YOU SENDING PEOPLE TO KILL US *BEFORE* YOU GAVE THAT DRAMATIC SPEECH.
ARE WE GOING TO BE *MORE* DEAD NOW?
WELL, IF NONE OF US CAN KILL HIM, M-MAYBE BETH COULD JUST NEUTER HIM? I MEAN, IT REALLY TOOK THE FIGHT OUT OF ME WHEN SHE TOOK *MY* BALLS.
IS THIS REALLY THE RIGHT TIME FOR THAT, JERRY?
IT'S NEVER THE RIGHT TIME TO TALK ABOUT MY BALLS, IS IT, BETH?
CH-CHECK THIS SOLUTION OUT!
I'M THE RESOLUTION MASTER, *BAYBAYYYYY!*

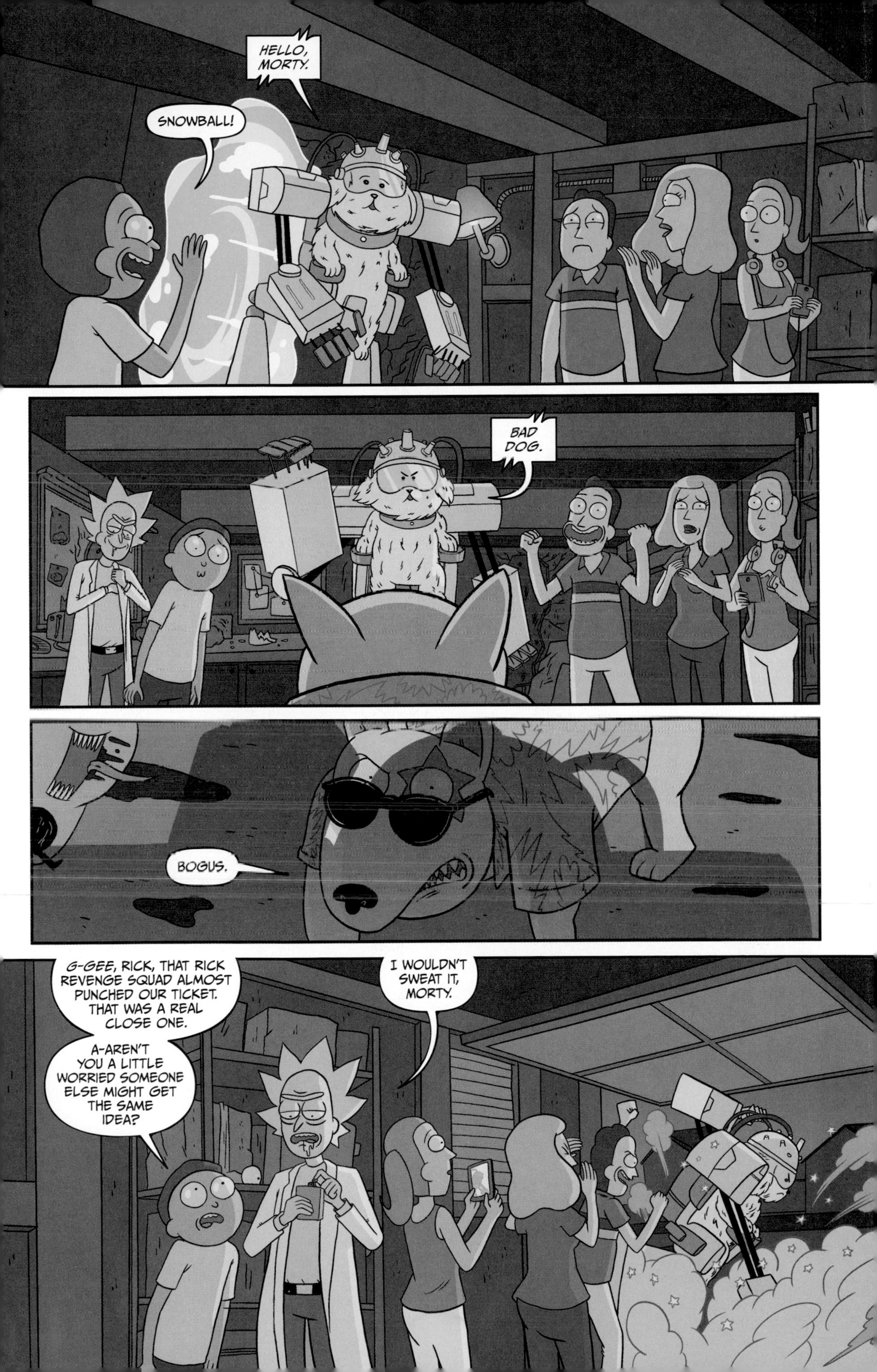

HELLO, MORTY.
SNOWBALL!
BAD DOG.
BOGUS.
G-GEE, RICK, THAT RICK REVENGE SQUAD ALMOST PUNCHED OUR TICKET. THAT WAS A REAL CLOSE ONE.
A-AREN'T YOU A LITTLE WORRIED SOMEONE ELSE MIGHT GET THE SAME IDEA?
I WOULDN'T SWEAT IT, MORTY.

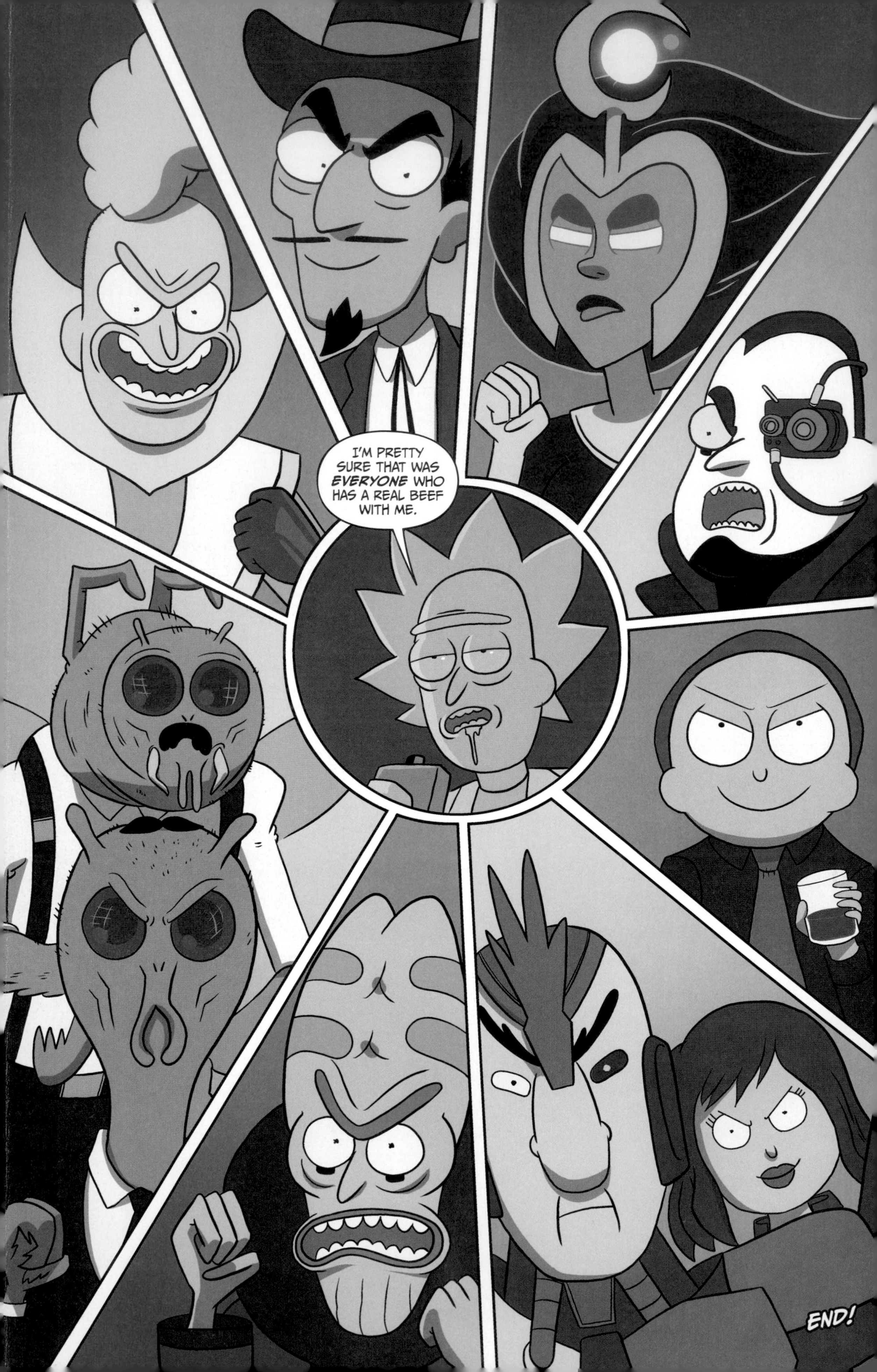
I'M PRETTY SURE THAT WAS EVERYONE WHO HAS A REAL BEEF WITH ME.
END!

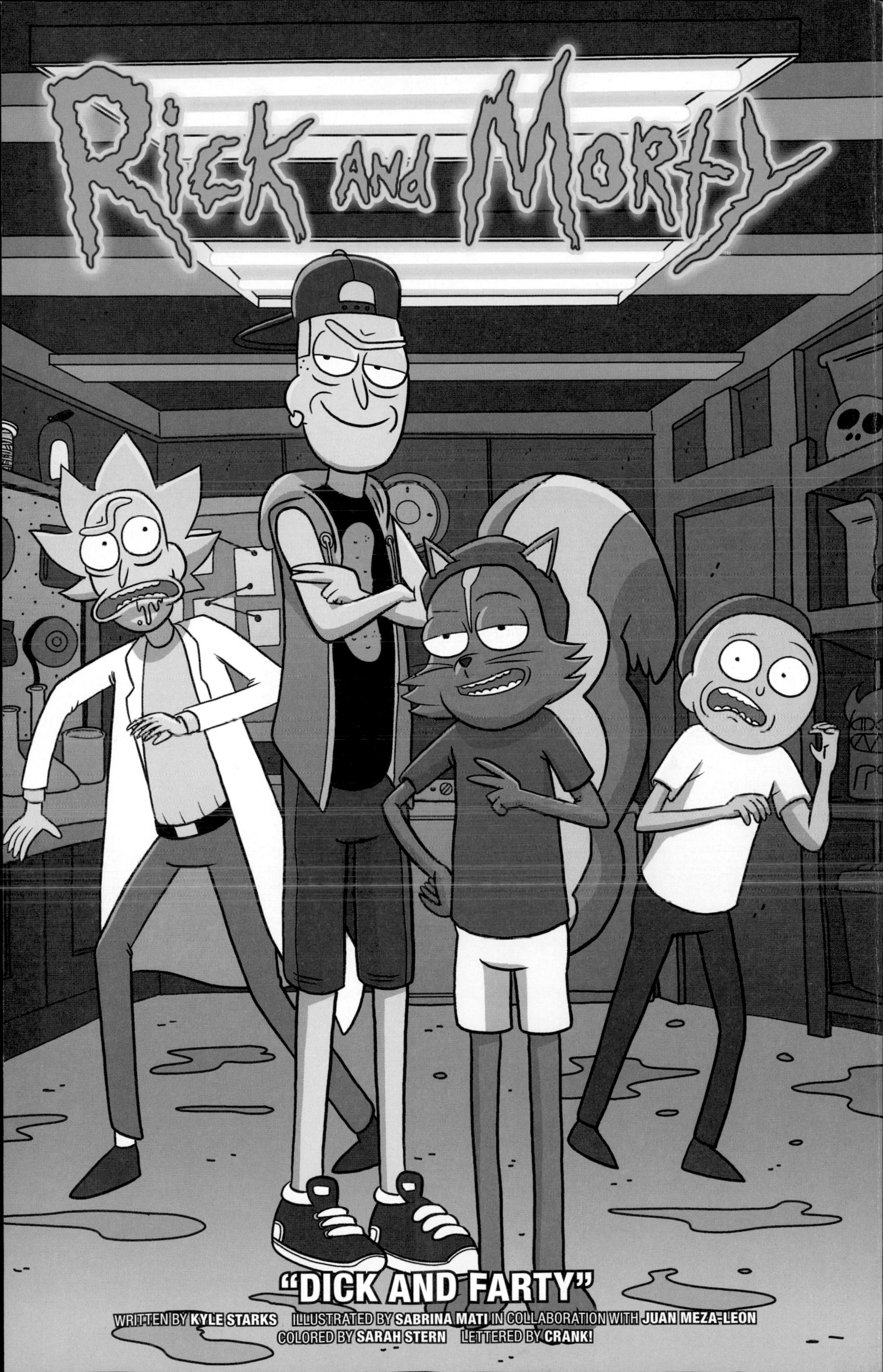
Rick and Morty

"DICK AND FARTY"

WRITTEN BY **KYLE STARKS** ILLUSTRATED BY **SABRINA MATI** IN COLLABORATION WITH **JUAN MEZA-LEON**
COLORED BY **SARAH STERN** LETTERED BY **CRANK!**

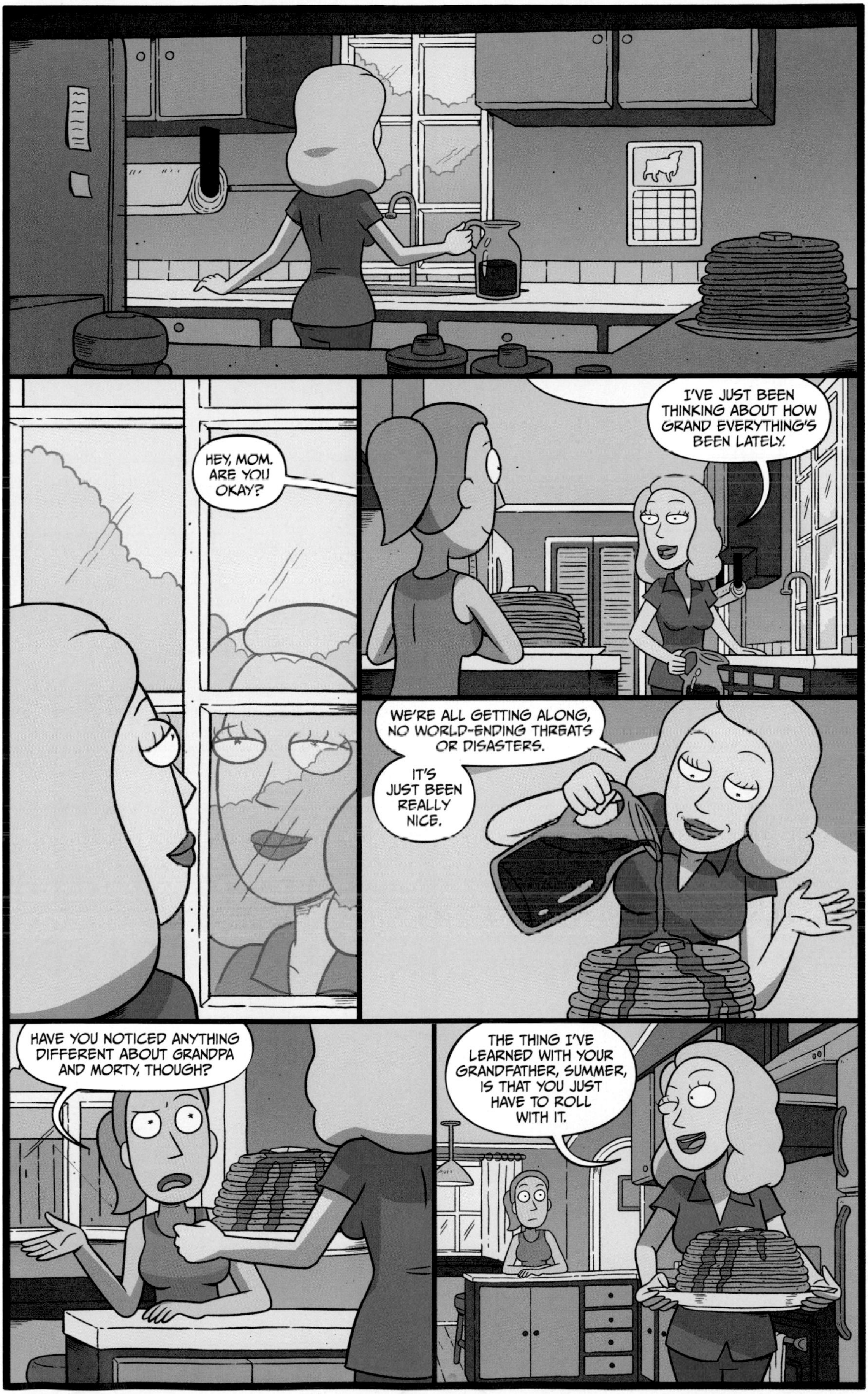
HEY, MOM. ARE YOU OKAY?
I'VE JUST BEEN THINKING ABOUT HOW GRAND EVERYTHING'S BEEN LATELY.
WE'RE ALL GETTING ALONG, NO WORLD-ENDING THREATS OR DISASTERS.
IT'S JUST BEEN REALLY NICE.
HAVE YOU NOTICED ANYTHING DIFFERENT ABOUT GRANDPA AND MORTY, THOUGH?
THE THING I'VE LEARNED WITH YOUR GRANDFATHER, SUMMER, IS THAT YOU JUST HAVE TO ROLL WITH IT.

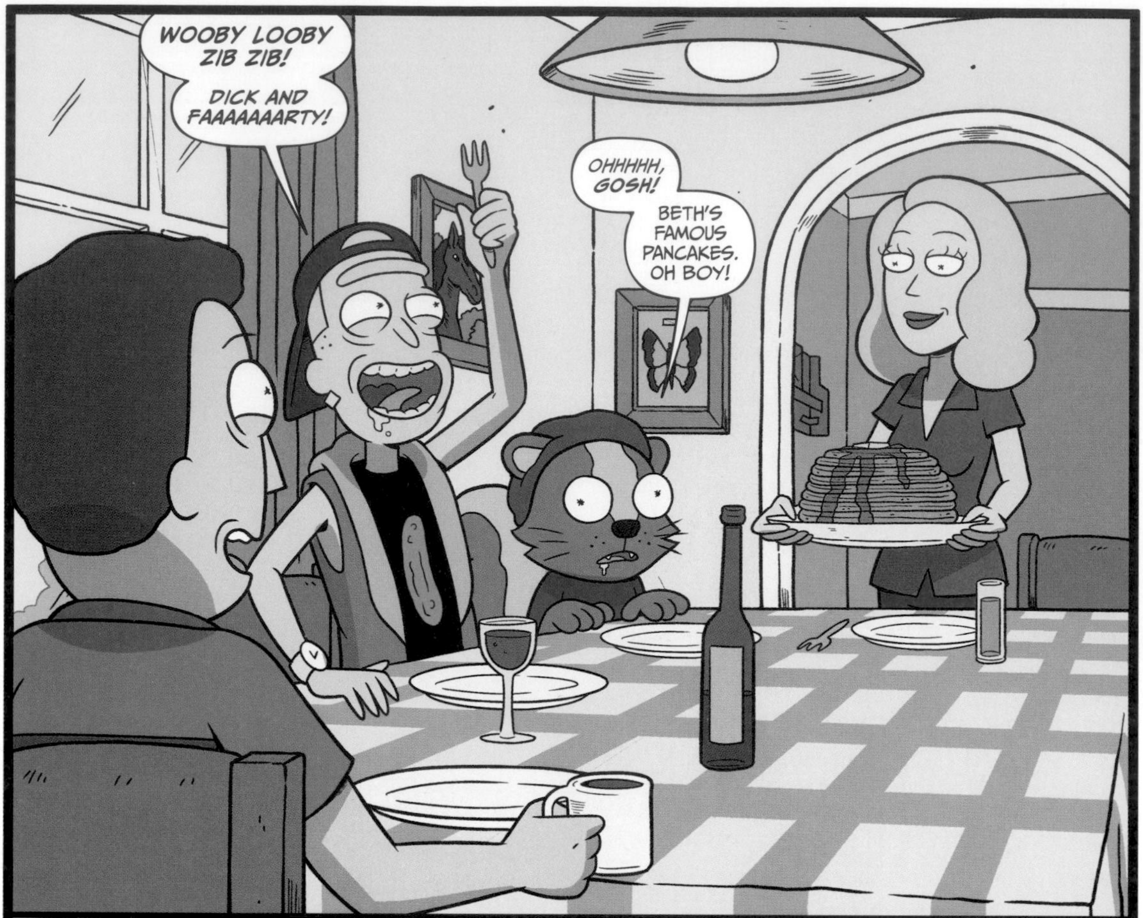
WOOBY LOOBY ZIB ZIB!
DICK AND FAAAAAAAARTY!
OHHHHH, GOSH!
BETH'S FAMOUS PANCAKES. OH BOY!
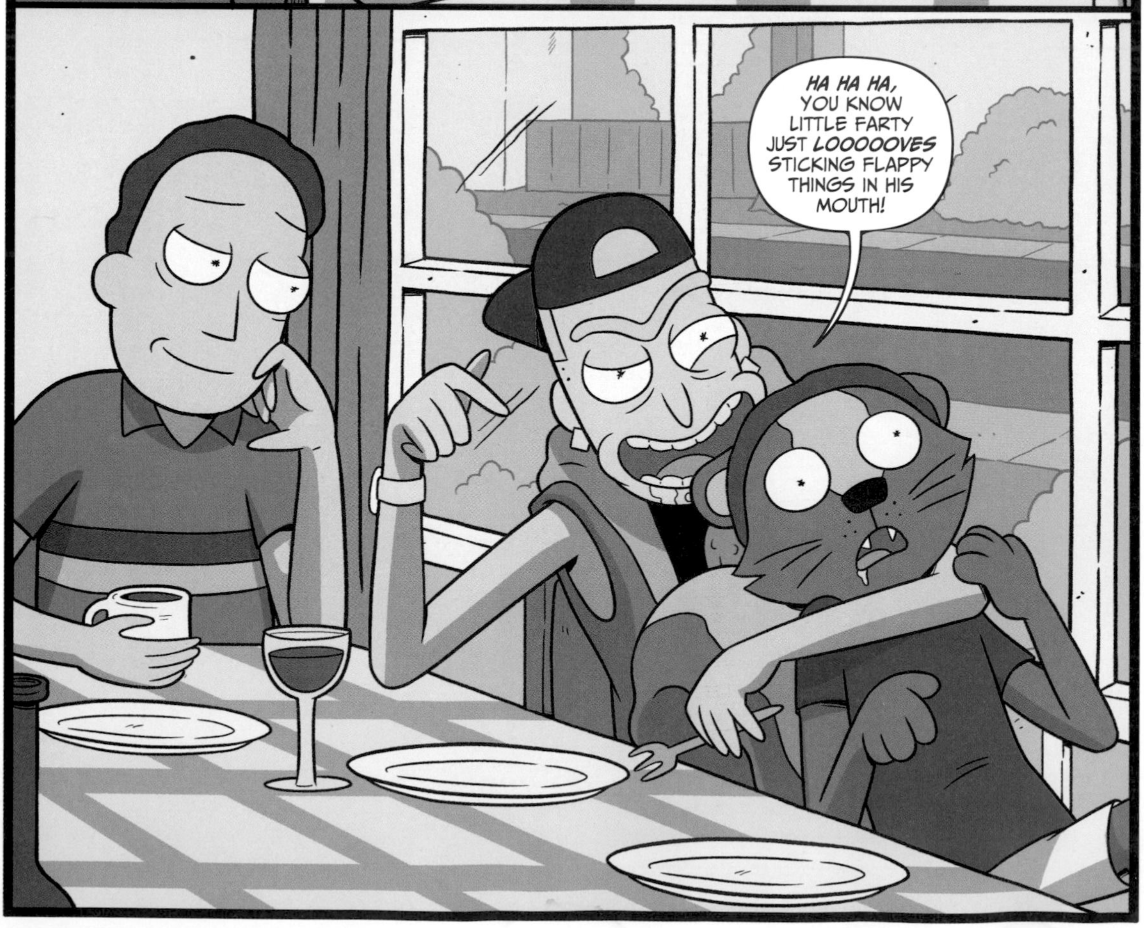
HA HA HA, YOU KNOW LITTLE FARTY JUST LOOOOOVES STICKING FLAPPY THINGS IN HIS MOUTH!

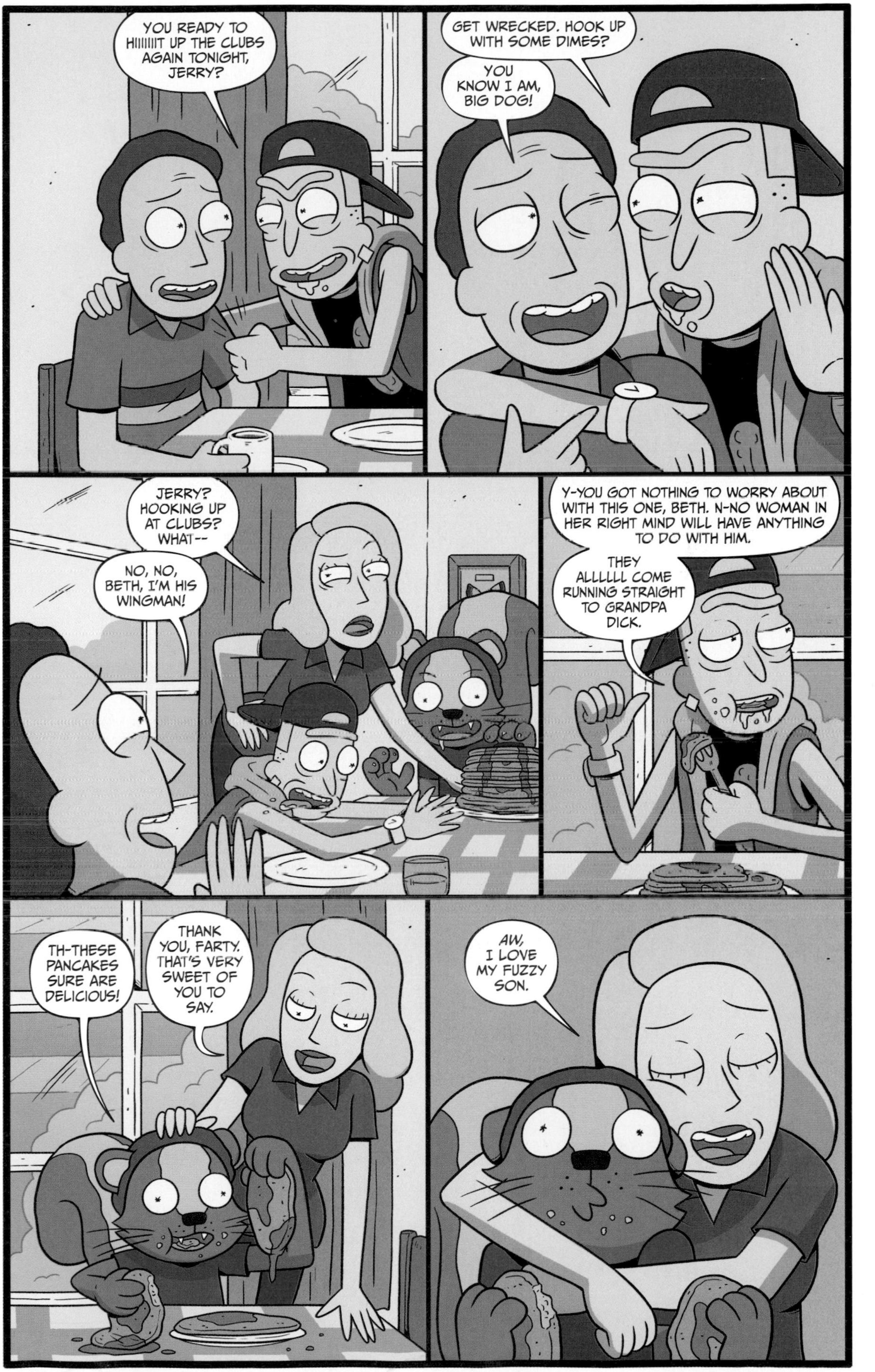
YOU READY TO HIIIIIIT UP THE CLUBS AGAIN TONIGHT, JERRY?
YOU KNOW I AM, BIG DOG!
GET WRECKED. HOOK UP WITH SOME DIMES?
JERRY? HOOKING UP AT CLUBS? WHAT--
NO, NO, BETH, I'M HIS WINGMAN!
Y-YOU GOT NOTHING TO WORRY ABOUT WITH THIS ONE, BETH. N-NO WOMAN IN HER RIGHT MIND WILL HAVE ANYTHING TO DO WITH HIM.
THEY ALLLLLL COME RUNNING STRAIGHT TO GRANDPA DICK.
TH-THESE PANCAKES SURE ARE DELICIOUS!
THANK YOU, FARTY. THAT'S VERY SWEET OF YOU TO SAY.
AW, I LOVE MY FUZZY SON.

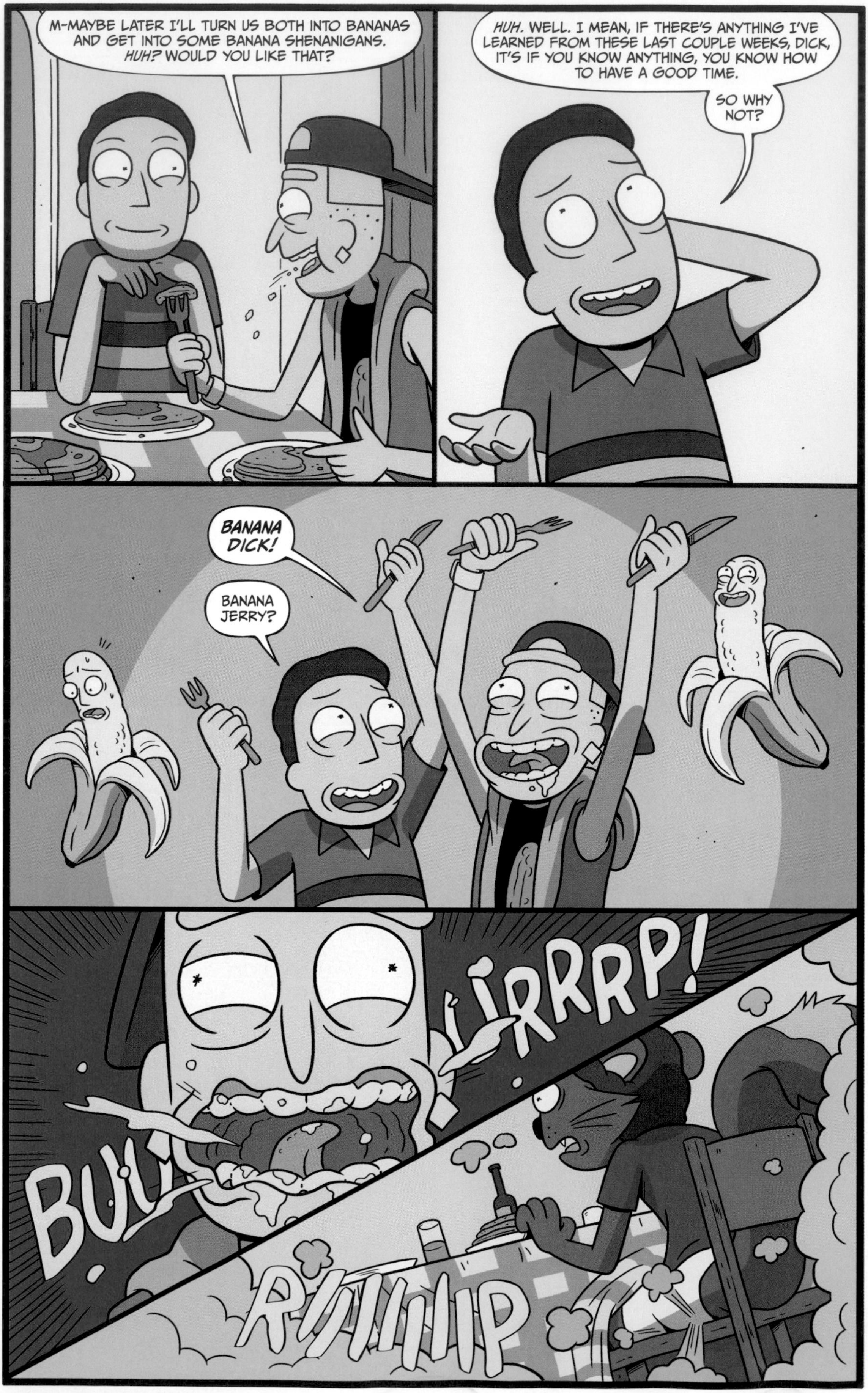
M-MAYBE LATER I'LL TURN US BOTH INTO BANANAS AND GET INTO SOME BANANA SHENANIGANS. *HUH?* WOULD YOU LIKE THAT?
HUH. WELL. I MEAN, IF THERE'S ANYTHING I'VE LEARNED FROM THESE LAST COUPLE WEEKS, DICK, IT'S IF YOU KNOW ANYTHING, YOU KNOW HOW TO HAVE A GOOD TIME.
SO WHY NOT?
BANANA DICK!
BANANA JERRY?
BUU
URRRP!
RUUUUUP

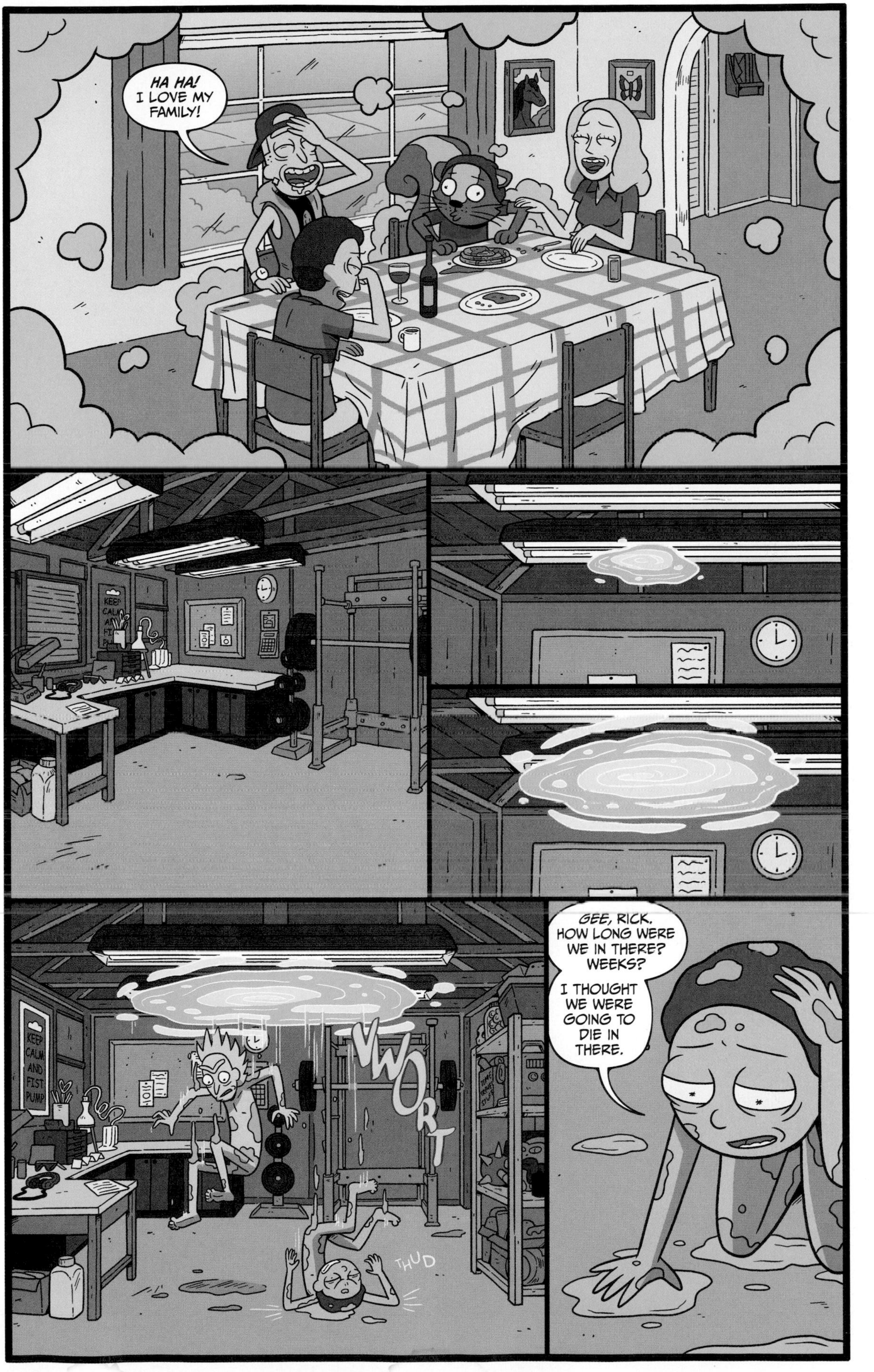
HA HA! I LOVE MY FAMILY!
KEEP CALM AND FIST PUMP
VWORT
THUD
GEE, RICK. HOW LONG WERE WE IN THERE? WEEKS?
I THOUGHT WE WERE GOING TO DIE IN THERE.

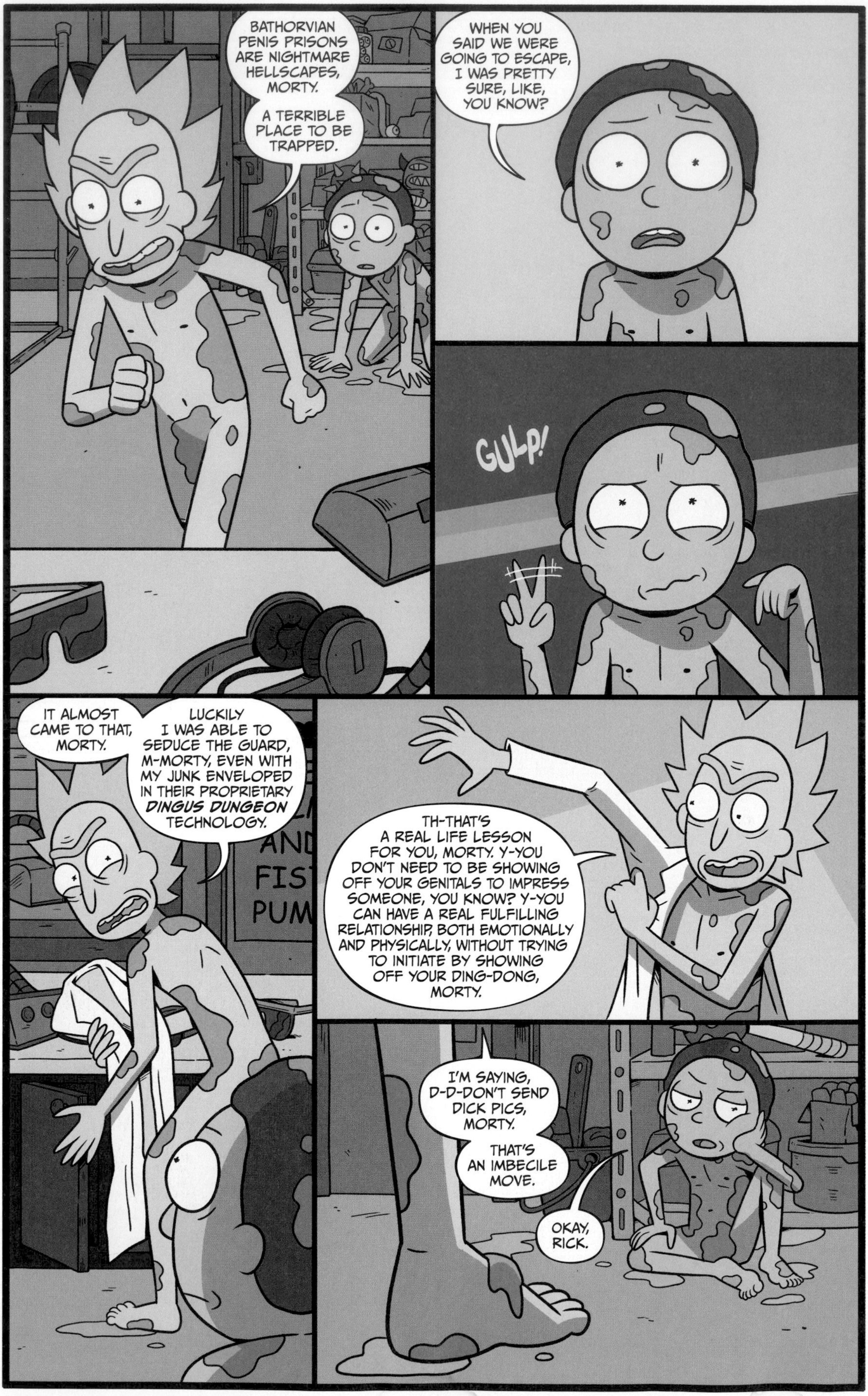
BATHORVIAN PENIS PRISONS ARE NIGHTMARE HELLSCAPES, MORTY.
A TERRIBLE PLACE TO BE TRAPPED.
WHEN YOU SAID WE WERE GOING TO ESCAPE, I WAS PRETTY SURE, LIKE, YOU KNOW?
GULP!
IT ALMOST CAME TO THAT, MORTY.
LUCKILY I WAS ABLE TO SEDUCE THE GUARD, M-MORTY, EVEN WITH MY JUNK ENVELOPED IN THEIR PROPRIETARY DINGUS DUNGEON TECHNOLOGY.
TH-THAT'S A REAL LIFE LESSON FOR YOU, MORTY. Y-YOU DON'T NEED TO BE SHOWING OFF YOUR GENITALS TO IMPRESS SOMEONE, YOU KNOW? Y-YOU CAN HAVE A REAL FULFILLING RELATIONSHIP, BOTH EMOTIONALLY AND PHYSICALLY, WITHOUT TRYING TO INITIATE BY SHOWING OFF YOUR DING-DONG, MORTY.
I'M SAYING, D-D-DON'T SEND DICK PICS, MORTY.
THAT'S AN IMBECILE MOVE.
OKAY, RICK.

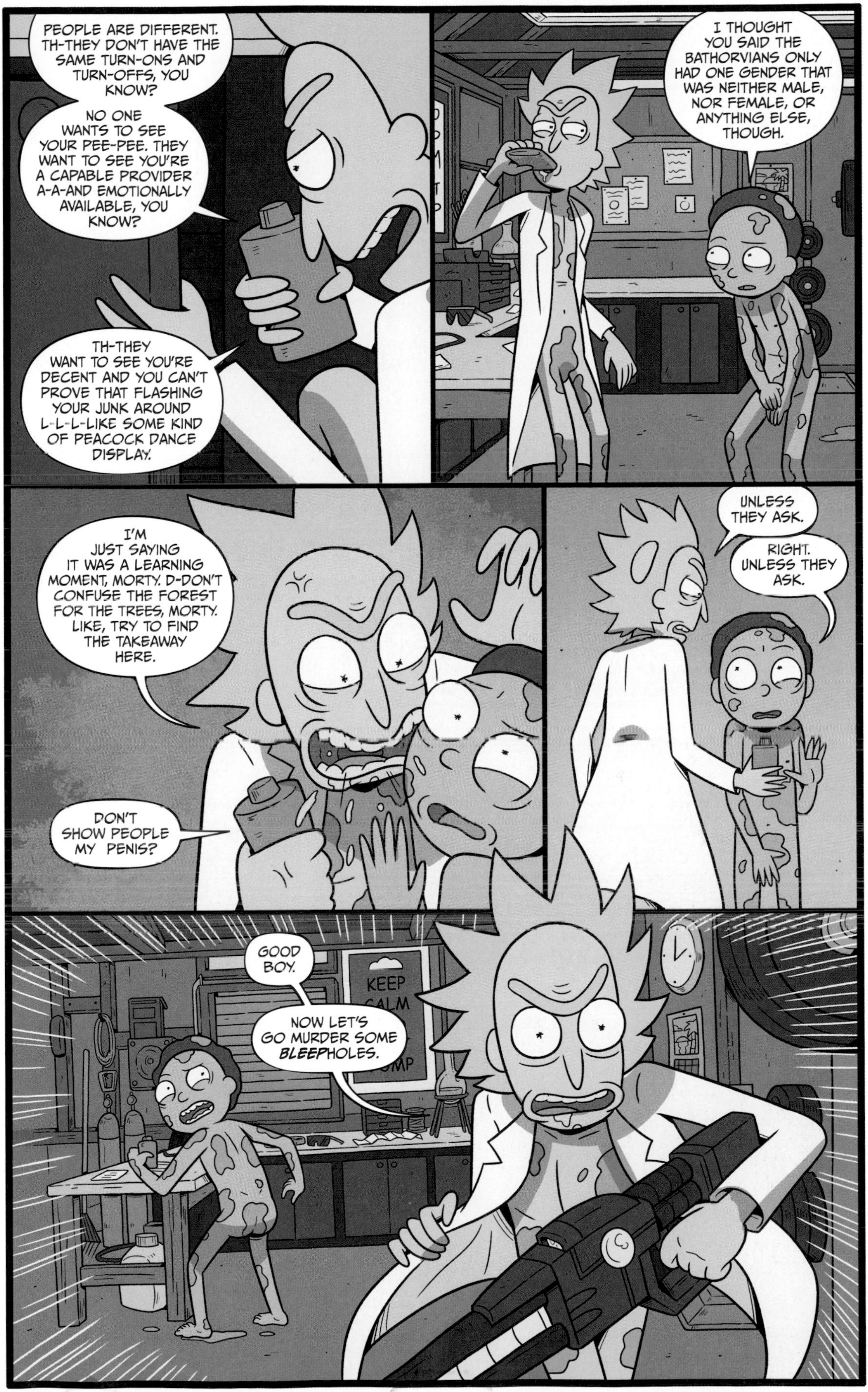
PEOPLE ARE DIFFERENT. TH-THEY DON'T HAVE THE SAME TURN-ONS AND TURN-OFFS, YOU KNOW?
NO ONE WANTS TO SEE YOUR PEE-PEE. THEY WANT TO SEE YOU'RE A CAPABLE PROVIDER A-A-AND EMOTIONALLY AVAILABLE, YOU KNOW?
TH-THEY WANT TO SEE YOU'RE DECENT AND YOU CAN'T PROVE THAT FLASHING YOUR JUNK AROUND L-L-L-LIKE SOME KIND OF PEACOCK DANCE DISPLAY.
I THOUGHT YOU SAID THE BATHORVIANS ONLY HAD ONE GENDER THAT WAS NEITHER MALE, NOR FEMALE, OR ANYTHING ELSE, THOUGH.
I'M JUST SAYING IT WAS A LEARNING MOMENT, MORTY. D-DON'T CONFUSE THE FOREST FOR THE TREES, MORTY. LIKE, TRY TO FIND THE TAKEAWAY HERE.
DON'T SHOW PEOPLE MY PENIS?
UNLESS THEY ASK.
RIGHT. UNLESS THEY ASK.
GOOD BOY.
NOW LET'S GO MURDER SOME *BLEEP*HOLES.

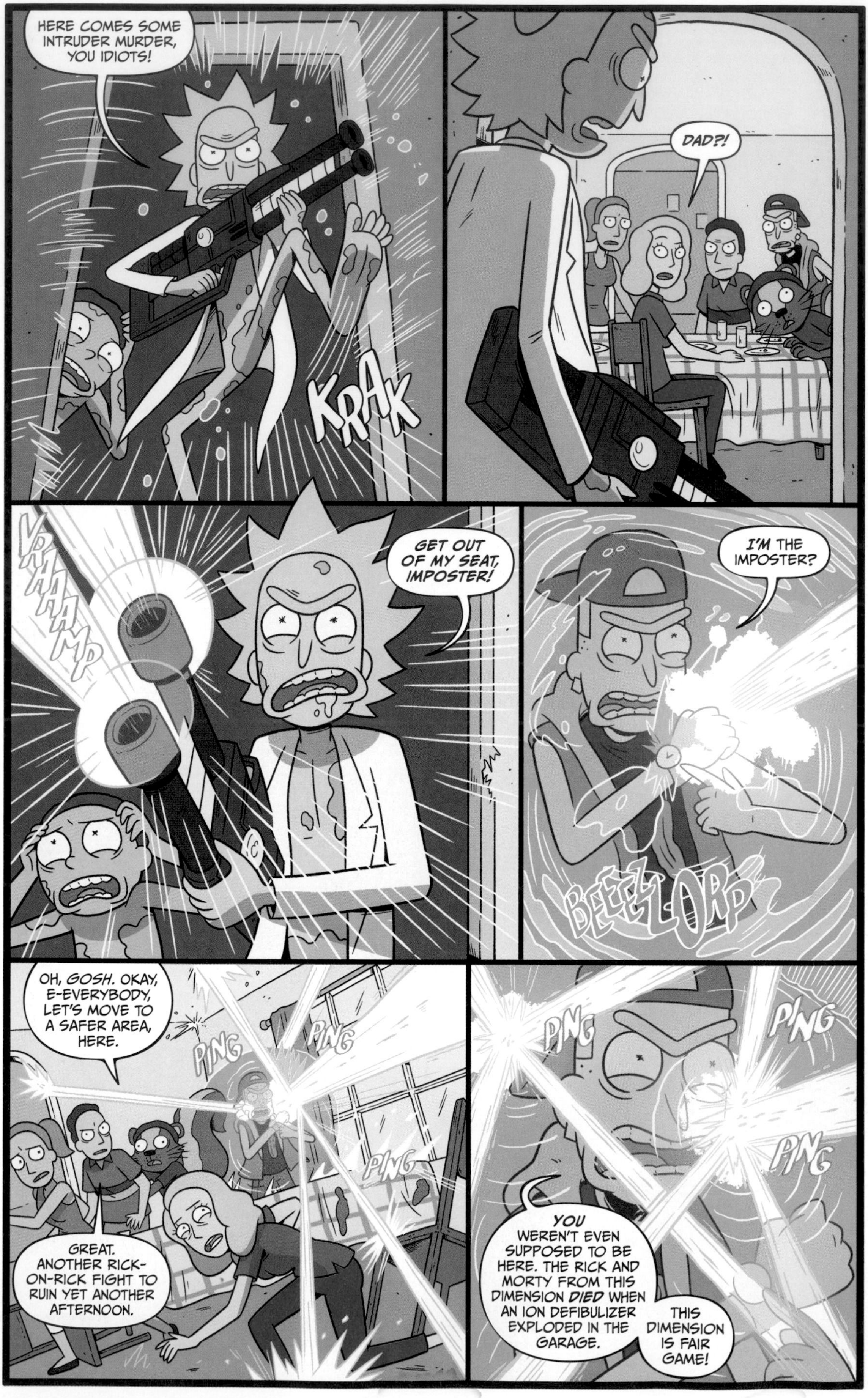
HERE COMES SOME INTRUDER MURDER, YOU IDIOTS!
KRAK
DAD?!
VRAAAAMP
GET OUT OF MY SEAT, IMPOSTER!
I'M THE IMPOSTER?
BEEEZLORP
OH, GOSH. OKAY, E-EVERYBODY, LET'S MOVE TO A SAFER AREA, HERE.
PING
PING
PING
GREAT. ANOTHER RICK-ON-RICK FIGHT TO RUIN YET ANOTHER AFTERNOON.
PING
PING
PING
YOU WEREN'T EVEN SUPPOSED TO BE HERE. THE RICK AND MORTY FROM THIS DIMENSION DIED WHEN AN ION DEFIBULIZER EXPLODED IN THE GARAGE.
THIS DIMENSION IS FAIR GAME!

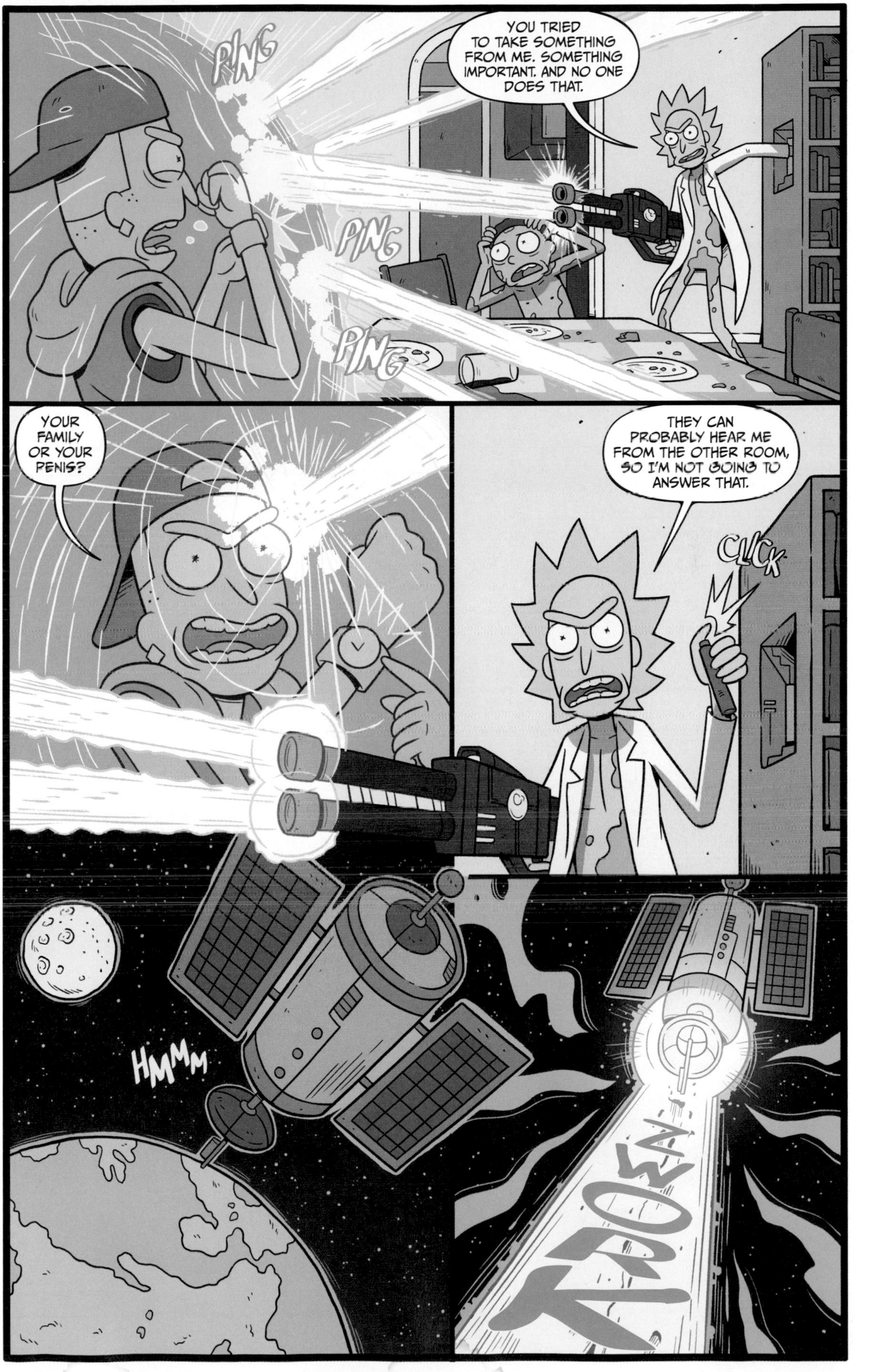
PING
YOU TRIED TO TAKE SOMETHING FROM ME. SOMETHING IMPORTANT. AND NO ONE DOES THAT.
PING
PING
YOUR FAMILY OR YOUR PENIS?
THEY CAN PROBABLY HEAR ME FROM THE OTHER ROOM, SO I'M NOT GOING TO ANSWER THAT.
CLICK
HMMM
ZWORK

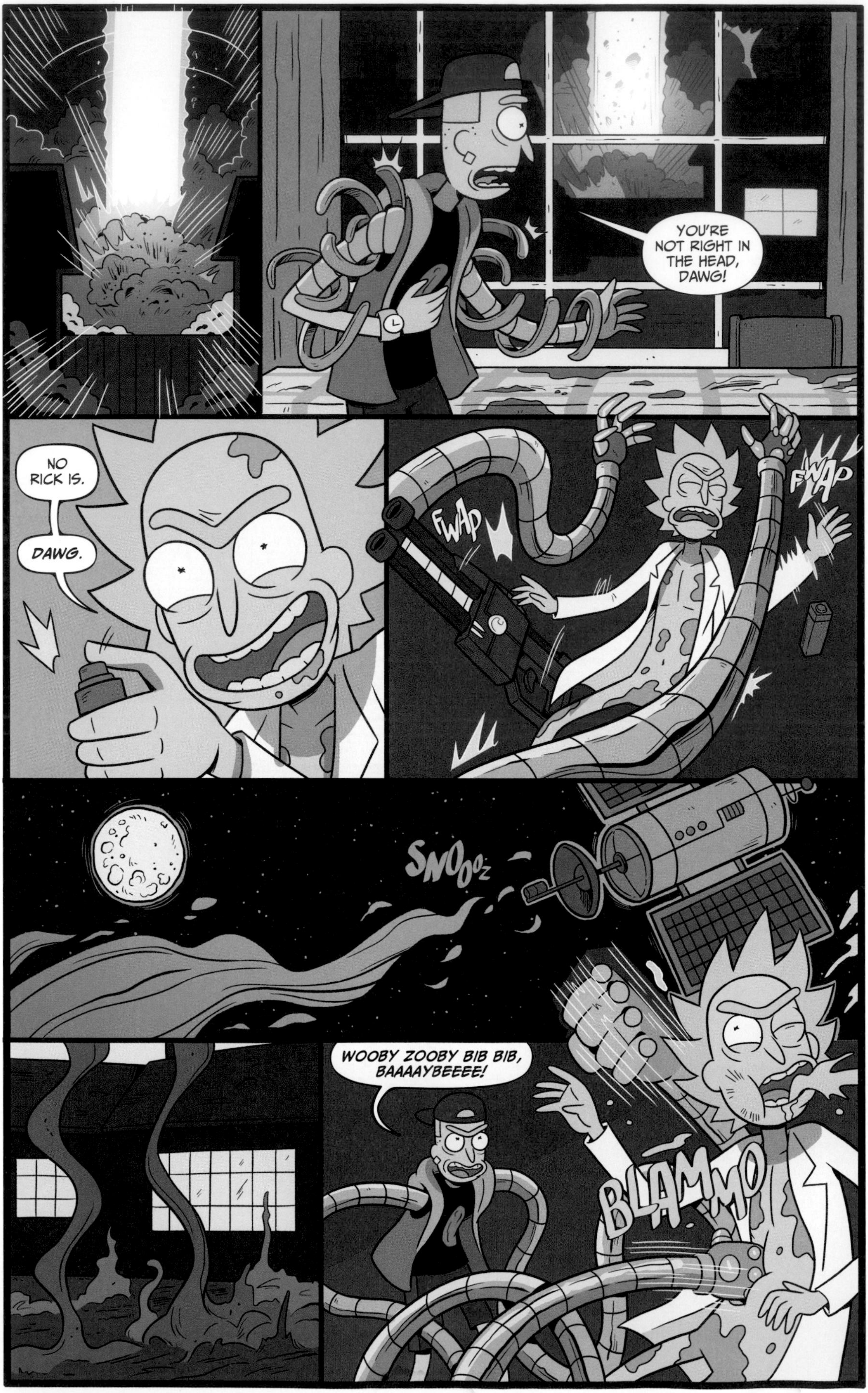
YOU'RE NOT RIGHT IN THE HEAD, DAWG!
NO RICK IS.
DAWG.
FWAP
FWAP
SNOOOZ
WOOBY ZOOBY BIB BIB, BAAAAYBEEEE!
BLAMMO

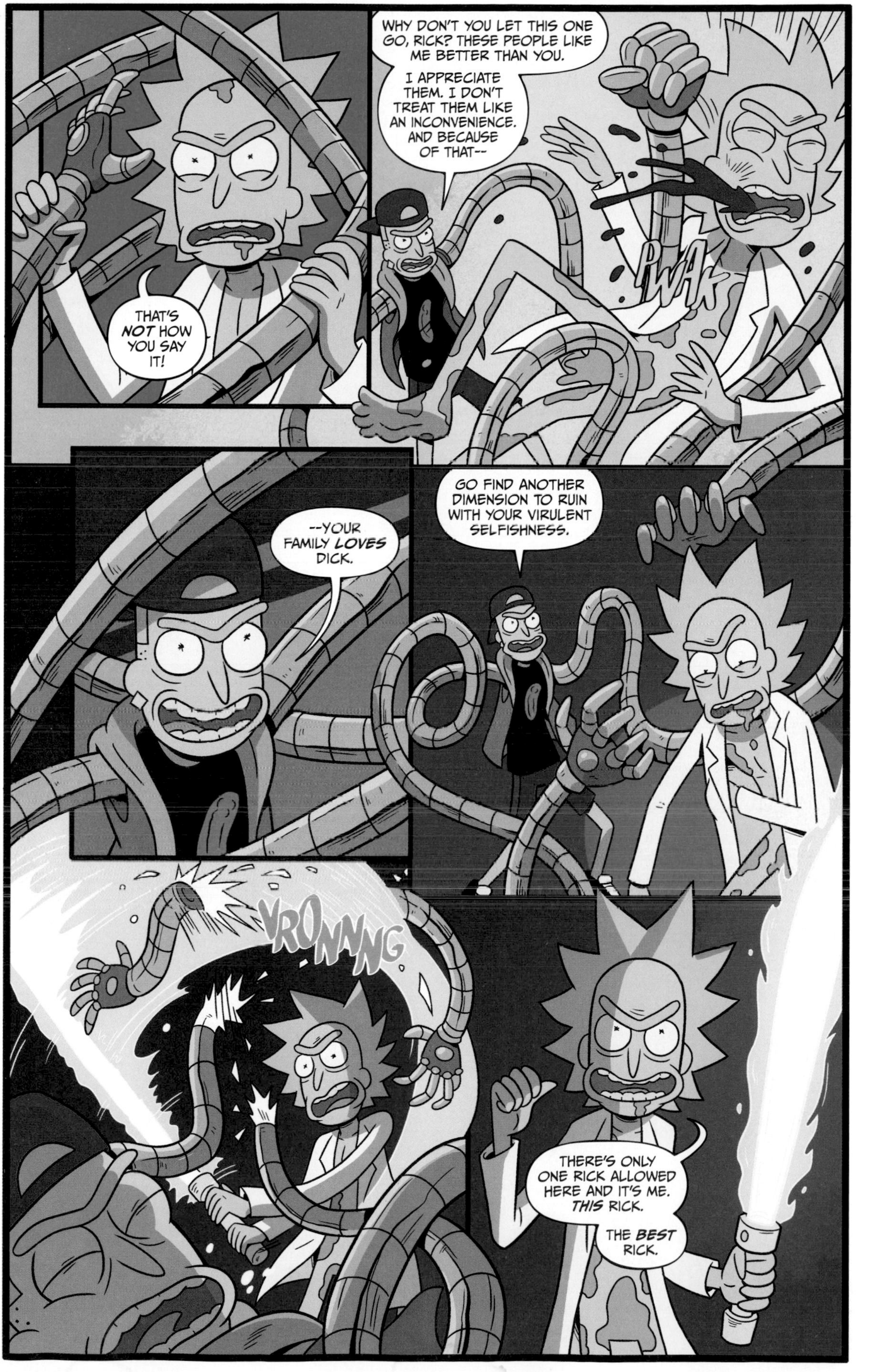
THAT'S NOT HOW YOU SAY IT!
WHY DON'T YOU LET THIS ONE GO, RICK? THESE PEOPLE LIKE ME BETTER THAN YOU.
I APPRECIATE THEM. I DON'T TREAT THEM LIKE AN INCONVENIENCE. AND BECAUSE OF THAT--
PWAK
--YOUR FAMILY LOVES DICK.
GO FIND ANOTHER DIMENSION TO RUIN WITH YOUR VIRULENT SELFISHNESS.
VRONNNG
THERE'S ONLY ONE RICK ALLOWED HERE AND IT'S ME. THIS RICK.
THE BEST RICK.

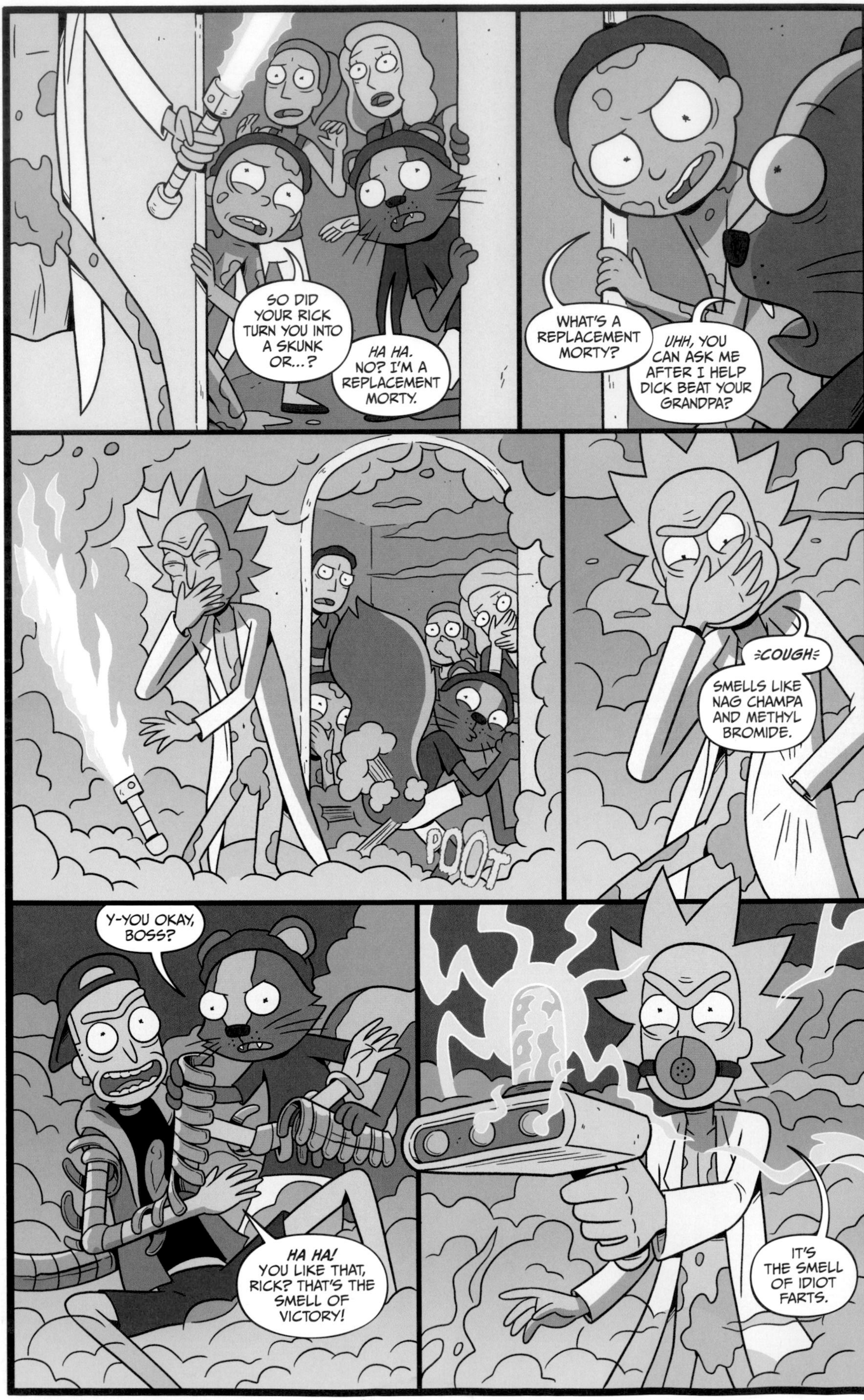
SO DID YOUR RICK TURN YOU INTO A SKUNK OR...?
HA HA. NO? I'M A REPLACEMENT MORTY.
WHAT'S A REPLACEMENT MORTY?
UHH, YOU CAN ASK ME AFTER I HELP DICK BEAT YOUR GRANDPA?
POOT
COUGH
SMELLS LIKE NAG CHAMPA AND METHYL BROMIDE.
Y-YOU OKAY, BOSS?
HA HA! YOU LIKE THAT, RICK? THAT'S THE SMELL OF VICTORY!
IT'S THE SMELL OF IDIOT FARTS.

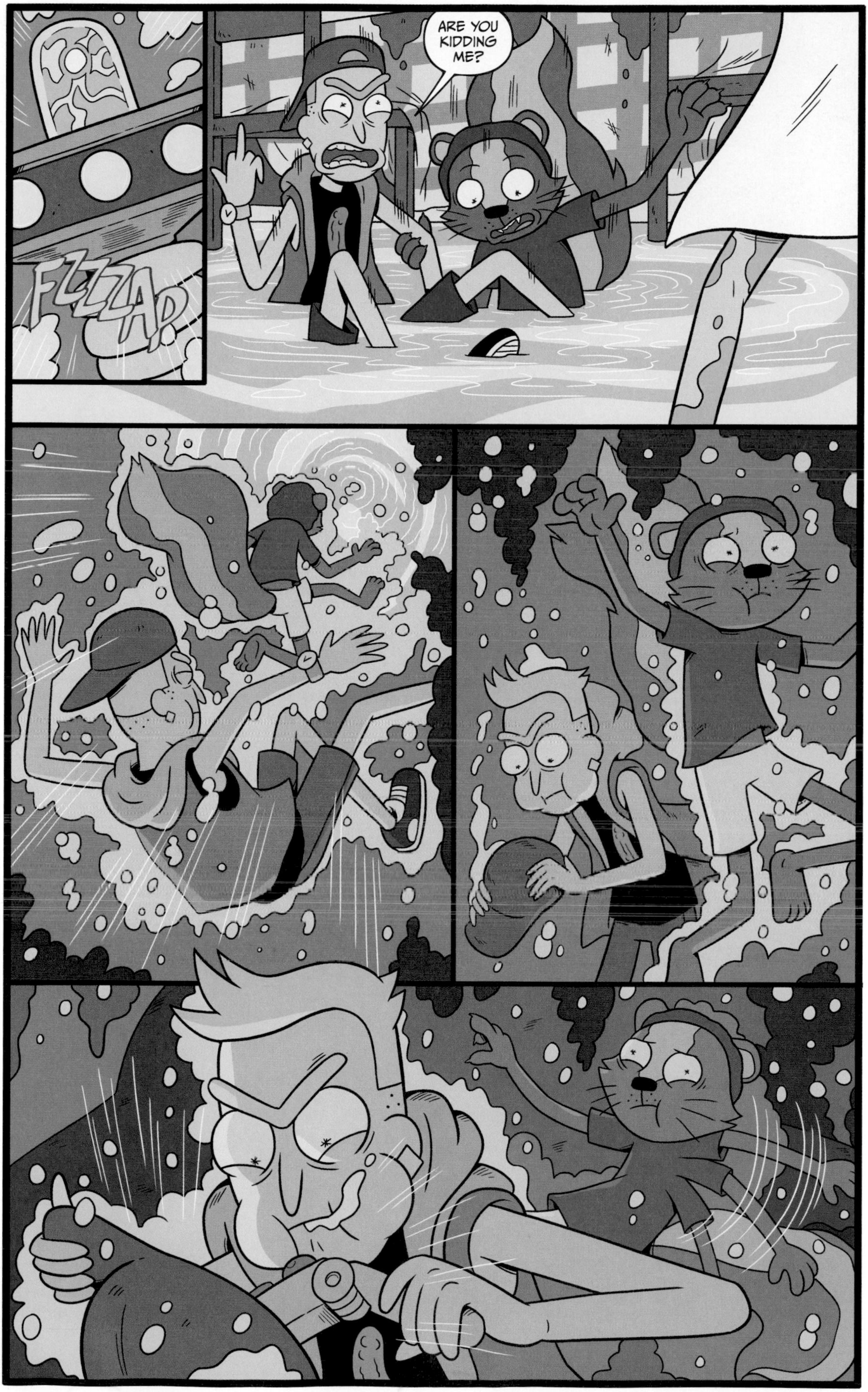
ARE YOU KIDDING ME?
FZZZAP!

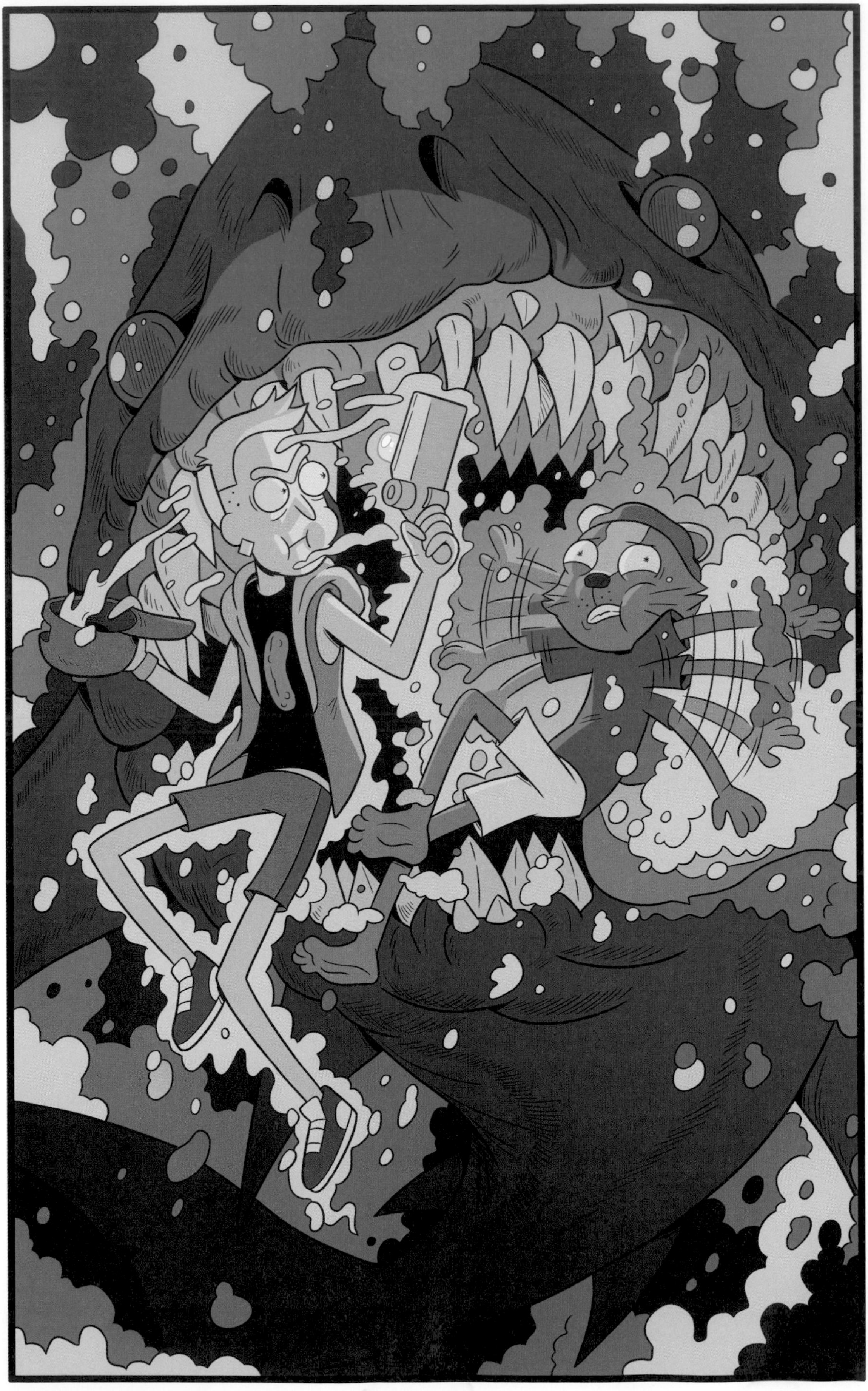

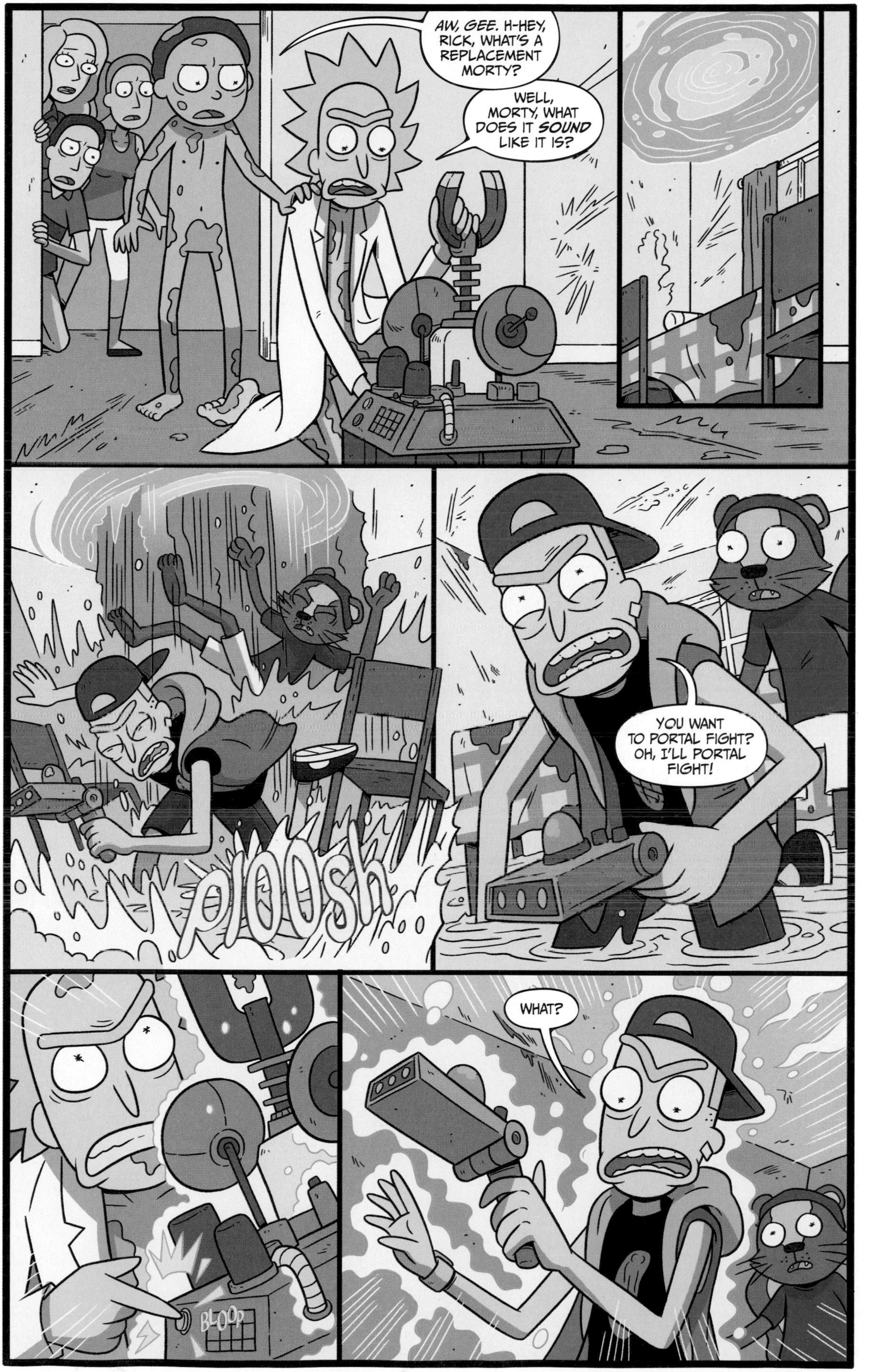

AW, GEE. H-HEY, RICK, WHAT'S A REPLACEMENT MORTY?
WELL, MORTY, WHAT DOES IT SOUND LIKE IT IS?
PLOOSH
YOU WANT TO PORTAL FIGHT? OH, I'LL PORTAL FIGHT!
BLOOP
WHAT?

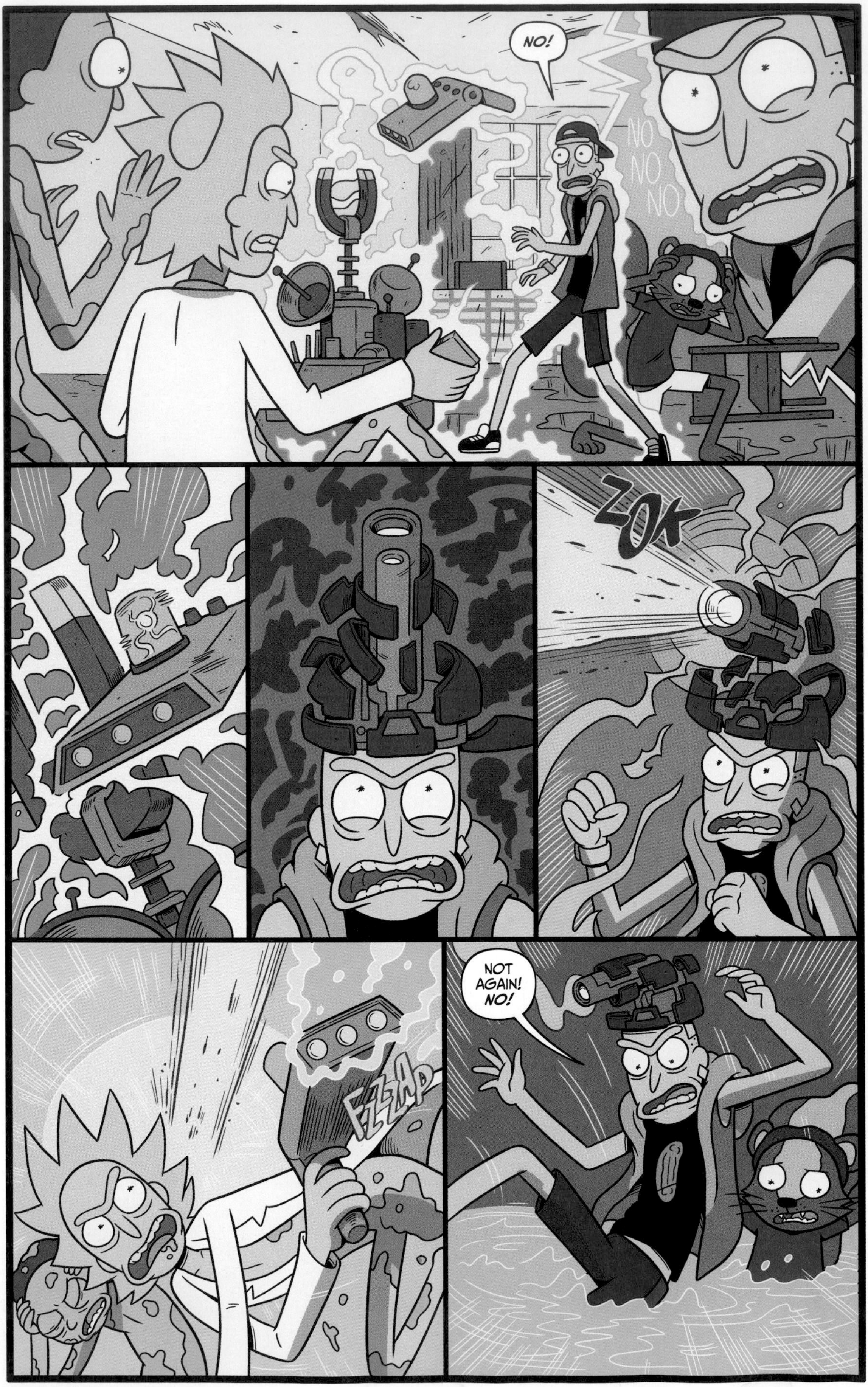
NO!
NO NO NO
ZOK
FZZAP
NOT AGAIN! NO!

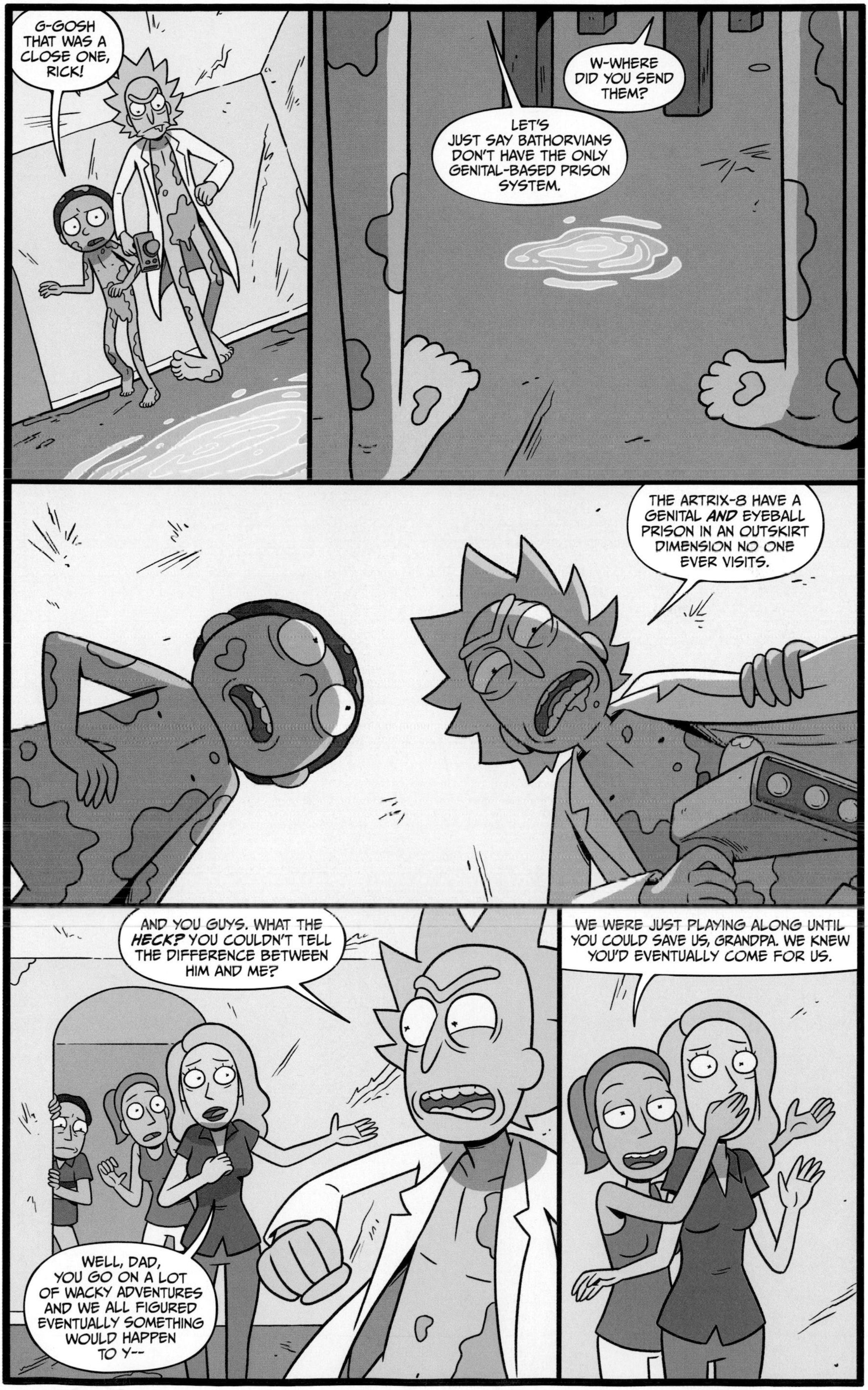
G-GOSH THAT WAS A CLOSE ONE, RICK!
W-WHERE DID YOU SEND THEM?
LET'S JUST SAY BATHORVIANS DON'T HAVE THE ONLY GENITAL-BASED PRISON SYSTEM.
THE ARTRIX-8 HAVE A GENITAL *AND* EYEBALL PRISON IN AN OUTSKIRT DIMENSION NO ONE EVER VISITS.
AND YOU GUYS. WHAT THE *HECK?* YOU COULDN'T TELL THE DIFFERENCE BETWEEN HIM AND ME?
WELL, DAD, YOU GO ON A LOT OF WACKY ADVENTURES AND WE ALL FIGURED EVENTUALLY SOMETHING WOULD HAPPEN TO Y--
WE WERE JUST PLAYING ALONG UNTIL YOU COULD SAVE US, GRANDPA. WE KNEW YOU'D EVENTUALLY COME FOR US.

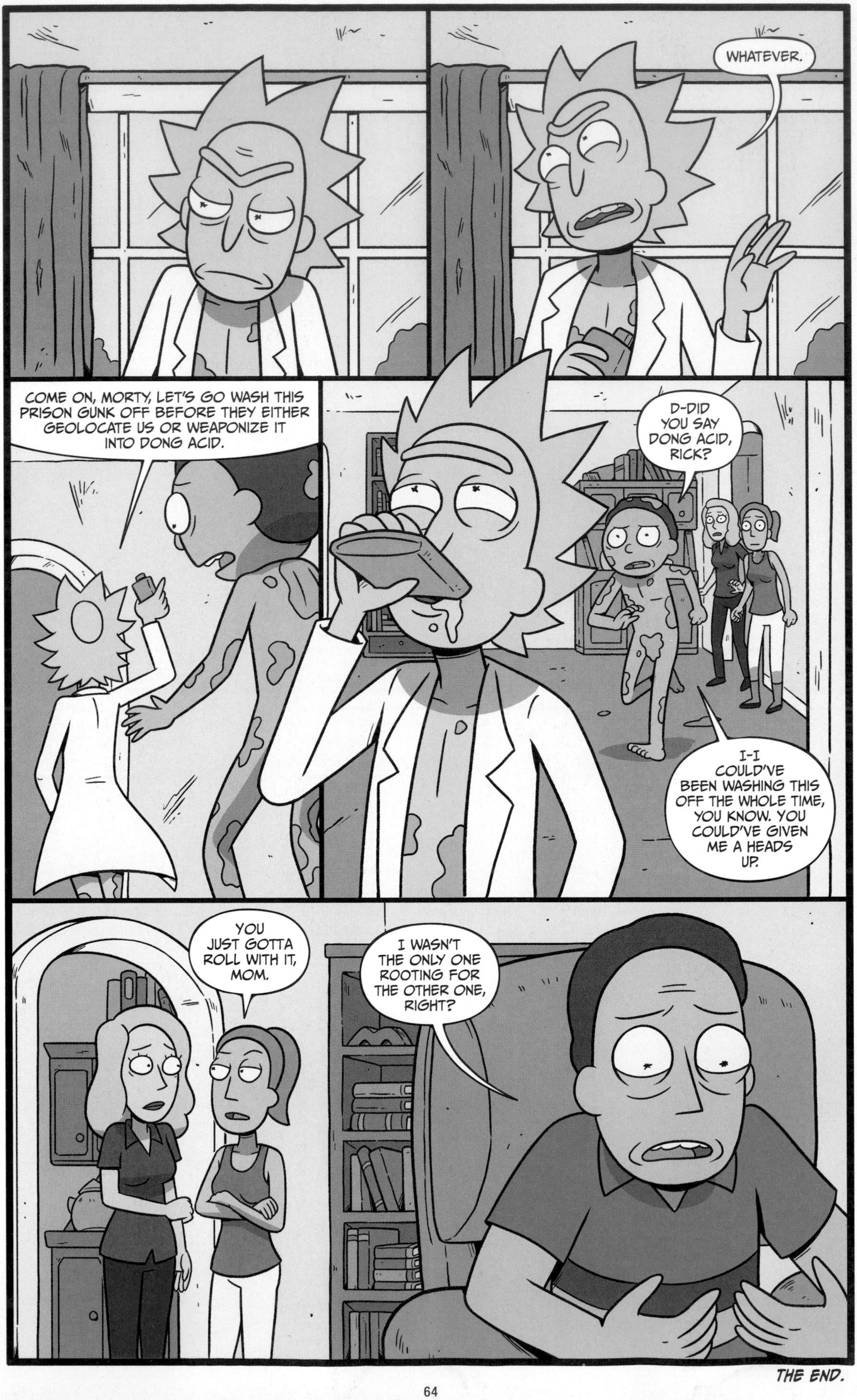
WHATEVER.
COME ON, MORTY, LET'S GO WASH THIS PRISON GUNK OFF BEFORE THEY EITHER GEOLOCATE US OR WEAPONIZE IT INTO DONG ACID.
D-DID YOU SAY DONG ACID, RICK?
I-I COULD'VE BEEN WASHING THIS OFF THE WHOLE TIME, YOU KNOW. YOU COULD'VE GIVEN ME A HEADS UP.
YOU JUST GOTTA ROLL WITH IT, MOM.
I WASN'T THE ONLY ONE ROOTING FOR THE OTHER ONE, RIGHT?

THE END.

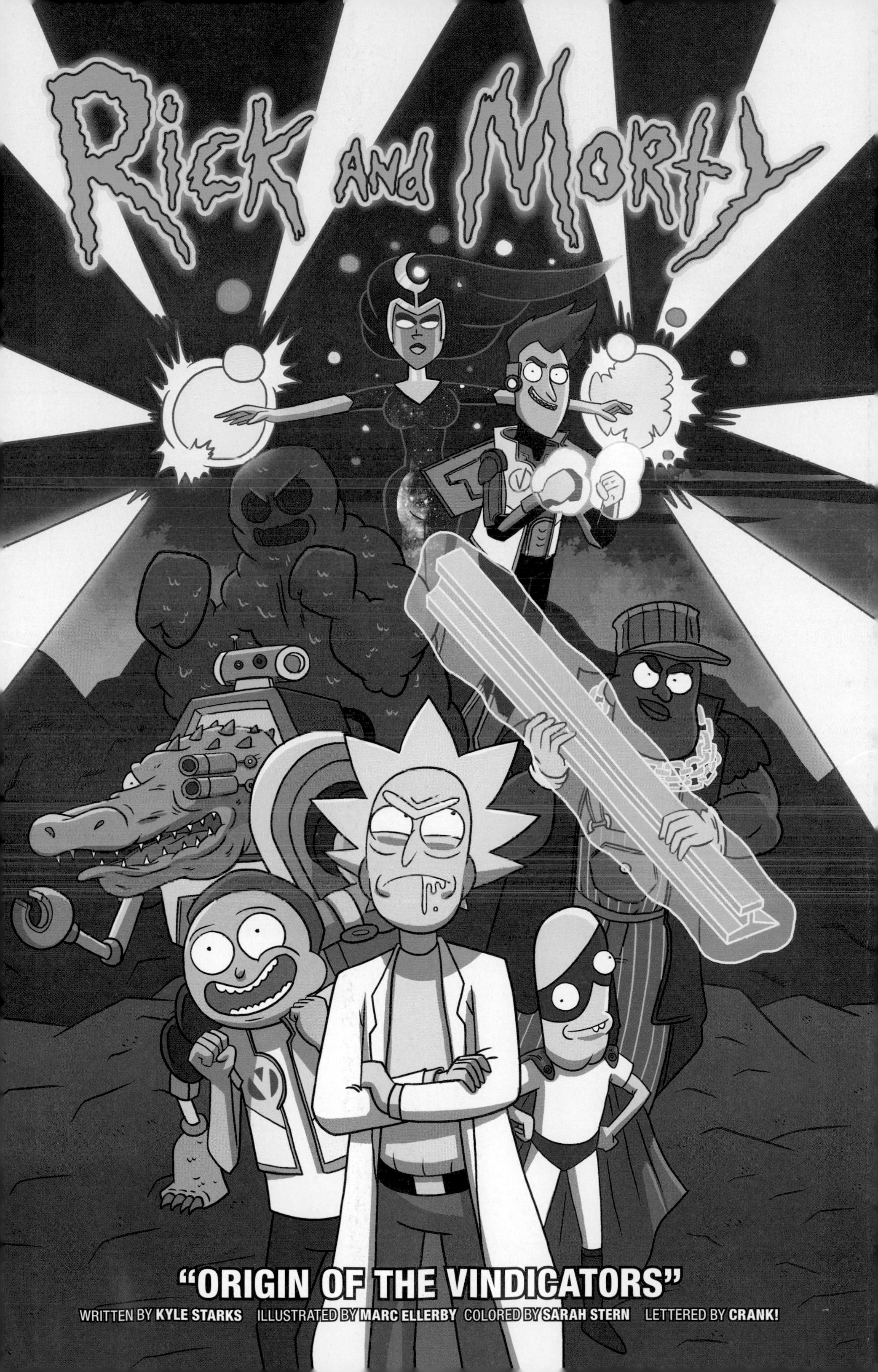
Rick and Morty
"ORIGIN OF THE VINDICATORS"
WRITTEN BY KYLE STARKS ILLUSTRATED BY MARC ELLERBY COLORED BY SARAH STERN LETTERED BY CRANK!

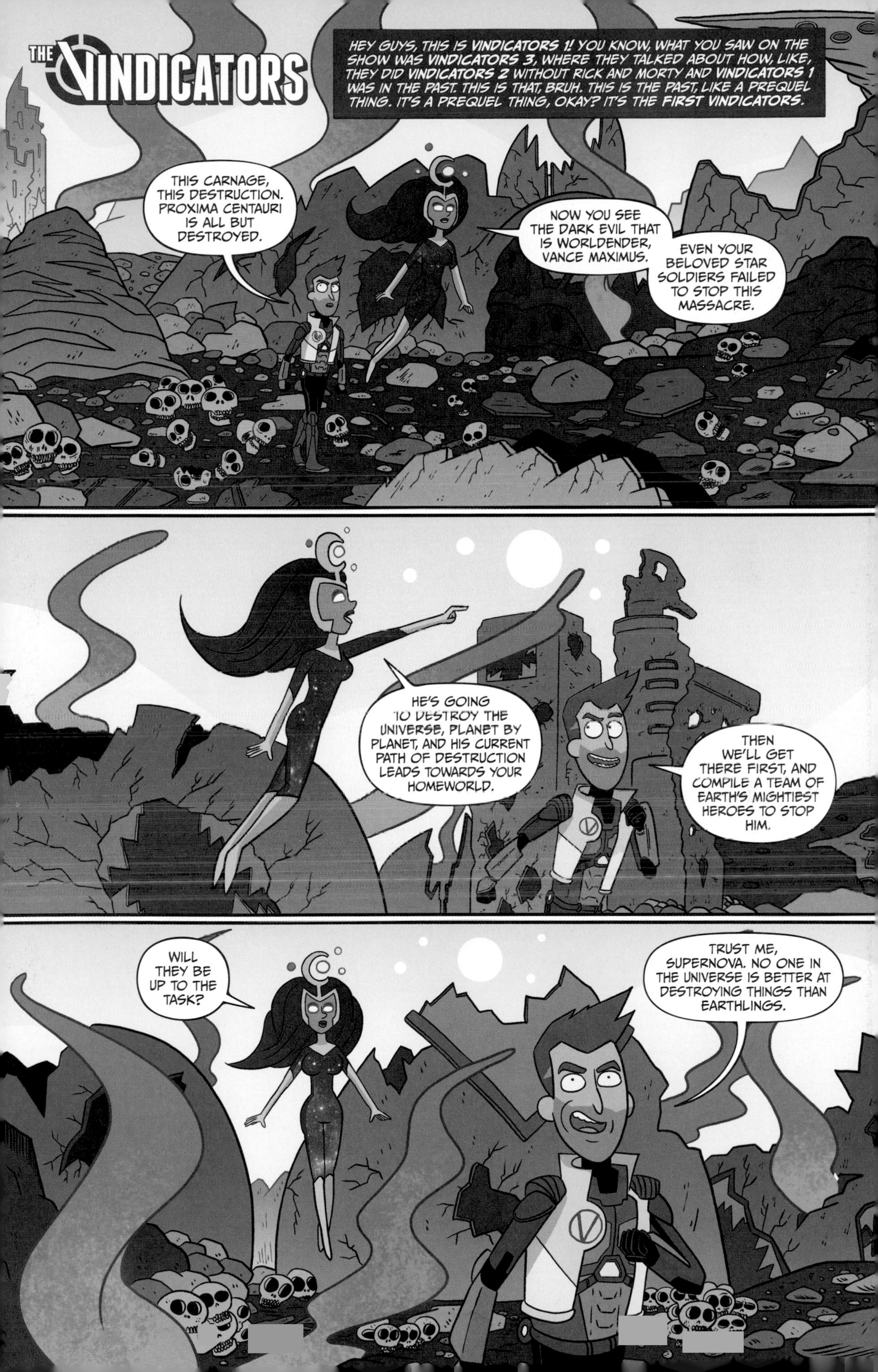
THE VINDICATORS
HEY GUYS, THIS IS VINDICATORS 1! YOU KNOW, WHAT YOU SAW ON THE SHOW WAS VINDICATORS 3, WHERE THEY TALKED ABOUT HOW, LIKE, THEY DID VINDICATORS 2 WITHOUT RICK AND MORTY AND VINDICATORS 1 WAS IN THE PAST. THIS IS THAT, BRUH. THIS IS THE PAST, LIKE A PREQUEL THING. IT'S A PREQUEL THING, OKAY? IT'S THE FIRST VINDICATORS.
THIS CARNAGE, THIS DESTRUCTION. PROXIMA CENTAURI IS ALL BUT DESTROYED.
NOW YOU SEE THE DARK EVIL THAT IS WORLDENDER, VANCE MAXIMUS.
EVEN YOUR BELOVED STAR SOLDIERS FAILED TO STOP THIS MASSACRE.
HE'S GOING TO DESTROY THE UNIVERSE, PLANET BY PLANET, AND HIS CURRENT PATH OF DESTRUCTION LEADS TOWARDS YOUR HOMEWORLD.
THEN WE'LL GET THERE FIRST, AND COMPILE A TEAM OF EARTH'S MIGHTIEST HEROES TO STOP HIM.
WILL THEY BE UP TO THE TASK?
TRUST ME, SUPERNOVA. NO ONE IN THE UNIVERSE IS BETTER AT DESTROYING THINGS THAN EARTHLINGS.

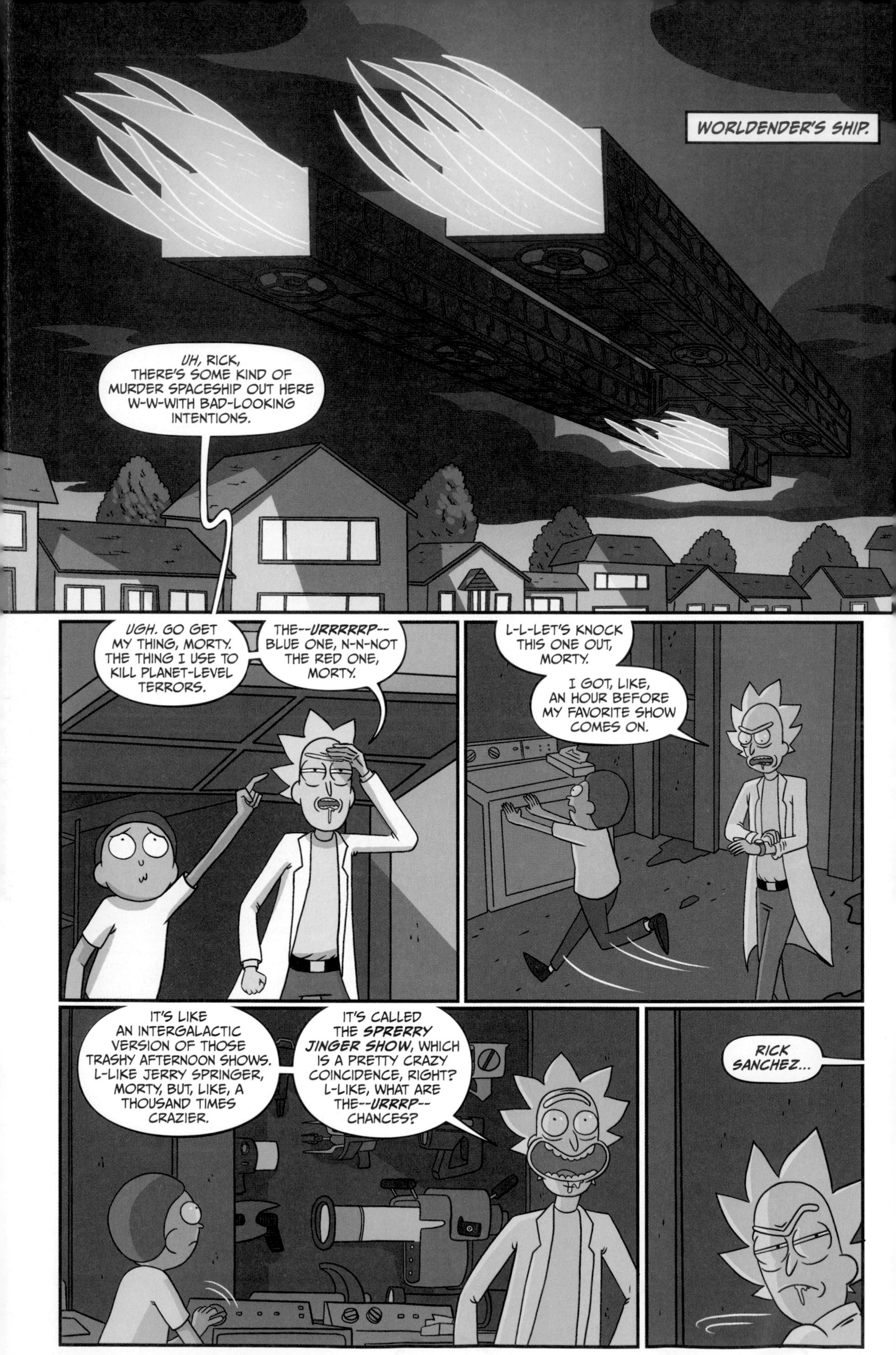
WORLDENDER'S SHIP.
UH, RICK, THERE'S SOME KIND OF MURDER SPACESHIP OUT HERE W-W-WITH BAD-LOOKING INTENTIONS.
UGH. GO GET MY THING, MORTY. THE THING I USE TO KILL PLANET-LEVEL TERRORS.
THE--URRRRRP--BLUE ONE, N-N-NOT THE RED ONE, MORTY.
L-L-LET'S KNOCK THIS ONE OUT, MORTY.
I GOT, LIKE, AN HOUR BEFORE MY FAVORITE SHOW COMES ON.
IT'S LIKE AN INTERGALACTIC VERSION OF THOSE TRASHY AFTERNOON SHOWS. L-LIKE JERRY SPRINGER, MORTY, BUT, LIKE, A THOUSAND TIMES CRAZIER.
IT'S CALLED THE SPRERRY JINGER SHOW, WHICH IS A PRETTY CRAZY COINCIDENCE, RIGHT? L-LIKE, WHAT ARE THE--URRRP--CHANCES?
RICK SANCHEZ...

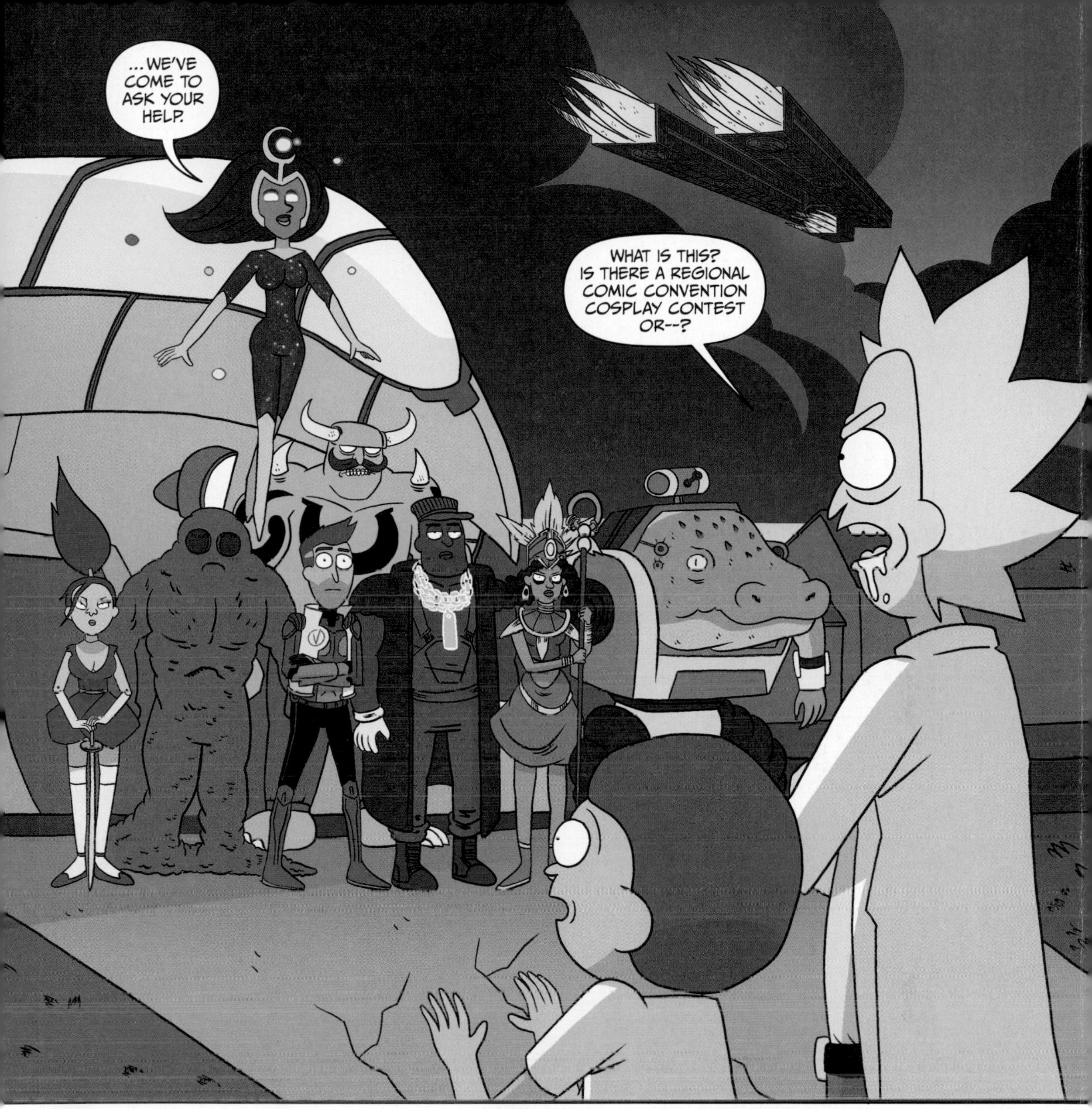
...WE'VE COME TO ASK YOUR HELP.
WHAT IS THIS? IS THERE A REGIONAL COMIC CONVENTION COSPLAY CONTEST OR--?

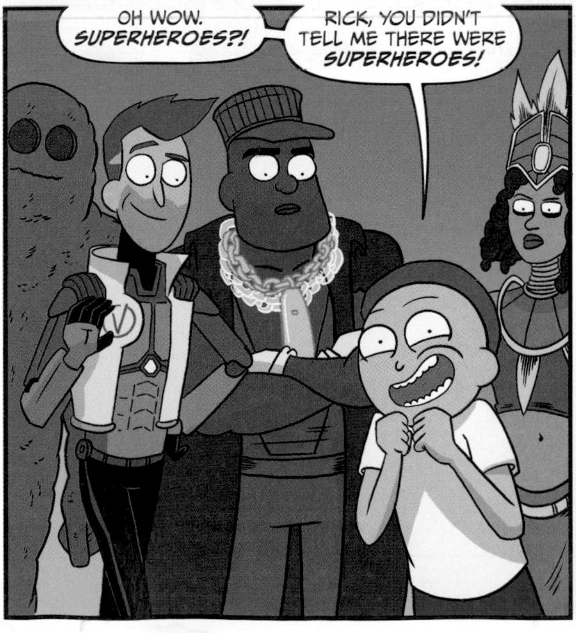
OH WOW. *SUPERHEROES?!*
RICK, YOU DIDN'T TELL ME THERE WERE *SUPERHEROES!*

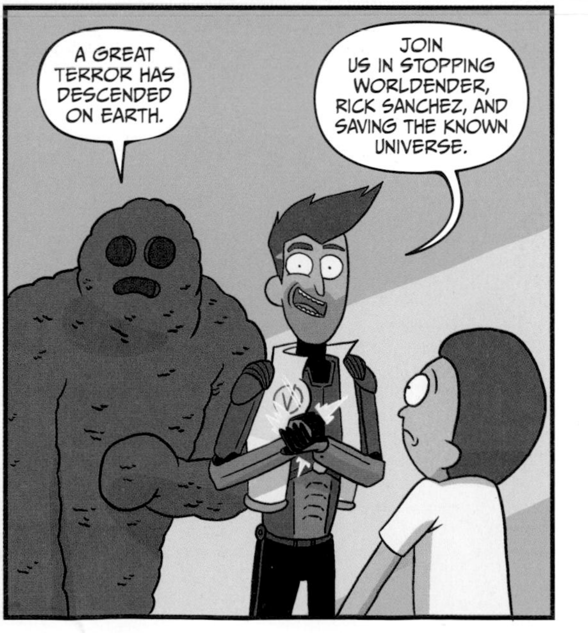
A GREAT TERROR HAS DESCENDED ON EARTH.
JOIN US IN STOPPING WORLDENDER, RICK SANCHEZ, AND SAVING THE KNOWN UNIVERSE.

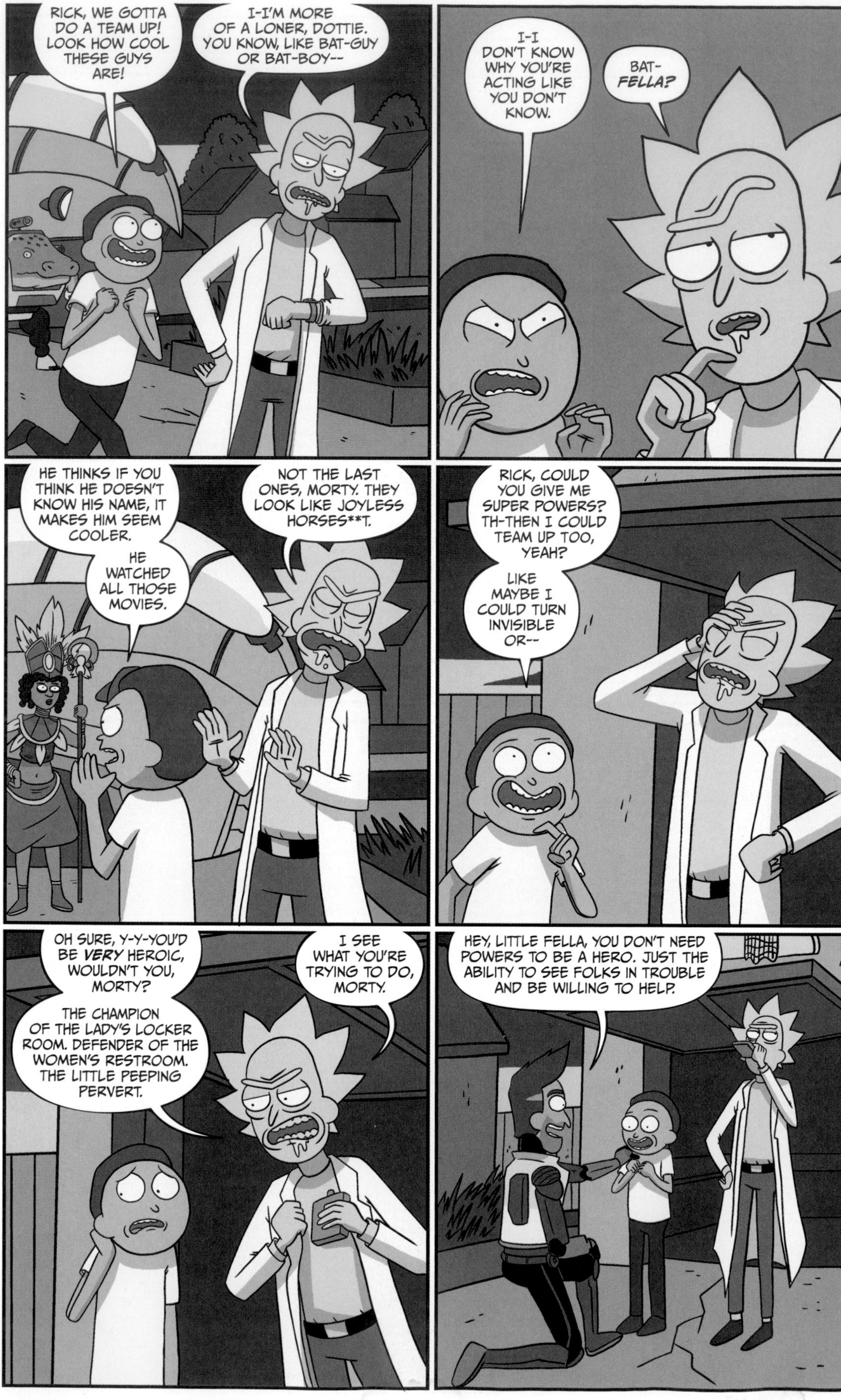
RICK, WE GOTTA DO A TEAM UP! LOOK HOW COOL THESE GUYS ARE!
I-I'M MORE OF A LONER, DOTTIE. YOU KNOW, LIKE BAT-GUY OR BAT-BOY--
I-I DON'T KNOW WHY YOU'RE ACTING LIKE YOU DON'T KNOW.
BAT-FELLA?
HE THINKS IF YOU THINK HE DOESN'T KNOW HIS NAME, IT MAKES HIM SEEM COOLER.
HE WATCHED ALL THOSE MOVIES.
NOT THE LAST ONES, MORTY. THEY LOOK LIKE JOYLESS HORSES**T.
RICK, COULD YOU GIVE ME SUPER POWERS? TH-THEN I COULD TEAM UP TOO, YEAH?
LIKE MAYBE I COULD TURN INVISIBLE OR--
OH SURE, Y-Y-YOU'D BE VERY HEROIC, WOULDN'T YOU, MORTY?
THE CHAMPION OF THE LADY'S LOCKER ROOM. DEFENDER OF THE WOMEN'S RESTROOM. THE LITTLE PEEPING PERVERT.
I SEE WHAT YOU'RE TRYING TO DO, MORTY.
HEY, LITTLE FELLA, YOU DON'T NEED POWERS TO BE A HERO. JUST THE ABILITY TO SEE FOLKS IN TROUBLE AND BE WILLING TO HELP.

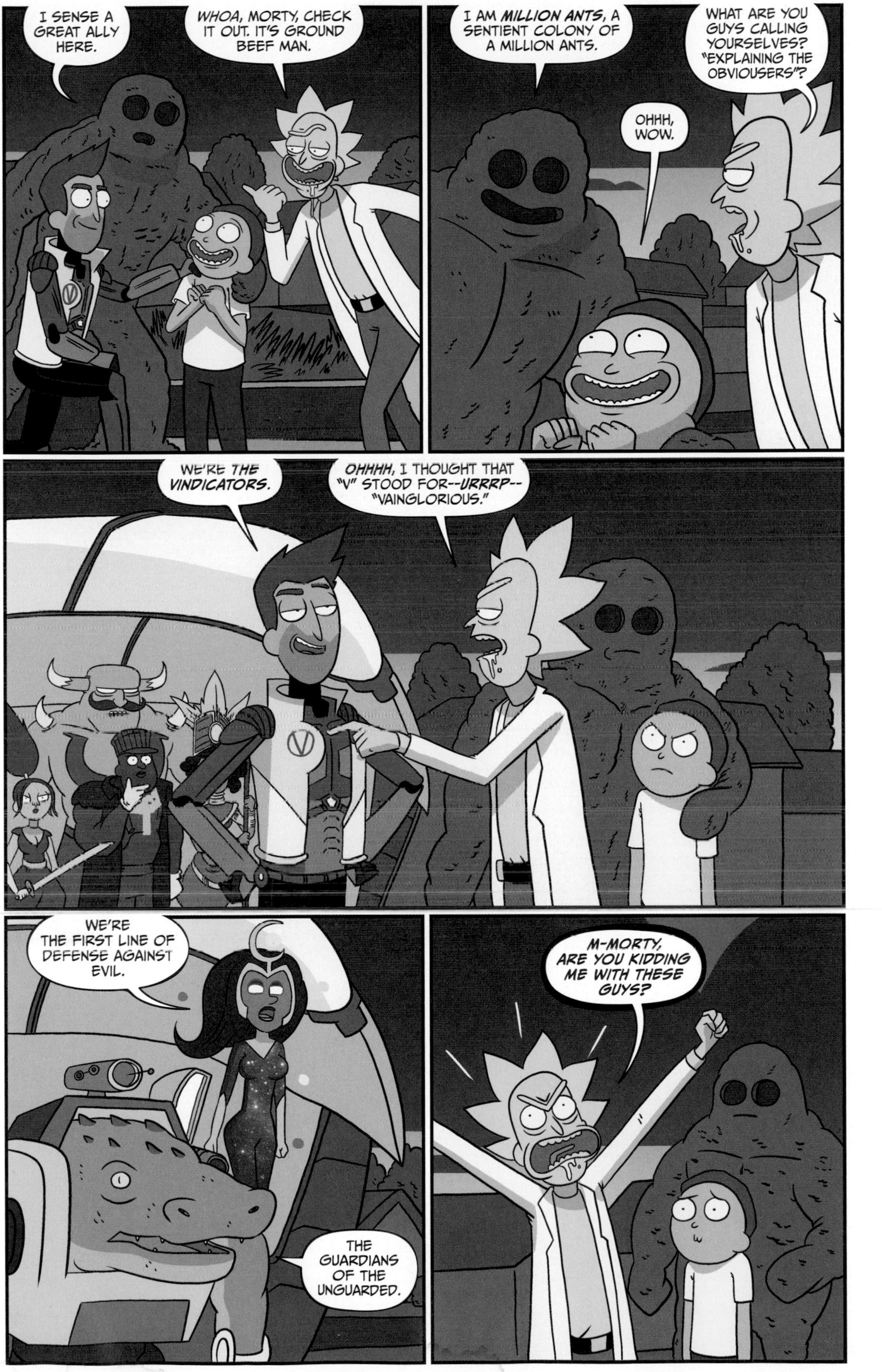
I SENSE A GREAT ALLY HERE.
WHOA, MORTY, CHECK IT OUT. IT'S GROUND BEEF MAN.
I AM MILLION ANTS, A SENTIENT COLONY OF A MILLION ANTS.
OHHH, WOW.
WHAT ARE YOU GUYS CALLING YOURSELVES? "EXPLAINING THE OBVIOUSERS"?
WE'RE THE VINDICATORS.
OHHHH, I THOUGHT THAT "V" STOOD FOR--URRRP-- "VAINGLORIOUS."
WE'RE THE FIRST LINE OF DEFENSE AGAINST EVIL.
THE GUARDIANS OF THE UNGUARDED.
M-MORTY, ARE YOU KIDDING ME WITH THESE GUYS?

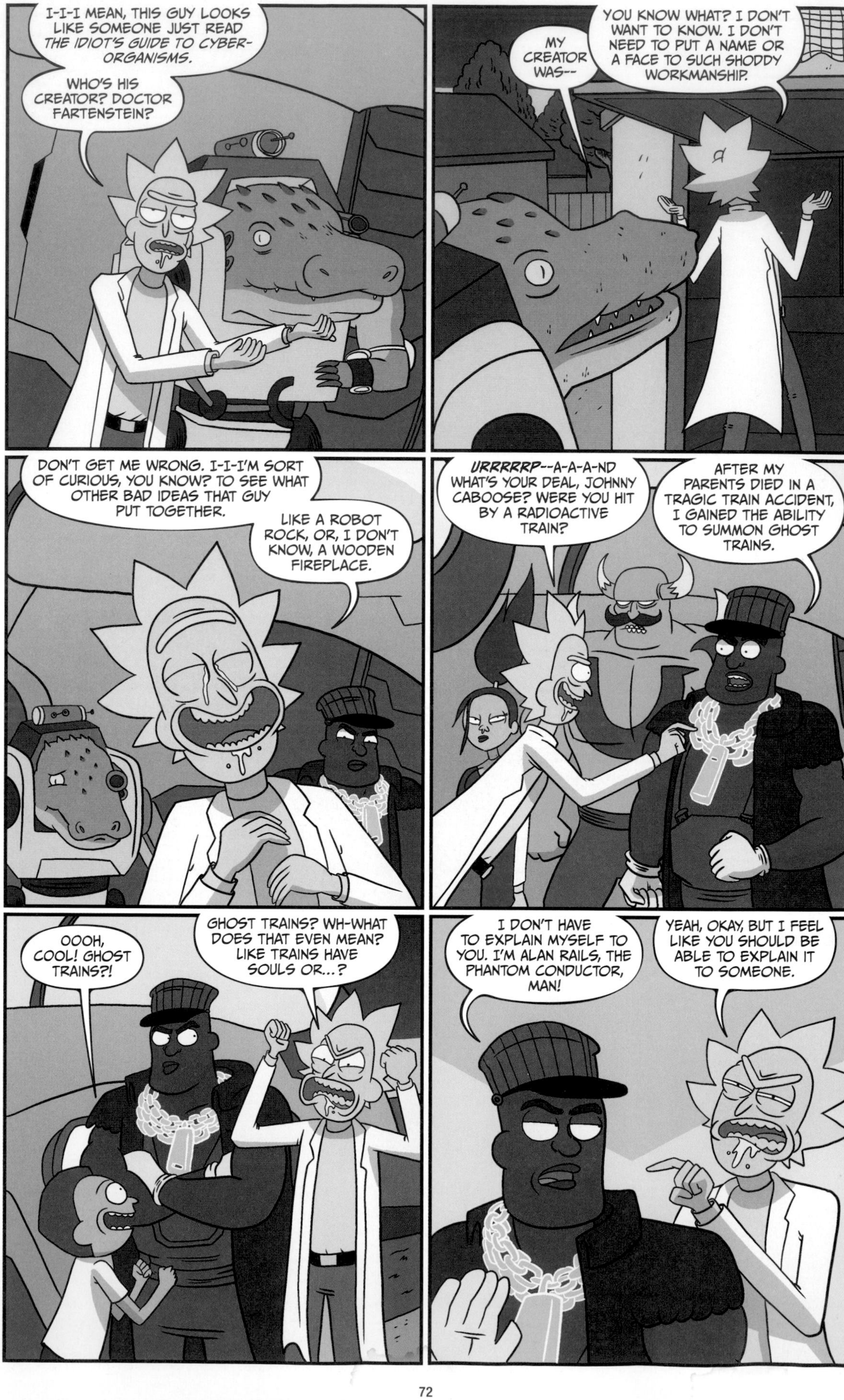
I-I-I MEAN, THIS GUY LOOKS LIKE SOMEONE JUST READ *THE IDIOT'S GUIDE TO CYBER-ORGANISMS.*
WHO'S HIS CREATOR? DOCTOR FARTENSTEIN?
MY CREATOR WAS--
YOU KNOW WHAT? I DON'T WANT TO KNOW. I DON'T NEED TO PUT A NAME OR A FACE TO SUCH SHODDY WORKMANSHIP.
DON'T GET ME WRONG. I-I-I'M SORT OF CURIOUS, YOU KNOW? TO SEE WHAT OTHER BAD IDEAS THAT GUY PUT TOGETHER.
LIKE A ROBOT ROCK, OR, I DON'T KNOW, A WOODEN FIREPLACE.
URRRRRP--A-A-A-ND WHAT'S YOUR DEAL, JOHNNY CABOOSE? WERE YOU HIT BY A RADIOACTIVE TRAIN?
AFTER MY PARENTS DIED IN A TRAGIC TRAIN ACCIDENT, I GAINED THE ABILITY TO SUMMON GHOST TRAINS.
OOOH, COOL! GHOST TRAINS?!
GHOST TRAINS? WH-WHAT DOES THAT EVEN MEAN? LIKE TRAINS HAVE SOULS OR...?
I DON'T HAVE TO EXPLAIN MYSELF TO YOU. I'M ALAN RAILS, THE PHANTOM CONDUCTOR, MAN!
YEAH, OKAY, BUT I FEEL LIKE YOU SHOULD BE ABLE TO EXPLAIN IT TO SOMEONE.

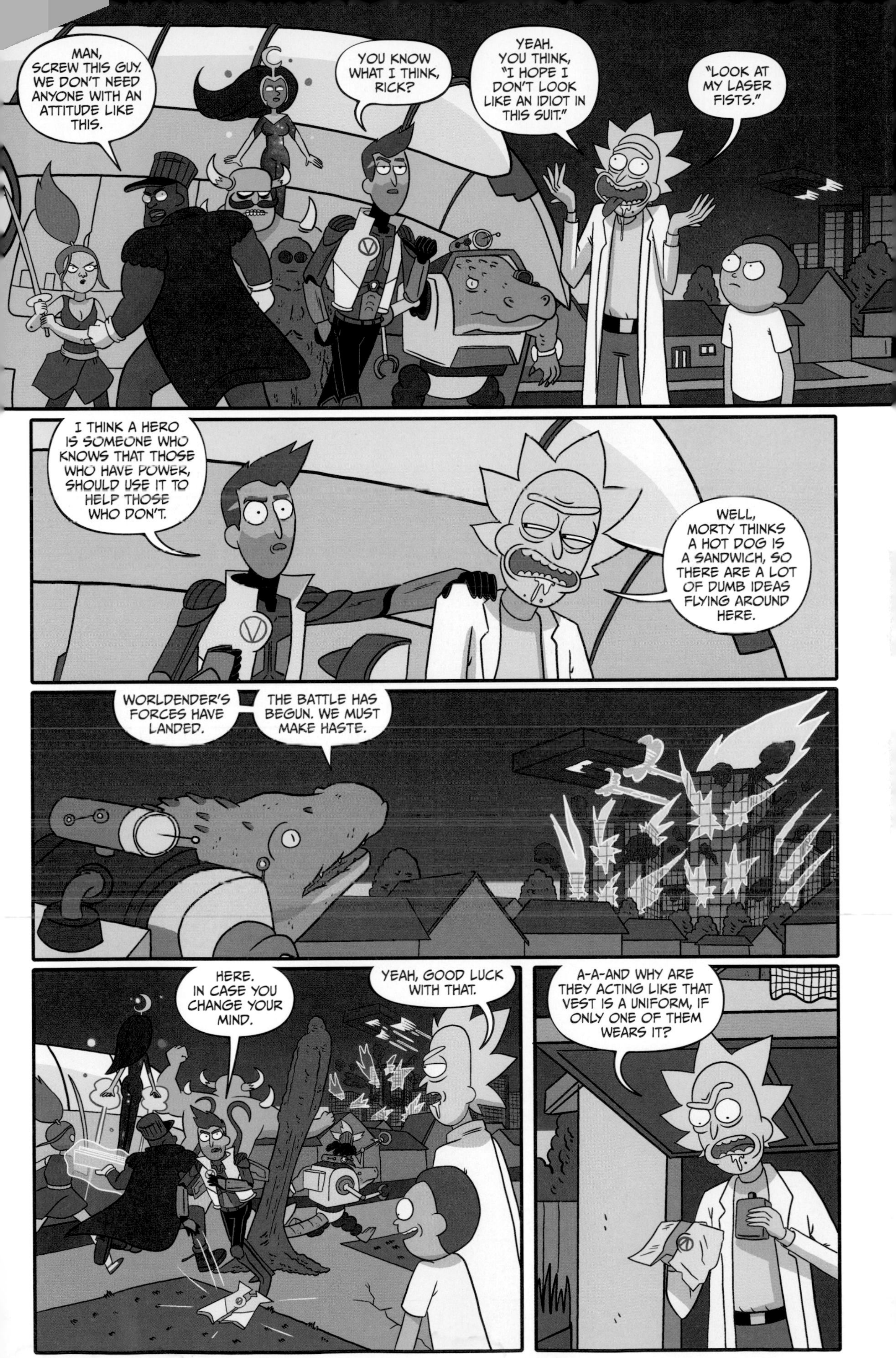
MAN, SCREW THIS GUY. WE DON'T NEED ANYONE WITH AN ATTITUDE LIKE THIS.
YOU KNOW WHAT I THINK, RICK?
YEAH. YOU THINK, "I HOPE I DON'T LOOK LIKE AN IDIOT IN THIS SUIT."
"LOOK AT MY LASER FISTS."
I THINK A HERO IS SOMEONE WHO KNOWS THAT THOSE WHO HAVE POWER, SHOULD USE IT TO HELP THOSE WHO DON'T.
WELL, MORTY THINKS A HOT DOG IS A SANDWICH, SO THERE ARE A LOT OF DUMB IDEAS FLYING AROUND HERE.
WORLDENDER'S FORCES HAVE LANDED.
THE BATTLE HAS BEGUN. WE MUST MAKE HASTE.
HERE. IN CASE YOU CHANGE YOUR MIND.
YEAH, GOOD LUCK WITH THAT.
A-A-AND WHY ARE THEY ACTING LIKE THAT VEST IS A UNIFORM, IF ONLY ONE OF THEM WEARS IT?

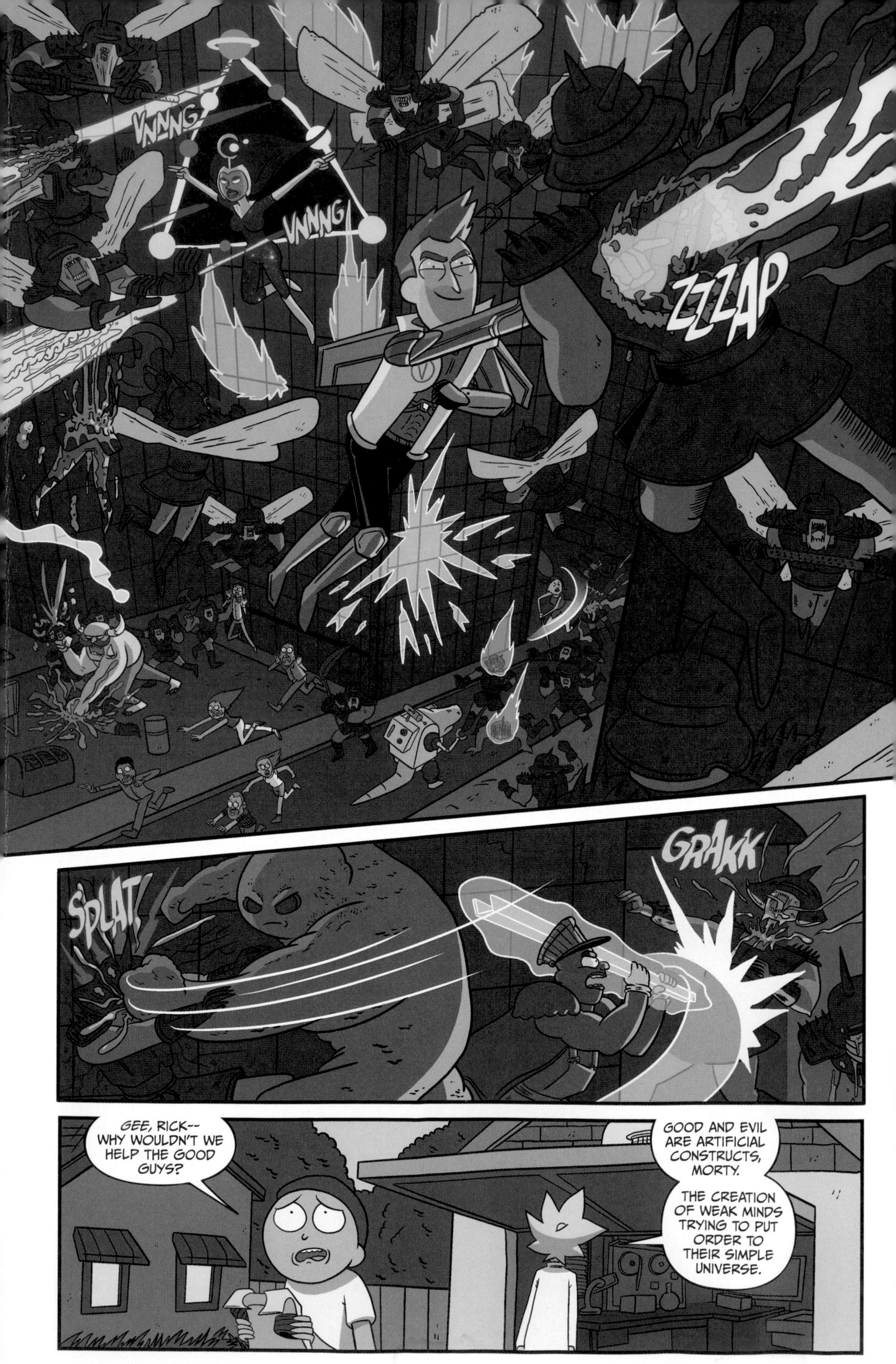
VNNNG
VNNNG
ZZZAP
SPLAT!
GRAKK
GEE, RICK-- WHY WOULDN'T WE HELP THE GOOD GUYS?
GOOD AND EVIL ARE ARTIFICIAL CONSTRUCTS, MORTY.
THE CREATION OF WEAK MINDS TRYING TO PUT ORDER TO THEIR SIMPLE UNIVERSE.

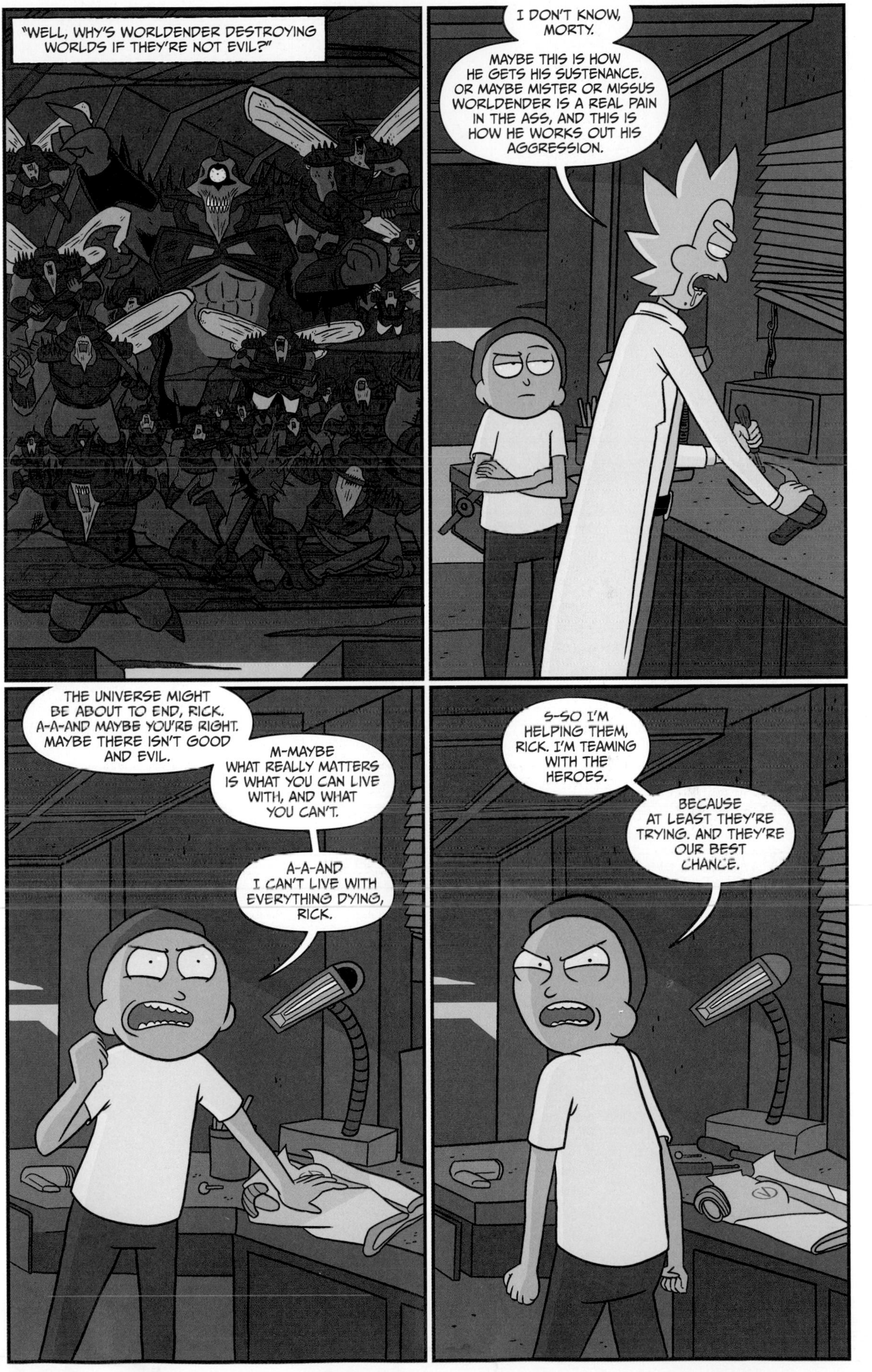
"WELL, WHY'S WORLDENDER DESTROYING WORLDS IF THEY'RE NOT EVIL?"
I DON'T KNOW, MORTY.
MAYBE THIS IS HOW HE GETS HIS SUSTENANCE. OR MAYBE MISTER OR MISSUS WORLDENDER IS A REAL PAIN IN THE ASS, AND THIS IS HOW HE WORKS OUT HIS AGGRESSION.
THE UNIVERSE MIGHT BE ABOUT TO END, RICK. A-A-AND MAYBE YOU'RE RIGHT. MAYBE THERE ISN'T GOOD AND EVIL.
M-MAYBE WHAT REALLY MATTERS IS WHAT YOU CAN LIVE WITH, AND WHAT YOU CAN'T.
A-A-AND I CAN'T LIVE WITH EVERYTHING DYING, RICK.
S-SO I'M HELPING THEM, RICK. I'M TEAMING WITH THE HEROES.
BECAUSE AT LEAST THEY'RE TRYING. AND THEY'RE OUR BEST CHANCE.

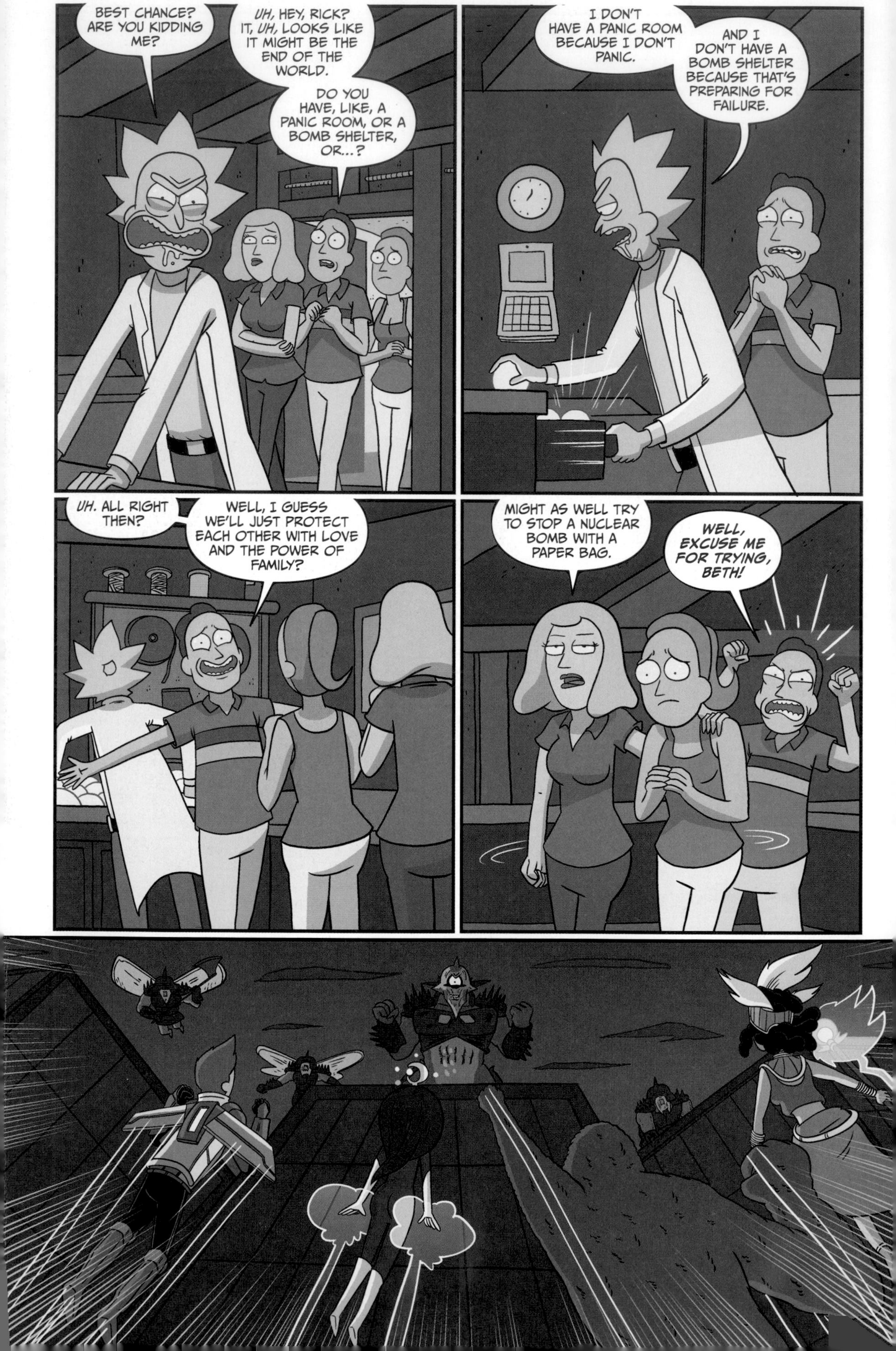
BEST CHANCE? ARE YOU KIDDING ME?
UH, HEY, RICK? IT, UH, LOOKS LIKE IT MIGHT BE THE END OF THE WORLD.
DO YOU HAVE, LIKE, A PANIC ROOM, OR A BOMB SHELTER, OR...?
I DON'T HAVE A PANIC ROOM BECAUSE I DON'T PANIC.
AND I DON'T HAVE A BOMB SHELTER BECAUSE THAT'S PREPARING FOR FAILURE.
UH. ALL RIGHT THEN?
WELL, I GUESS WE'LL JUST PROTECT EACH OTHER WITH LOVE AND THE POWER OF FAMILY?
MIGHT AS WELL TRY TO STOP A NUCLEAR BOMB WITH A PAPER BAG.
WELL, EXCUSE ME FOR TRYING, BETH!

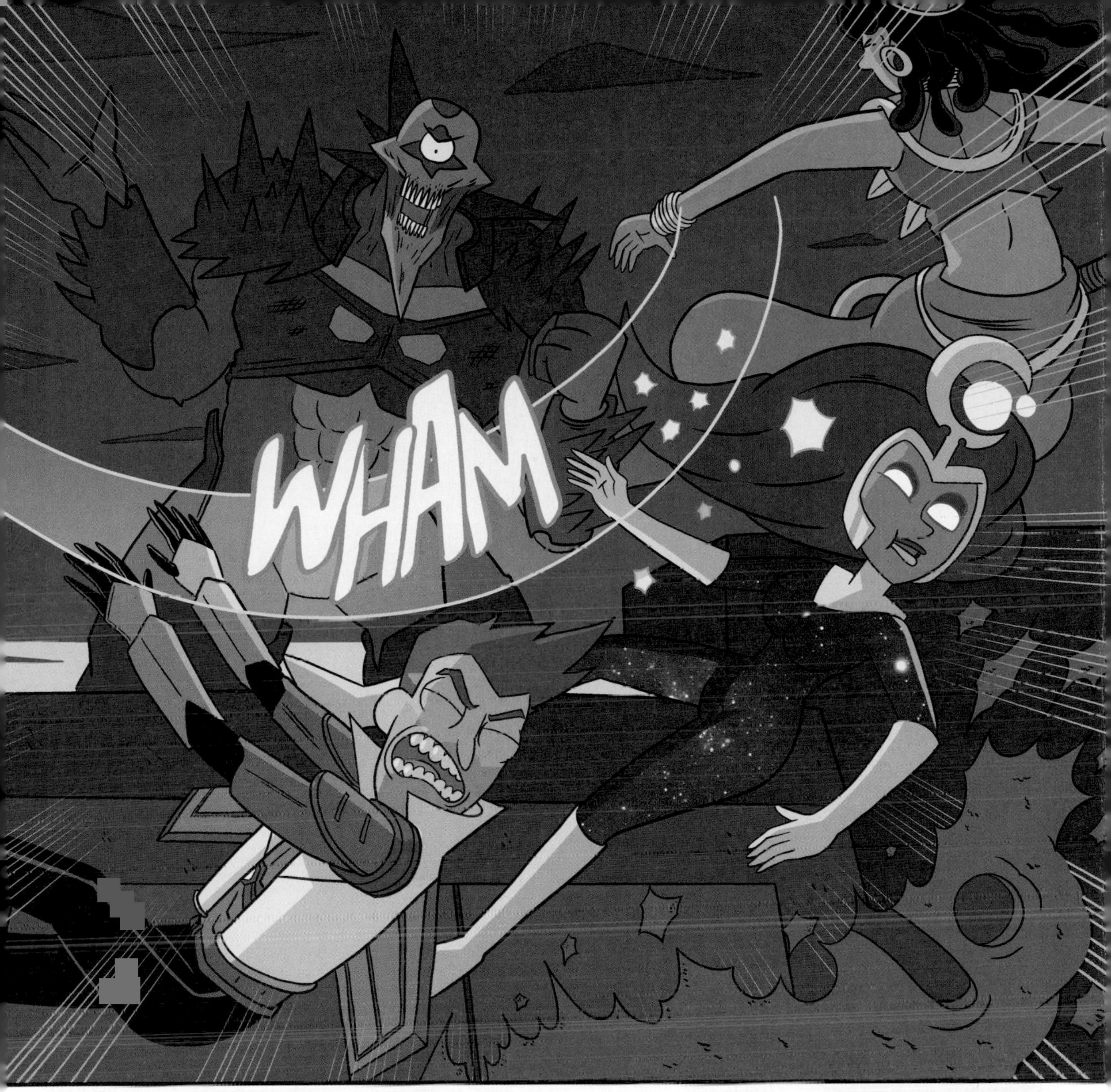
WHAM

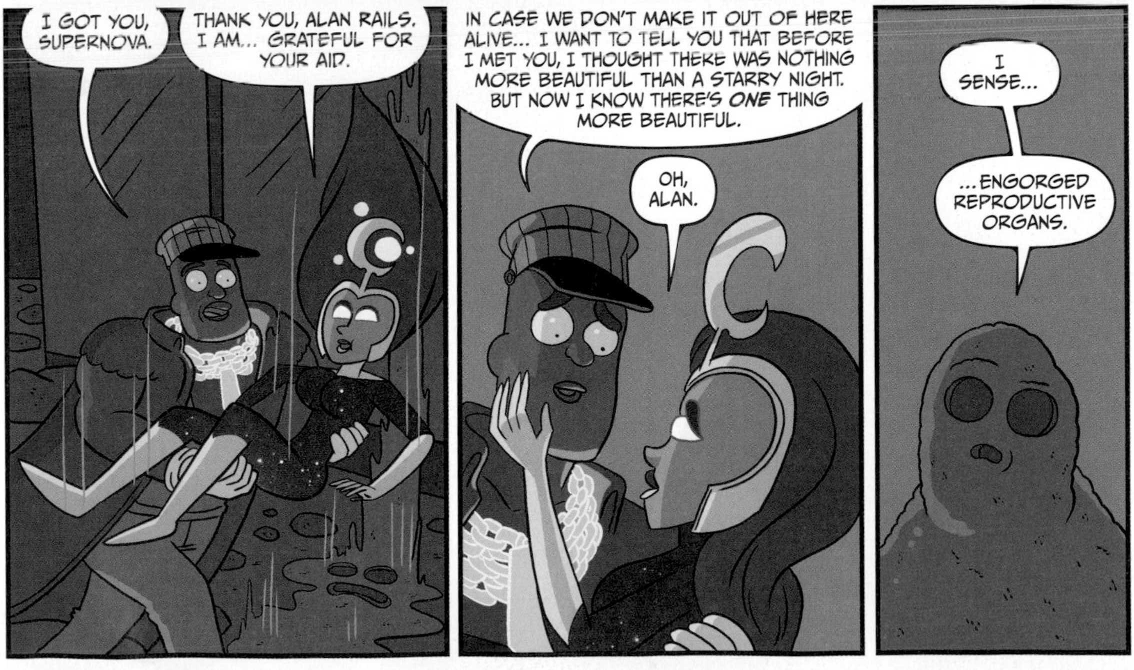
I GOT YOU, SUPERNOVA.
THANK YOU, ALAN RAILS. I AM... GRATEFUL FOR YOUR AID.
IN CASE WE DON'T MAKE IT OUT OF HERE ALIVE... I WANT TO TELL YOU THAT BEFORE I MET YOU, I THOUGHT THERE WAS NOTHING MORE BEAUTIFUL THAN A STARRY NIGHT. BUT NOW I KNOW THERE'S *ONE* THING MORE BEAUTIFUL.
OH, ALAN.
I SENSE...
...ENGORGED REPRODUCTIVE ORGANS.

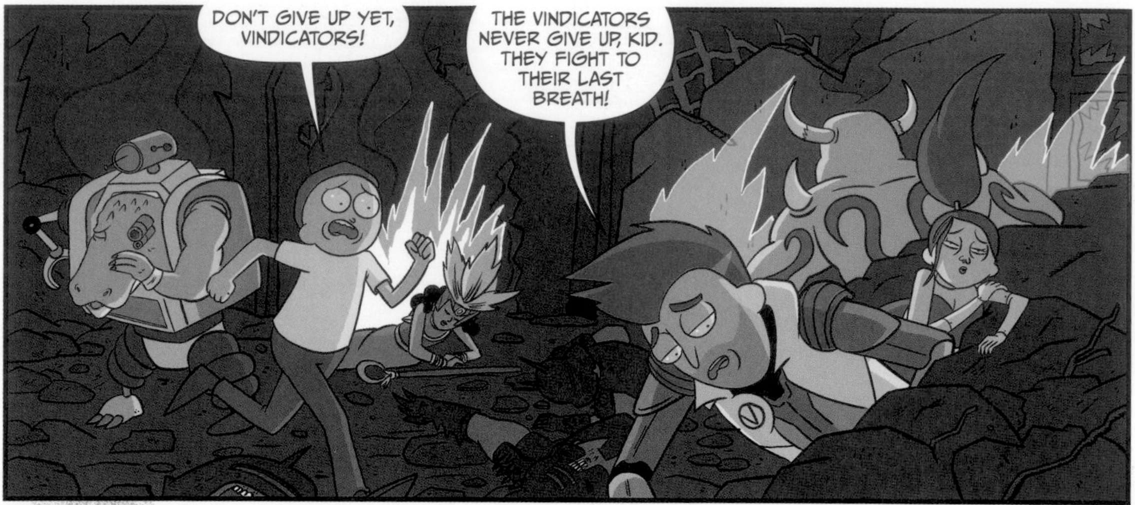
DON'T GIVE UP YET, VINDICATORS!
THE VINDICATORS NEVER GIVE UP, KID. THEY FIGHT TO THEIR LAST BREATH!

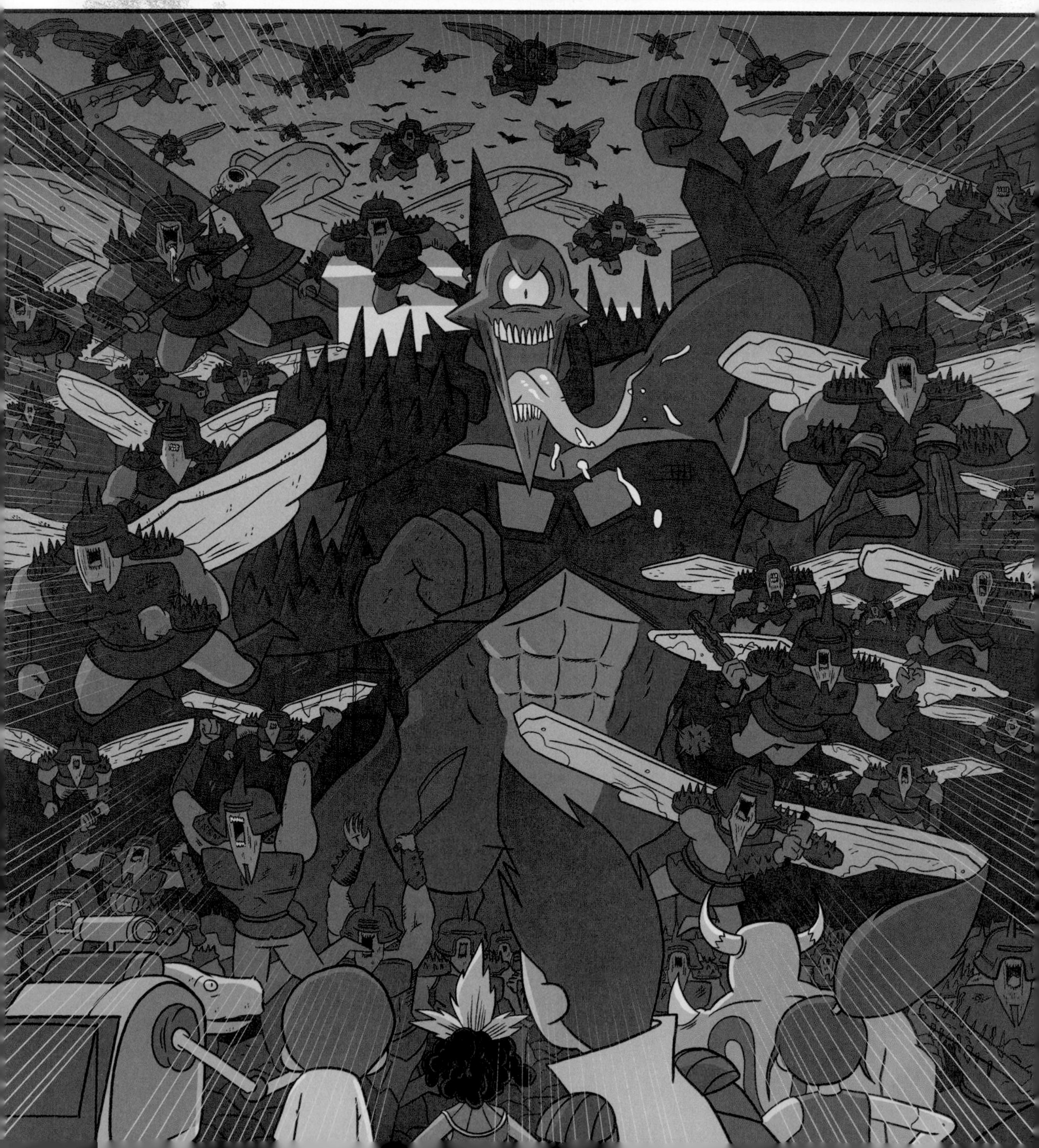

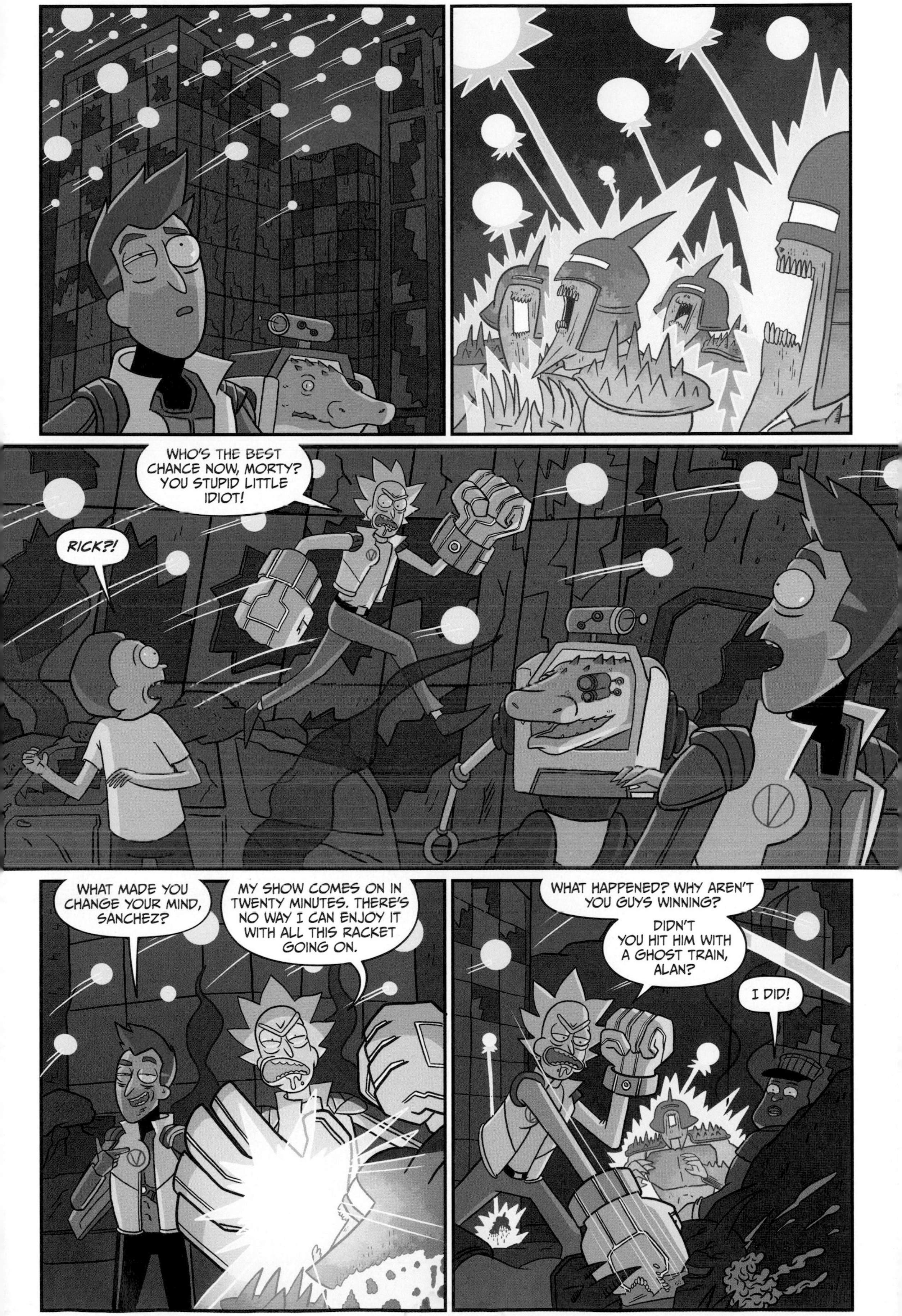
WHO'S THE BEST CHANCE NOW, MORTY? YOU STUPID LITTLE IDIOT!
RICK?!
WHAT MADE YOU CHANGE YOUR MIND, SANCHEZ?
MY SHOW COMES ON IN TWENTY MINUTES. THERE'S NO WAY I CAN ENJOY IT WITH ALL THIS RACKET GOING ON.
WHAT HAPPENED? WHY AREN'T YOU GUYS WINNING?
DIDN'T YOU HIT HIM WITH A GHOST TRAIN, ALAN?
I DID!

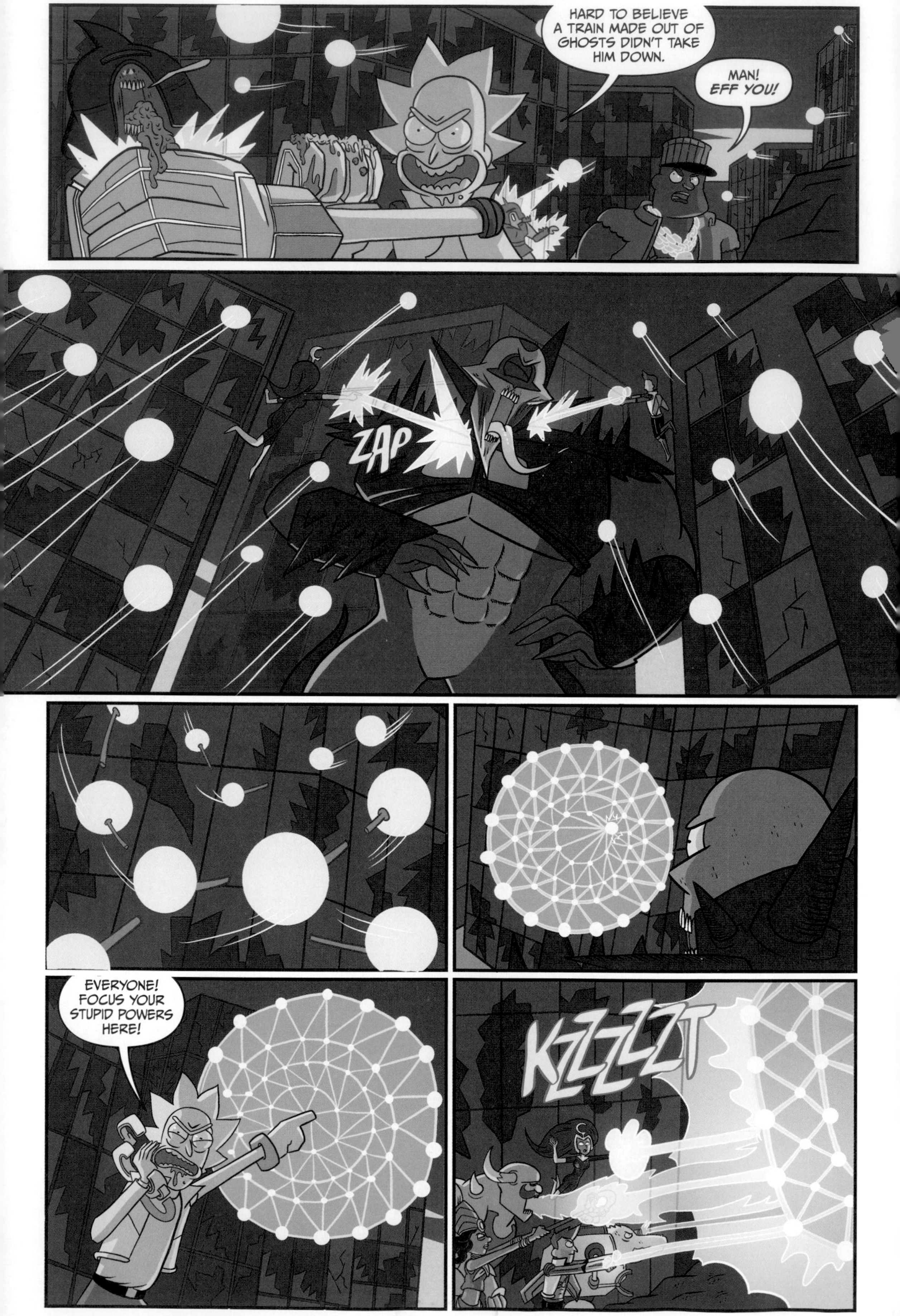
HARD TO BELIEVE A TRAIN MADE OUT OF GHOSTS DIDN'T TAKE HIM DOWN.
MAN! EFF YOU!
ZAP
EVERYONE! FOCUS YOUR STUPID POWERS HERE!
KZZZZZT

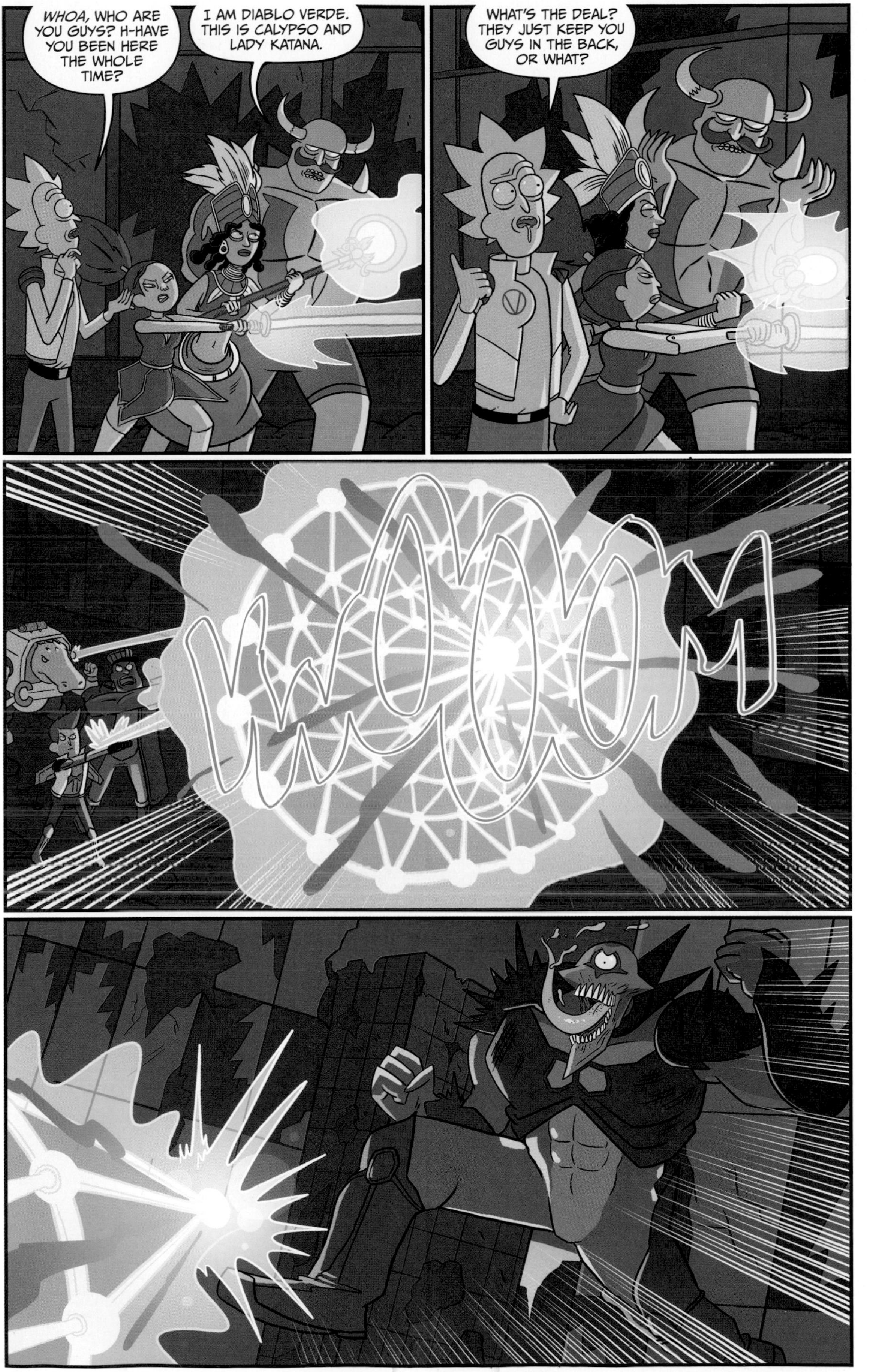
WHOA, WHO ARE YOU GUYS? H-HAVE YOU BEEN HERE THE WHOLE TIME?
I AM DIABLO VERDE. THIS IS CALYPSO AND LADY KATANA.
WHAT'S THE DEAL? THEY JUST KEEP YOU GUYS IN THE BACK, OR WHAT?
VWOOOOM

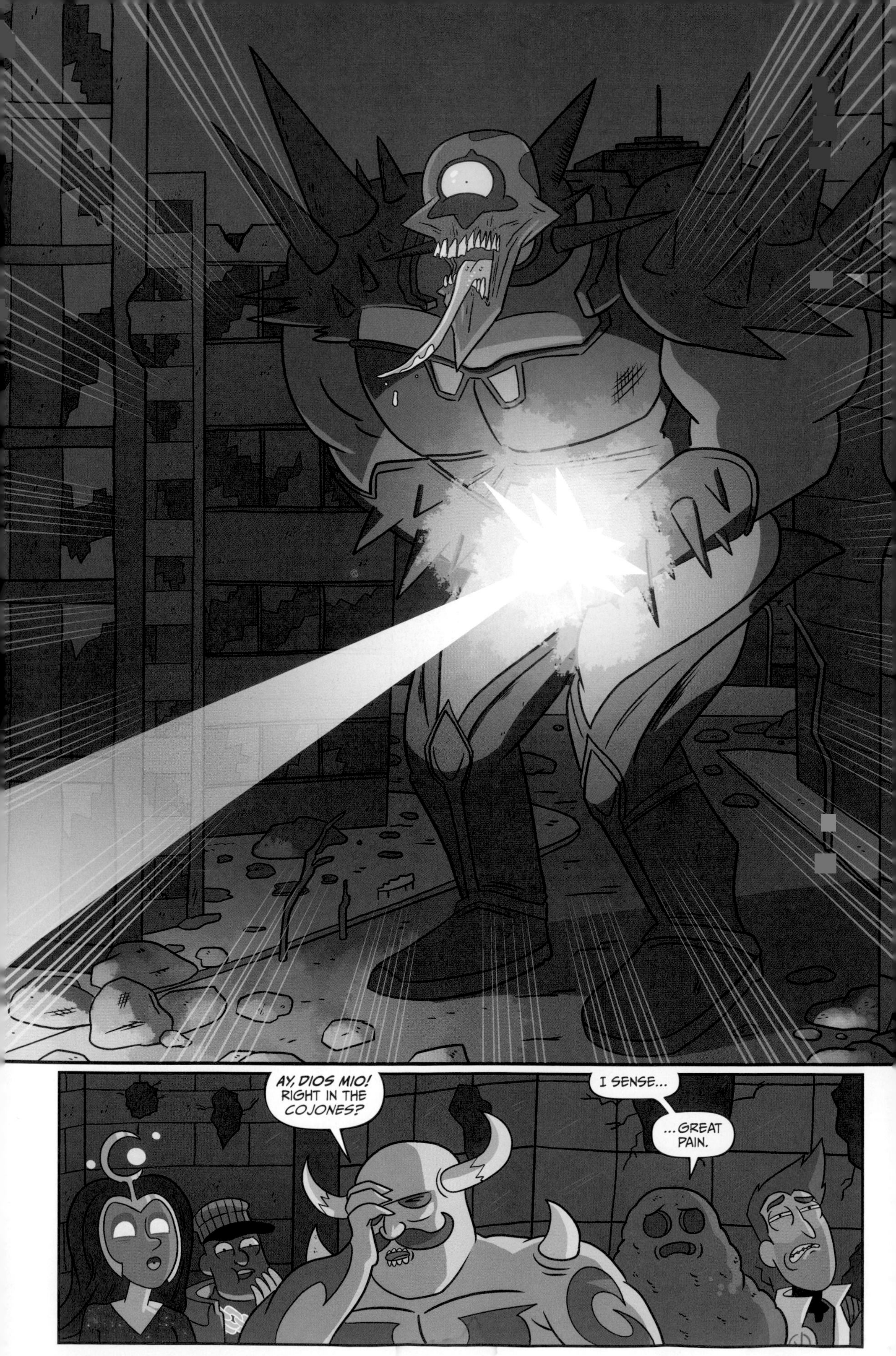
AY, DIOS MIO! RIGHT IN THE COJONES?
I SENSE...
...GREAT PAIN.

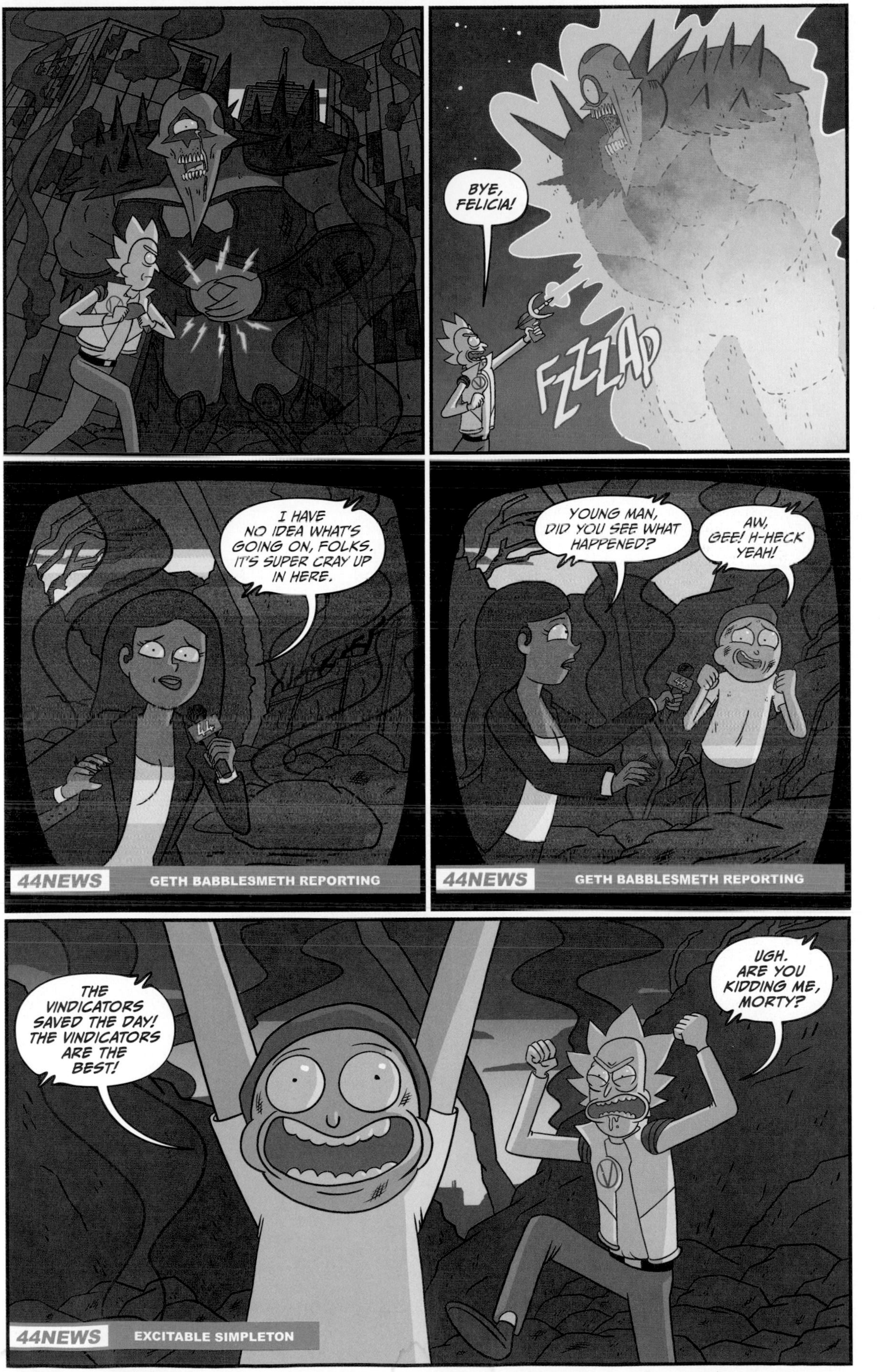
BYE, FELICIA!
FZZZAP
I HAVE NO IDEA WHAT'S GOING ON, FOLKS. IT'S SUPER CRAY UP IN HERE.
44NEWS
GETH BABBLESMETH REPORTING
YOUNG MAN, DID YOU SEE WHAT HAPPENED?
AW, GEE! H-HECK YEAH!
44NEWS
GETH BABBLESMETH REPORTING
THE VINDICATORS SAVED THE DAY! THE VINDICATORS ARE THE BEST!
UGH. ARE YOU KIDDING ME, MORTY?
44NEWS
EXCITABLE SIMPLETON

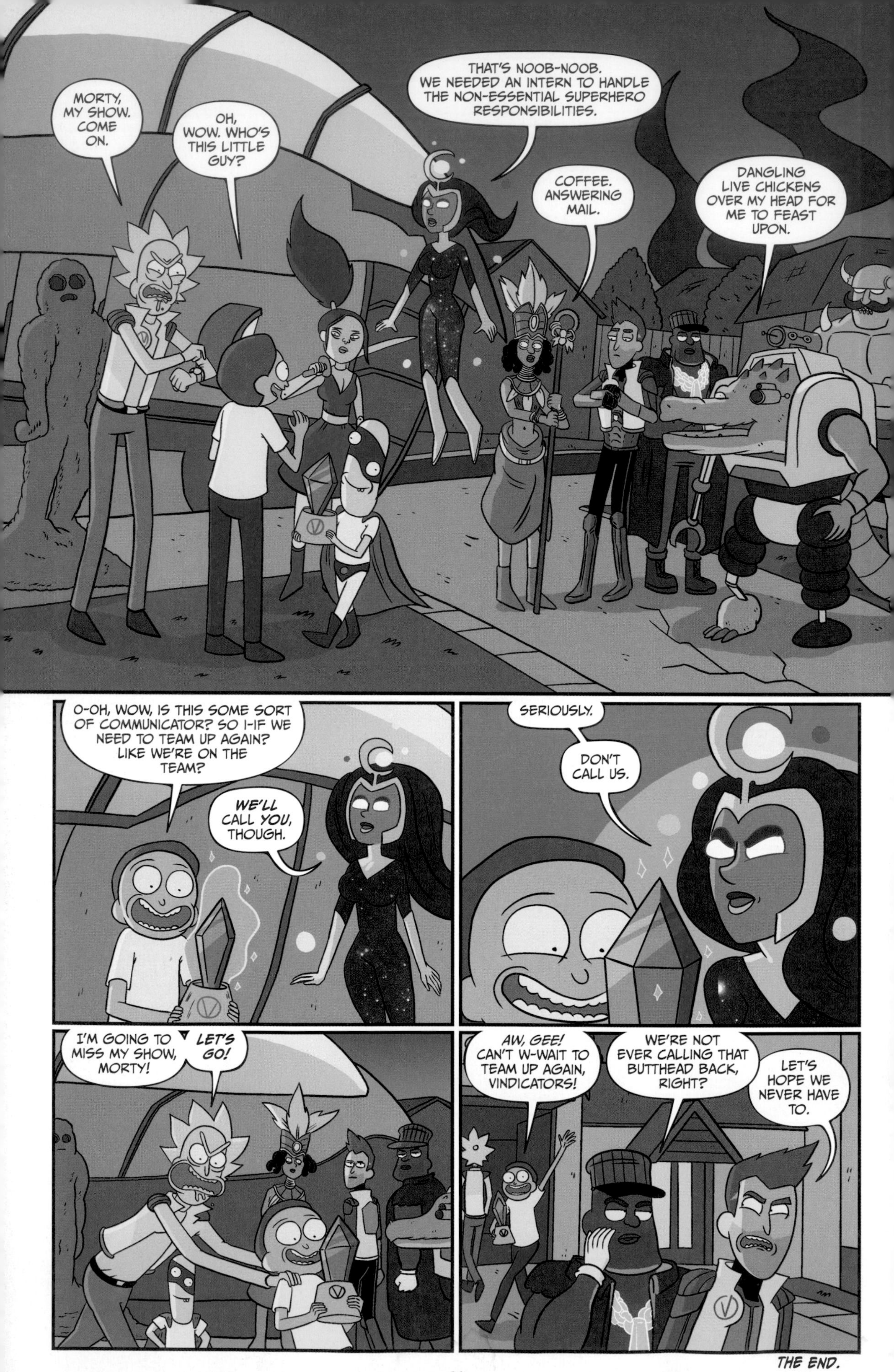

MORTY, MY SHOW. COME ON.
OH, WOW. WHO'S THIS LITTLE GUY?
THAT'S NOOB-NOOB. WE NEEDED AN INTERN TO HANDLE THE NON-ESSENTIAL SUPERHERO RESPONSIBILITIES.
COFFEE. ANSWERING MAIL.
DANGLING LIVE CHICKENS OVER MY HEAD FOR ME TO FEAST UPON.
O-OH, WOW, IS THIS SOME SORT OF COMMUNICATOR? SO I-IF WE NEED TO TEAM UP AGAIN? LIKE WE'RE ON THE TEAM?
WE'LL CALL YOU, THOUGH.
SERIOUSLY.
DON'T CALL US.
I'M GOING TO MISS MY SHOW, MORTY!
LET'S GO!
AW, GEE! CAN'T W-WAIT TO TEAM UP AGAIN, VINDICATORS!
WE'RE NOT EVER CALLING THAT BUTTHEAD BACK, RIGHT?
LET'S HOPE WE NEVER HAVE TO.

THE END.

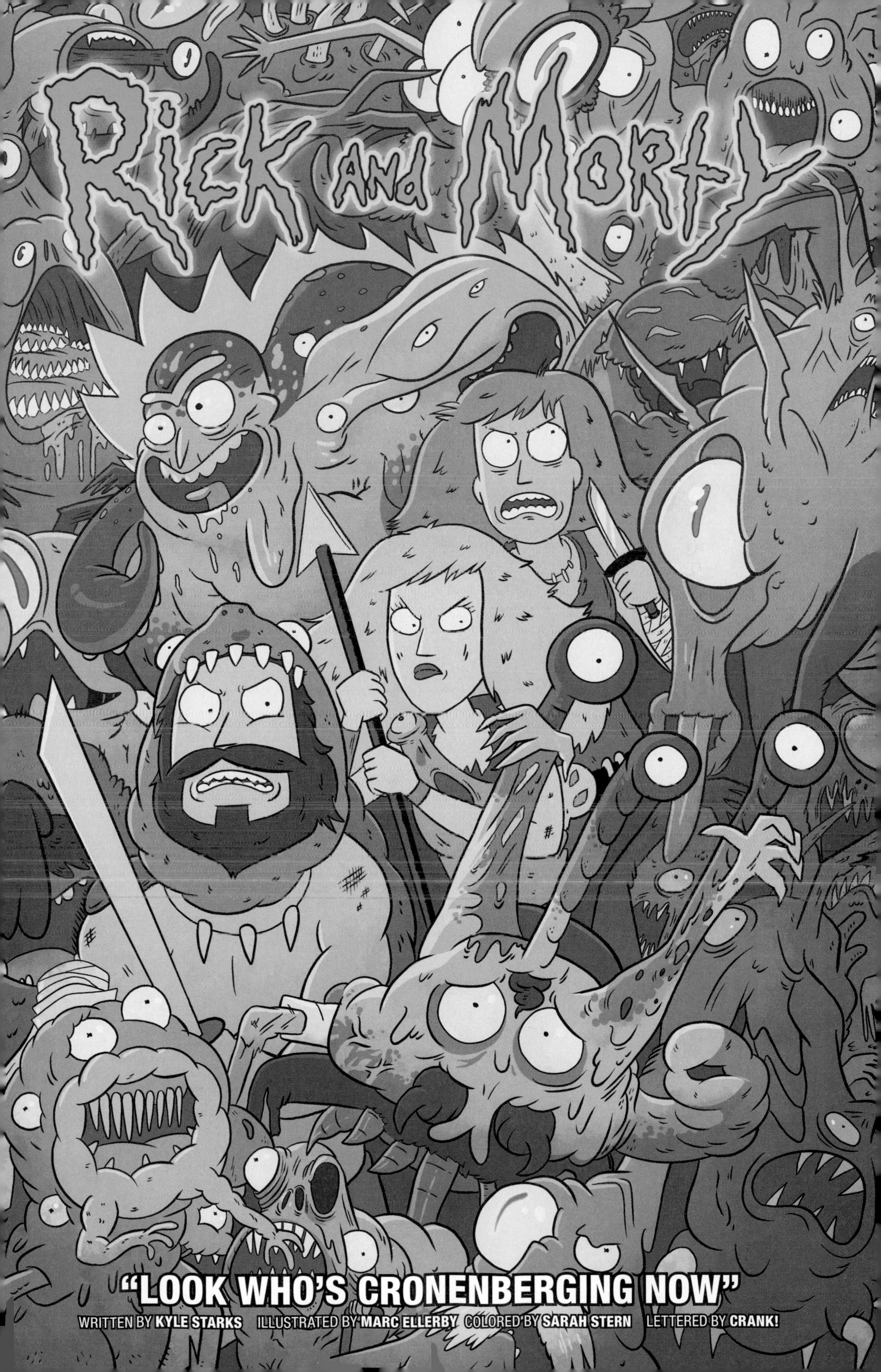
Rick and Morty™
"LOOK WHO'S CRONENBERGING NOW"
WRITTEN BY KYLE STARKS ILLUSTRATED BY MARC ELLERBY COLORED BY SARAH STERN LETTERED BY CRANK!

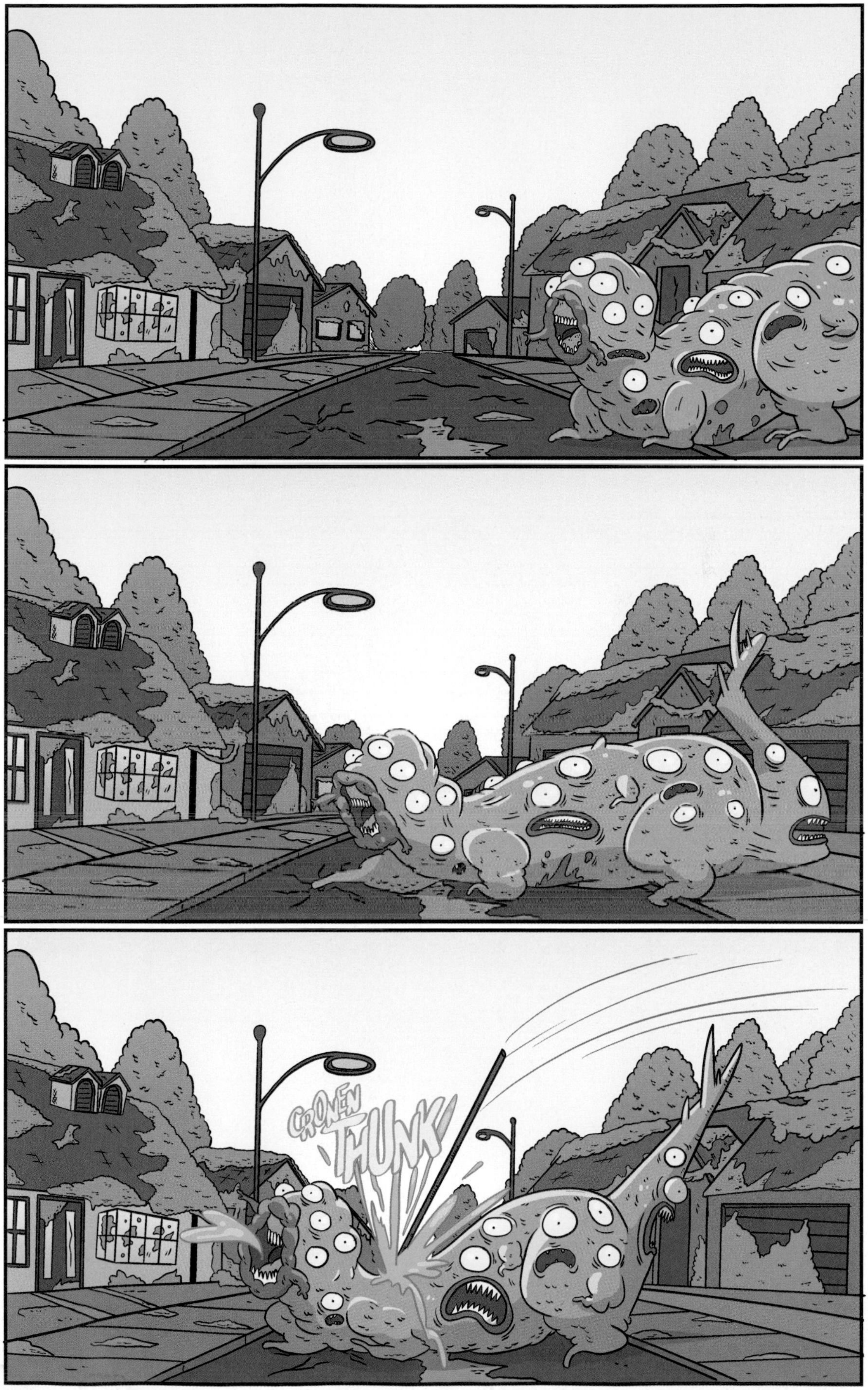
CRONEN
THUNK

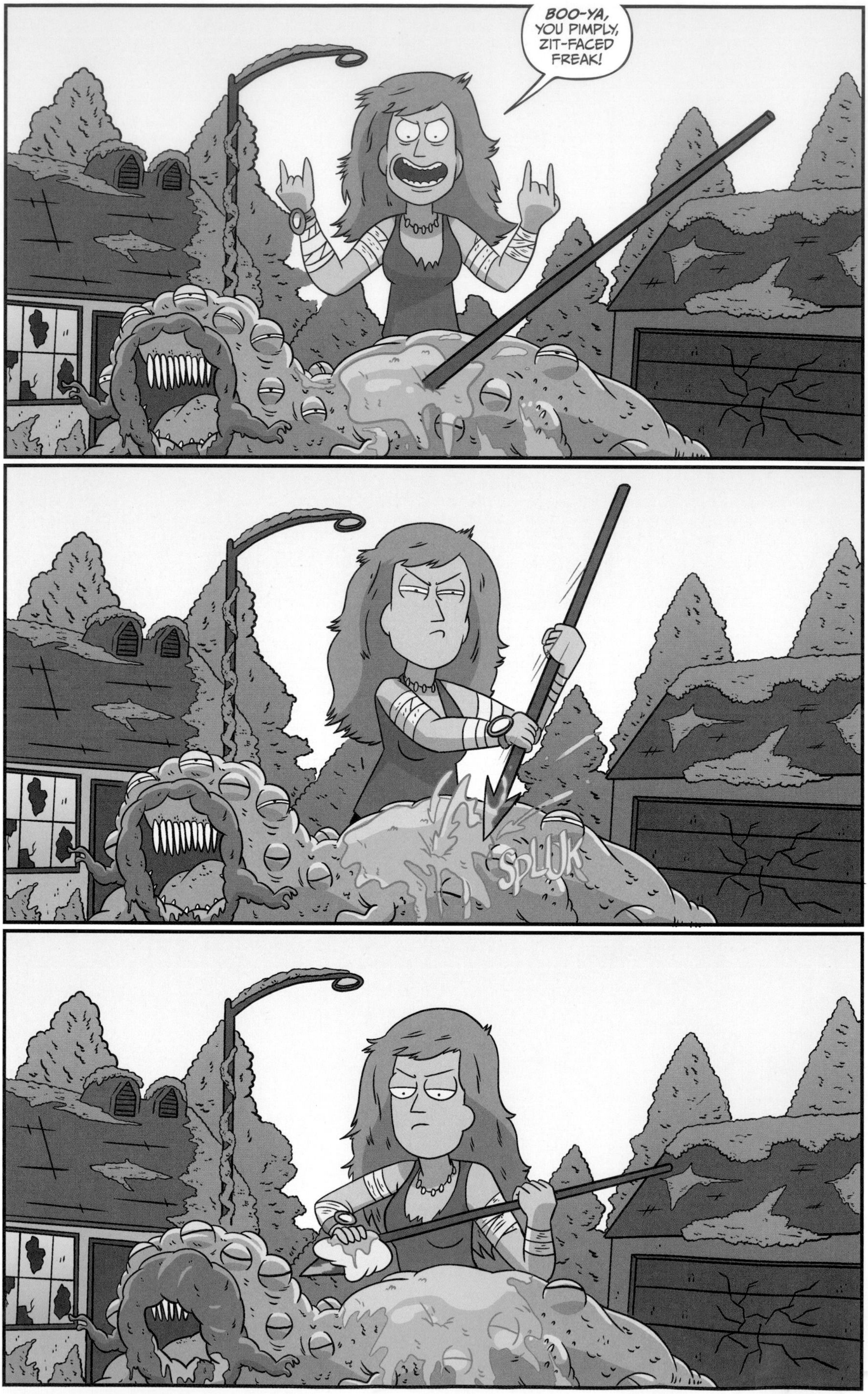
BOO-YA, YOU PIMPLY, ZIT-FACED FREAK!
SPLUK

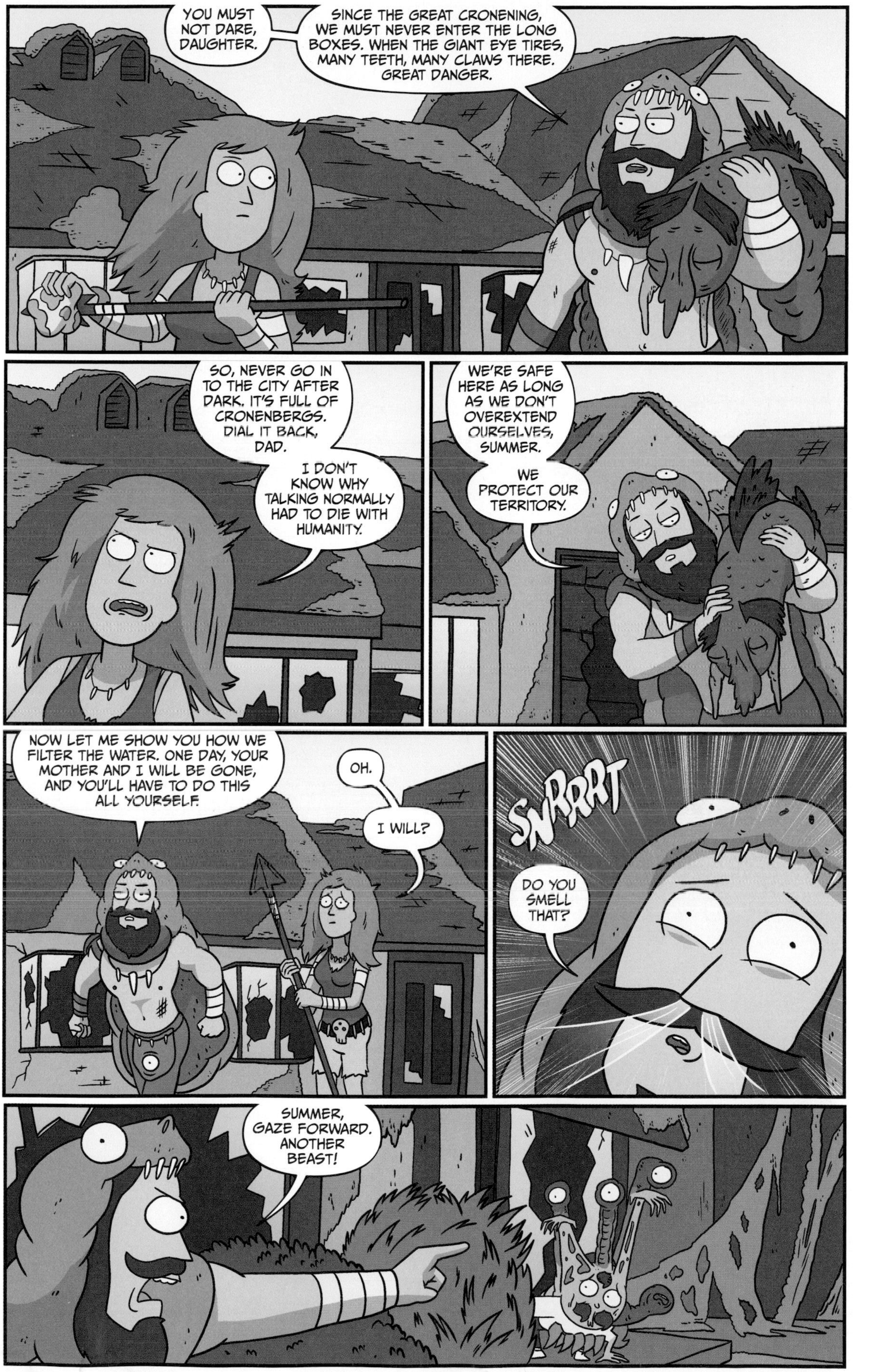
YOU MUST NOT DARE, DAUGHTER.
SINCE THE GREAT CRONENING, WE MUST NEVER ENTER THE LONG BOXES. WHEN THE GIANT EYE TIRES, MANY TEETH, MANY CLAWS THERE. GREAT DANGER.
SO, NEVER GO IN TO THE CITY AFTER DARK. IT'S FULL OF CRONENBERGS. DIAL IT BACK, DAD.
I DON'T KNOW WHY TALKING NORMALLY HAD TO DIE WITH HUMANITY.
WE'RE SAFE HERE AS LONG AS WE DON'T OVEREXTEND OURSELVES, SUMMER.
WE PROTECT OUR TERRITORY.
NOW LET ME SHOW YOU HOW WE FILTER THE WATER. ONE DAY, YOUR MOTHER AND I WILL BE GONE, AND YOU'LL HAVE TO DO THIS ALL YOURSELF.
OH.
I WILL?
SNRRRT
DO YOU SMELL THAT?
SUMMER, GAZE FORWARD. ANOTHER BEAST!

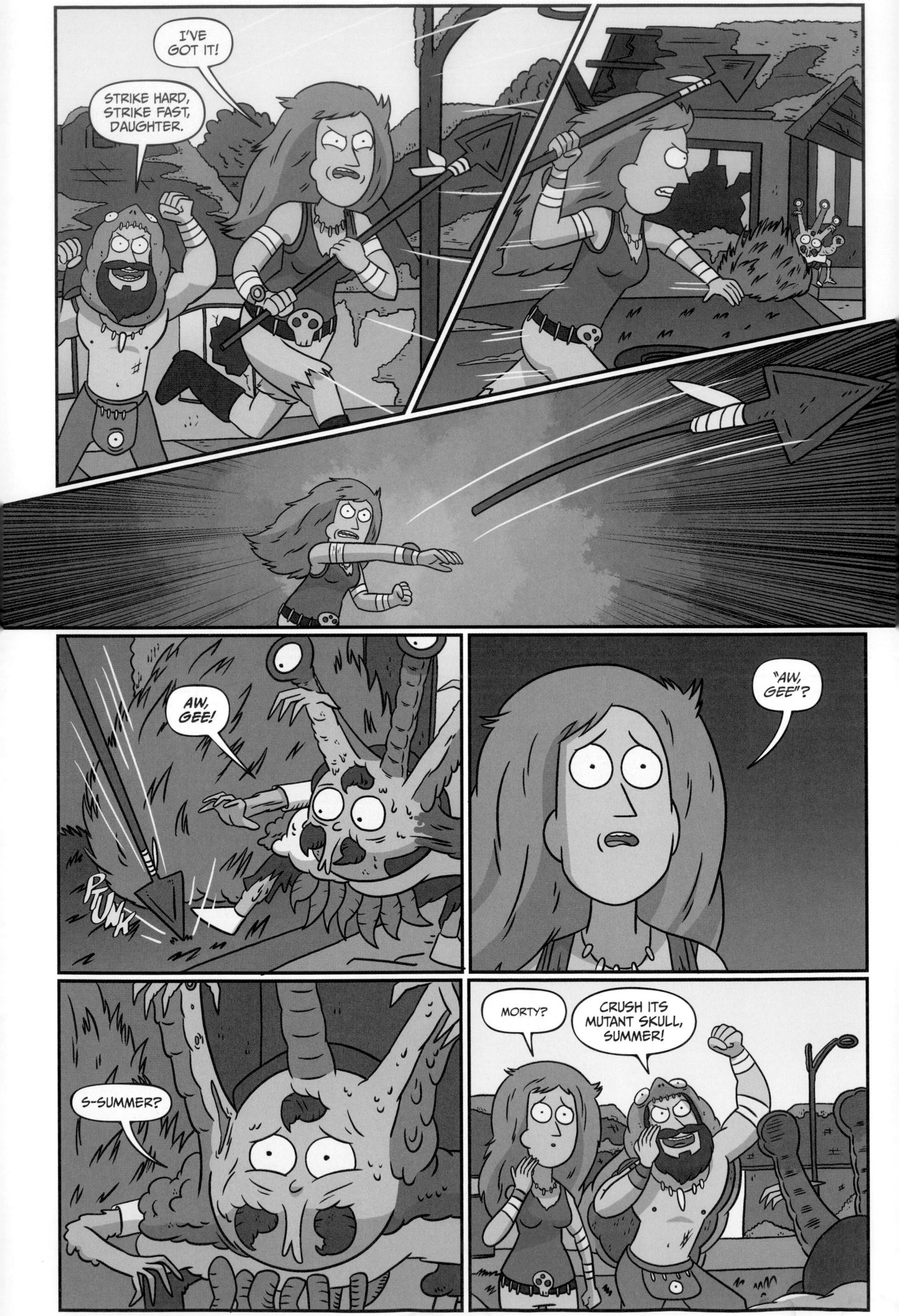

STRIKE HARD, STRIKE FAST, DAUGHTER.
I'VE GOT IT!
AW, GEE!
PTUNK
"AW, GEE"?
S-SUMMER?
MORTY?
CRUSH ITS MUTANT SKULL, SUMMER!

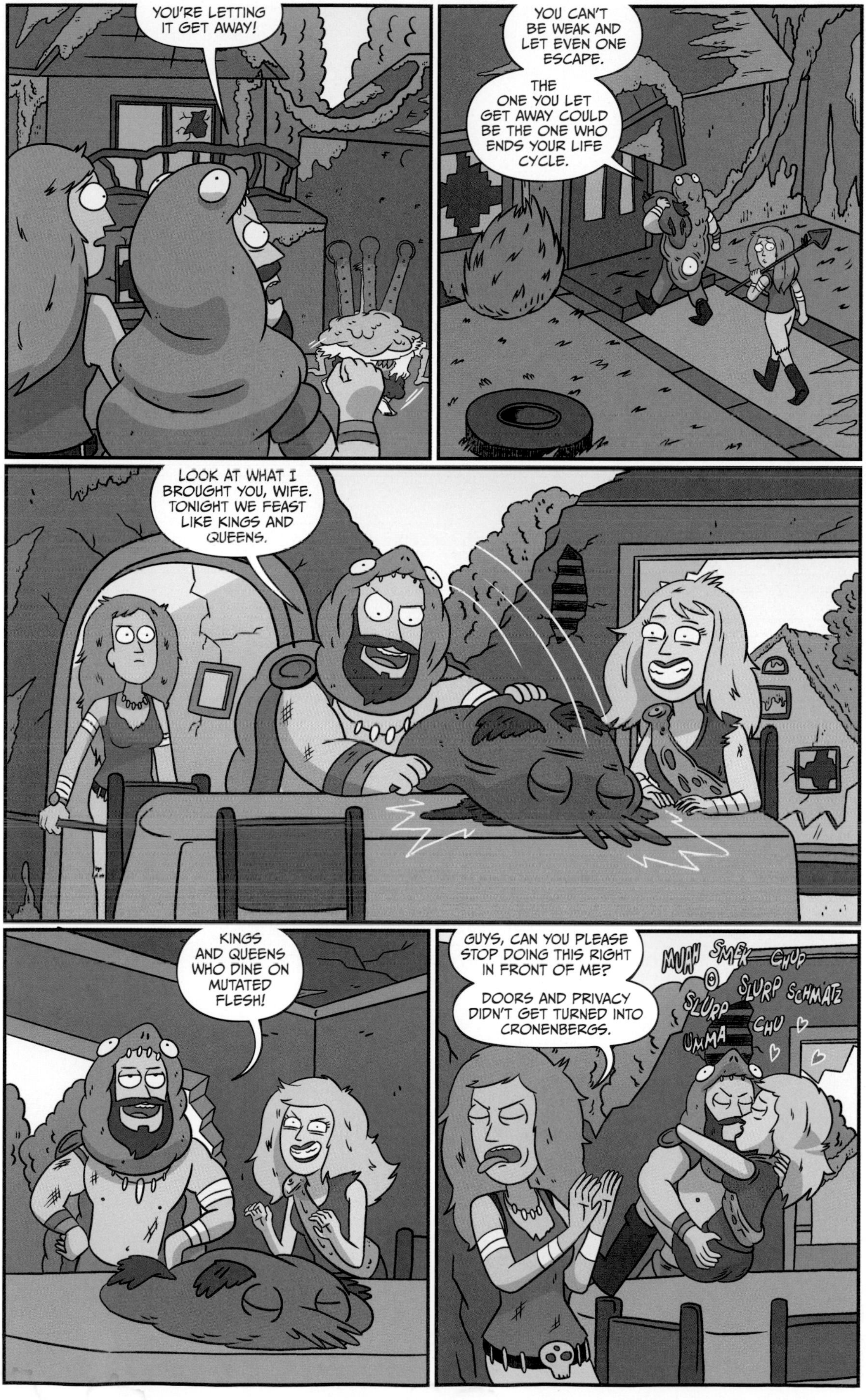
YOU'RE LETTING IT GET AWAY!
YOU CAN'T BE WEAK AND LET EVEN ONE ESCAPE.
THE ONE YOU LET GET AWAY COULD BE THE ONE WHO ENDS YOUR LIFE CYCLE.
LOOK AT WHAT I BROUGHT YOU, WIFE. TONIGHT WE FEAST LIKE KINGS AND QUEENS.
KINGS AND QUEENS WHO DINE ON MUTATED FLESH!
GUYS, CAN YOU PLEASE STOP DOING THIS RIGHT IN FRONT OF ME?
DOORS AND PRIVACY DIDN'T GET TURNED INTO CRONENBERGS.
MUAH SMEK CHUP
SLURP SCHMATZ
SLURP
CHU
UMMA

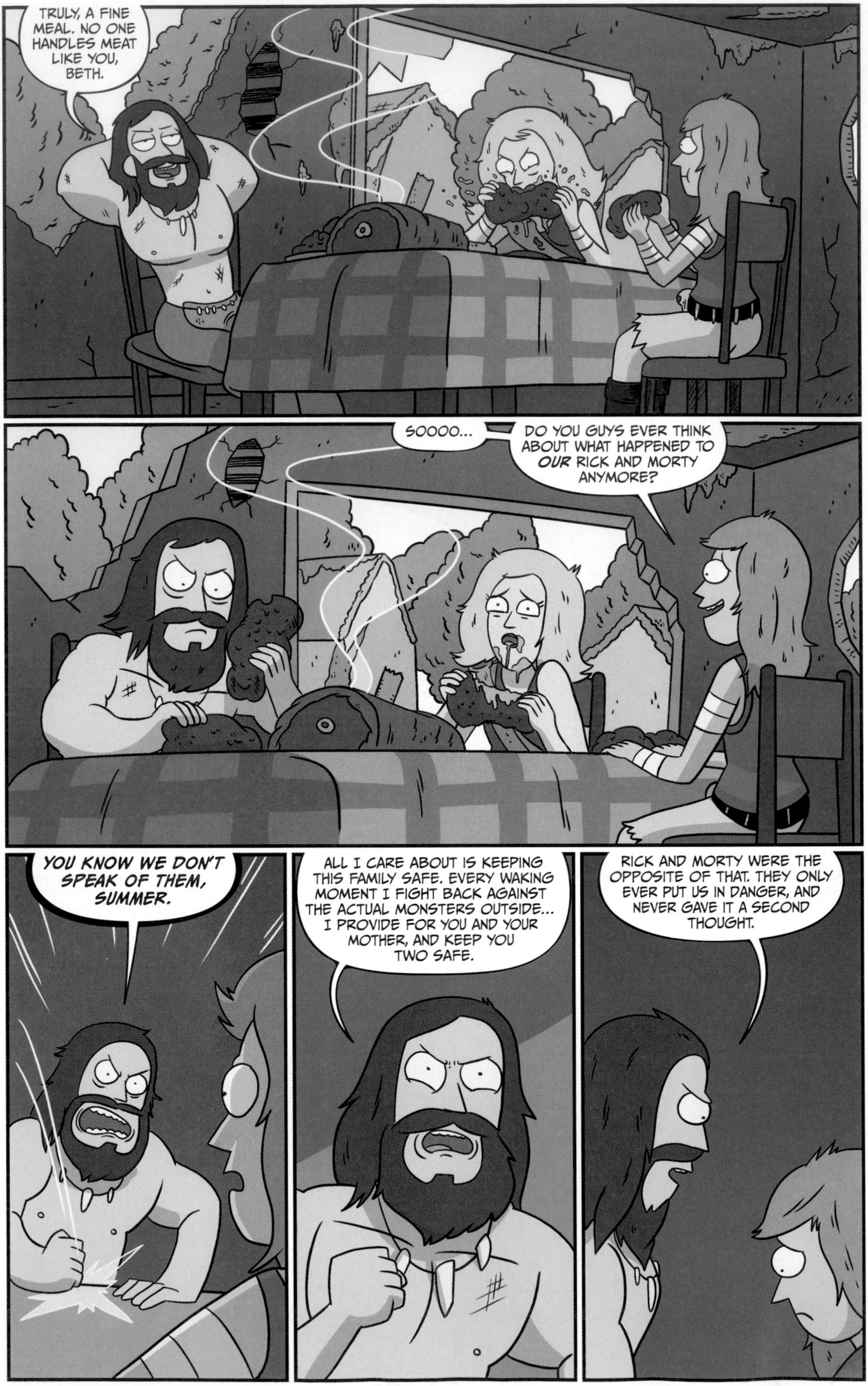
TRULY, A FINE MEAL. NO ONE HANDLES MEAT LIKE YOU, BETH.
SOOOO...
DO YOU GUYS EVER THINK ABOUT WHAT HAPPENED TO OUR RICK AND MORTY ANYMORE?
YOU KNOW WE DON'T SPEAK OF THEM, SUMMER.
ALL I CARE ABOUT IS KEEPING THIS FAMILY SAFE. EVERY WAKING MOMENT I FIGHT BACK AGAINST THE ACTUAL MONSTERS OUTSIDE... I PROVIDE FOR YOU AND YOUR MOTHER, AND KEEP YOU TWO SAFE.
RICK AND MORTY WERE THE OPPOSITE OF THAT. THEY ONLY EVER PUT US IN DANGER, AND NEVER GAVE IT A SECOND THOUGHT.

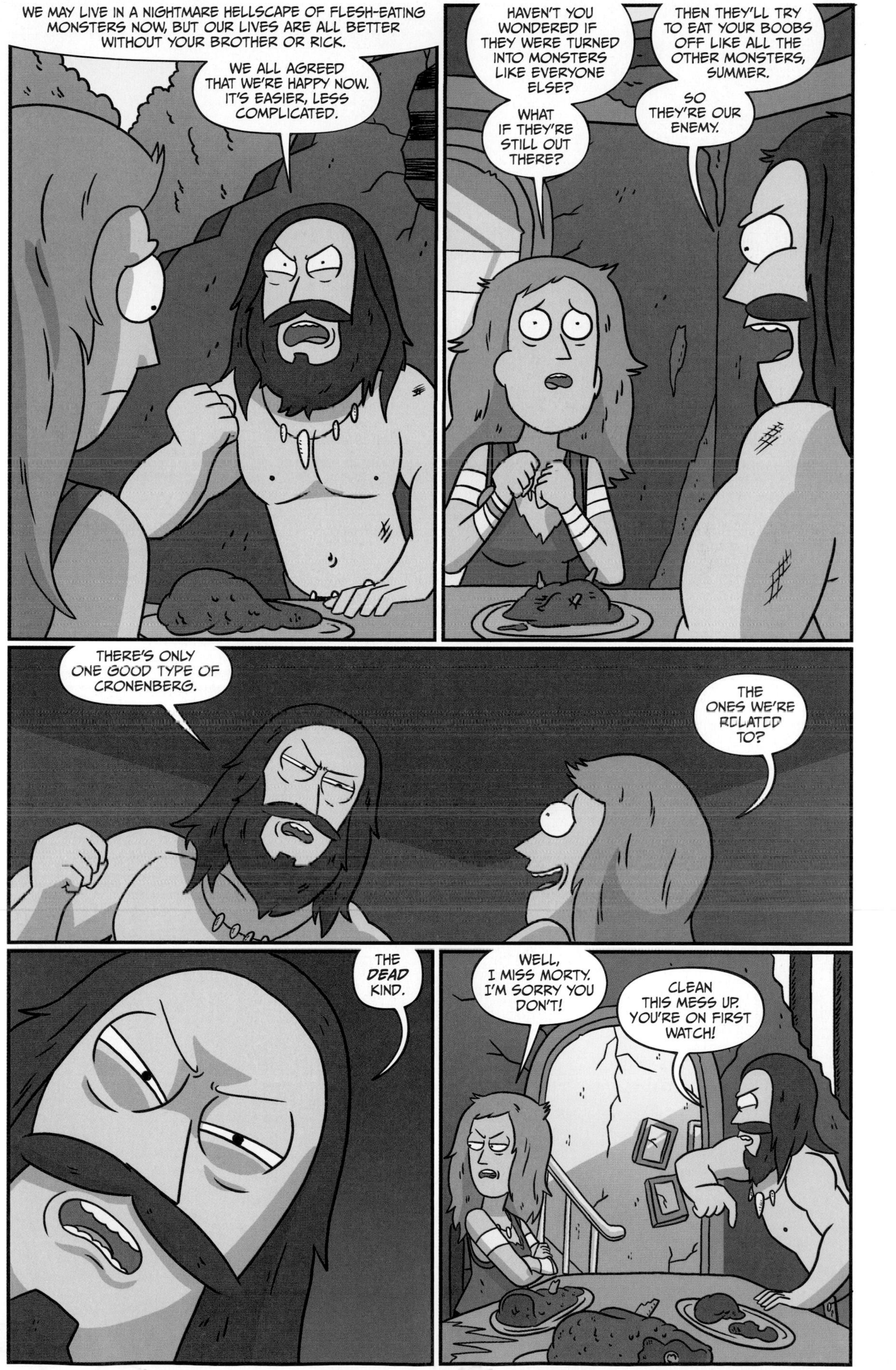
WE MAY LIVE IN A NIGHTMARE HELLSCAPE OF FLESH-EATING MONSTERS NOW, BUT OUR LIVES ARE ALL BETTER WITHOUT YOUR BROTHER OR RICK.
WE ALL AGREED THAT WE'RE HAPPY NOW. IT'S EASIER, LESS COMPLICATED.
HAVEN'T YOU WONDERED IF THEY WERE TURNED INTO MONSTERS LIKE EVERYONE ELSE?
WHAT IF THEY'RE STILL OUT THERE?
THEN THEY'LL TRY TO EAT YOUR BOOBS OFF LIKE ALL THE OTHER MONSTERS, SUMMER.
SO THEY'RE OUR ENEMY.
THERE'S ONLY ONE GOOD TYPE OF CRONENBERG.
THE ONES WE'RE RELATED TO?
THE ***DEAD*** KIND.
WELL, I MISS MORTY. I'M SORRY YOU DON'T!
CLEAN THIS MESS UP. YOU'RE ON FIRST WATCH!

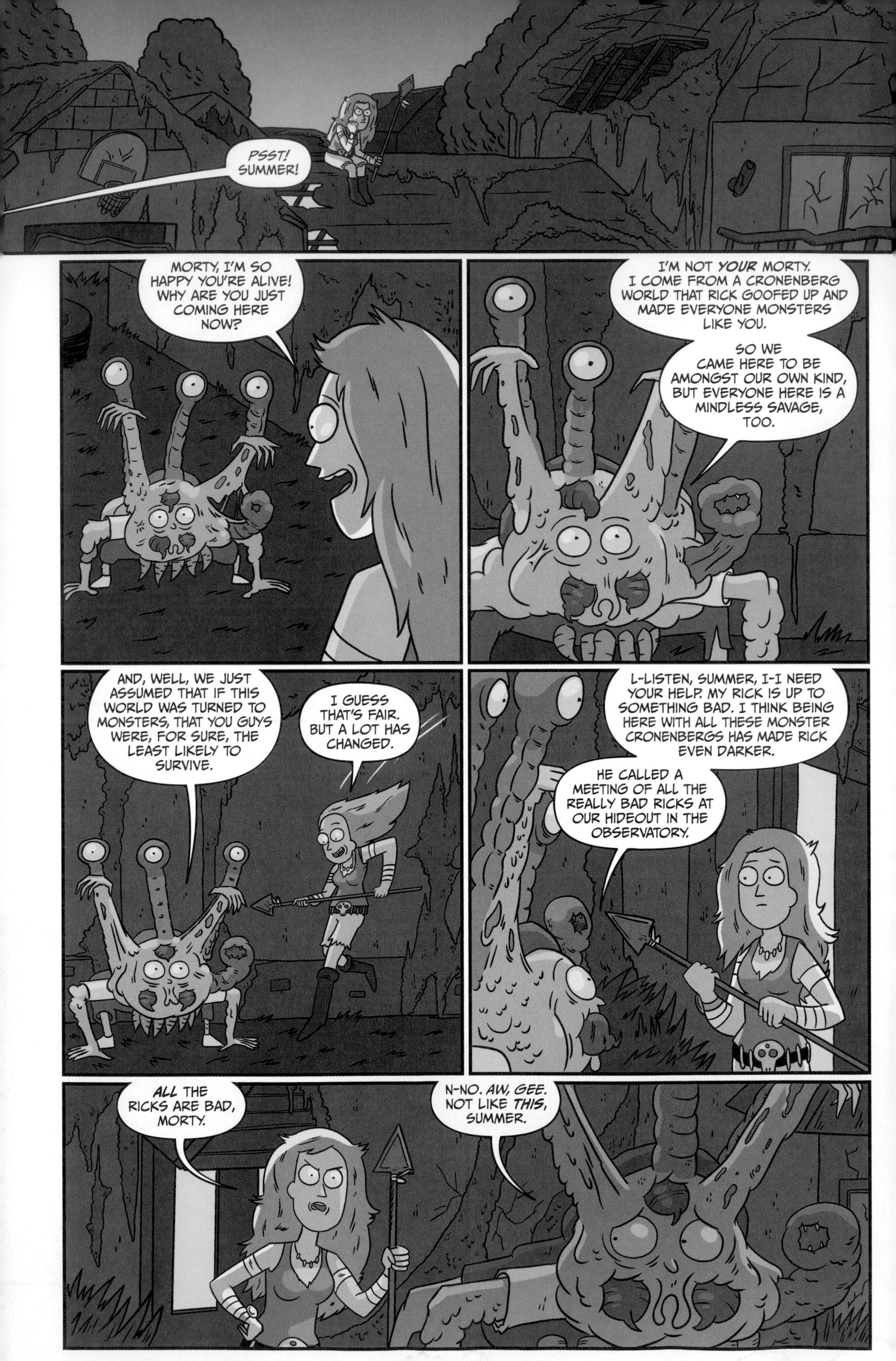
PSST! SUMMER!
MORTY, I'M SO HAPPY YOU'RE ALIVE! WHY ARE YOU JUST COMING HERE NOW?
I'M NOT *YOUR* MORTY. I COME FROM A CRONENBERG WORLD THAT RICK GOOFED UP AND MADE EVERYONE MONSTERS LIKE YOU.
SO WE CAME HERE TO BE AMONGST OUR OWN KIND, BUT EVERYONE HERE IS A MINDLESS SAVAGE, TOO.
AND, WELL, WE JUST ASSUMED THAT IF THIS WORLD WAS TURNED TO MONSTERS, THAT YOU GUYS WERE, FOR SURE, THE LEAST LIKELY TO SURVIVE.
I GUESS THAT'S FAIR. BUT A LOT HAS CHANGED.
L-LISTEN, SUMMER, I-I NEED YOUR HELP. MY RICK IS UP TO SOMETHING BAD. I THINK BEING HERE WITH ALL THESE MONSTER CRONENBERGS HAS MADE RICK EVEN DARKER.
HE CALLED A MEETING OF ALL THE REALLY BAD RICKS AT OUR HIDEOUT IN THE OBSERVATORY.
ALL THE RICKS ARE BAD, MORTY.
N-NO. *AW, GEE.* NOT LIKE *THIS*, SUMMER.

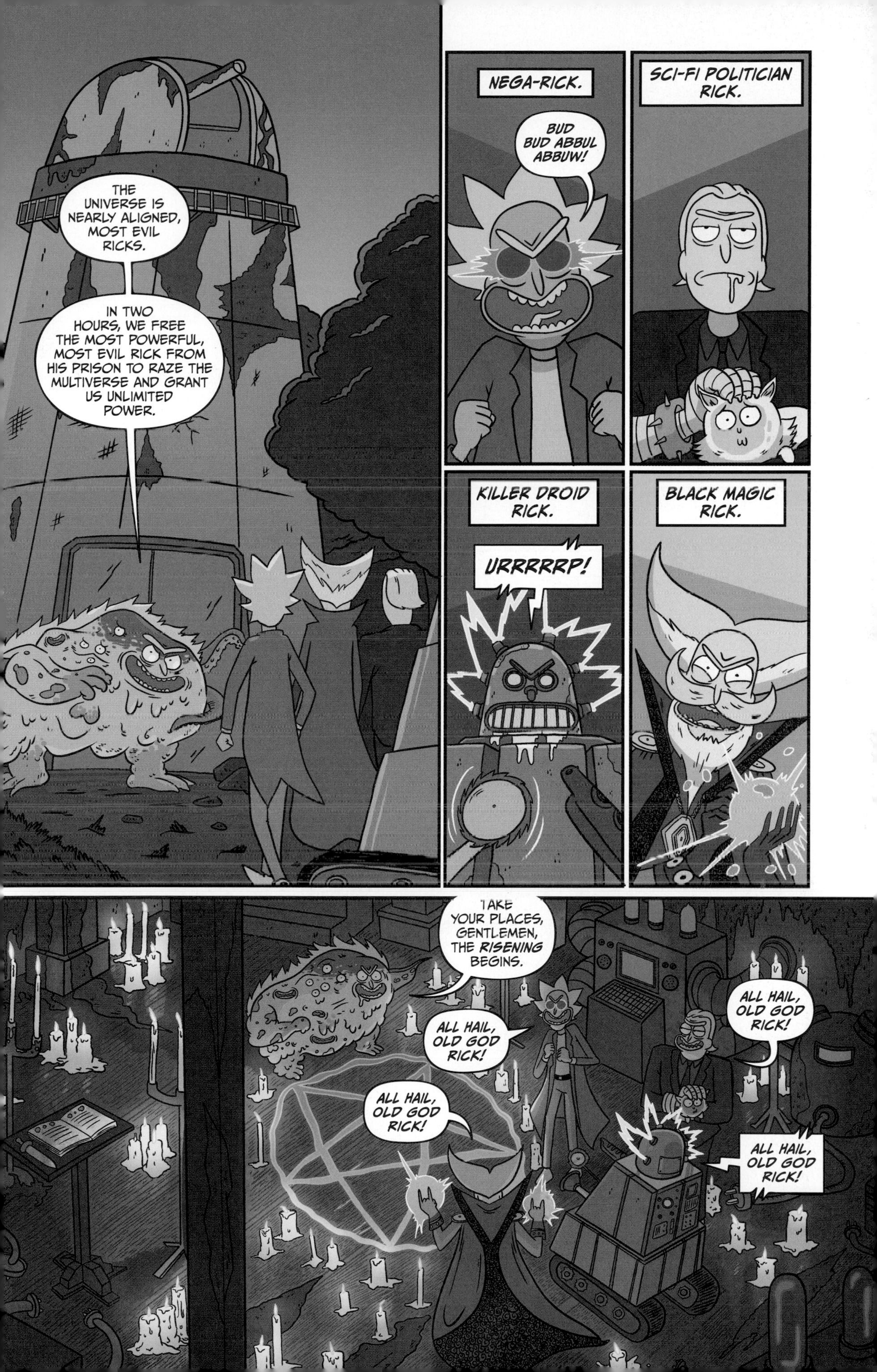
THE UNIVERSE IS NEARLY ALIGNED, MOST EVIL RICKS.
IN TWO HOURS, WE FREE THE MOST POWERFUL, MOST EVIL RICK FROM HIS PRISON TO RAZE THE MULTIVERSE AND GRANT US UNLIMITED POWER.
NEGA-RICK.
BUD BUD ABBUL ABBUW!
SCI-FI POLITICIAN RICK.
KILLER DROID RICK.
URRRRRP!
BLACK MAGIC RICK.
TAKE YOUR PLACES, GENTLEMEN, THE RISENING BEGINS.
ALL HAIL, OLD GOD RICK!
ALL HAIL, OLD GOD RICK!
ALL HAIL, OLD GOD RICK!
ALL HAIL, OLD GOD RICK!

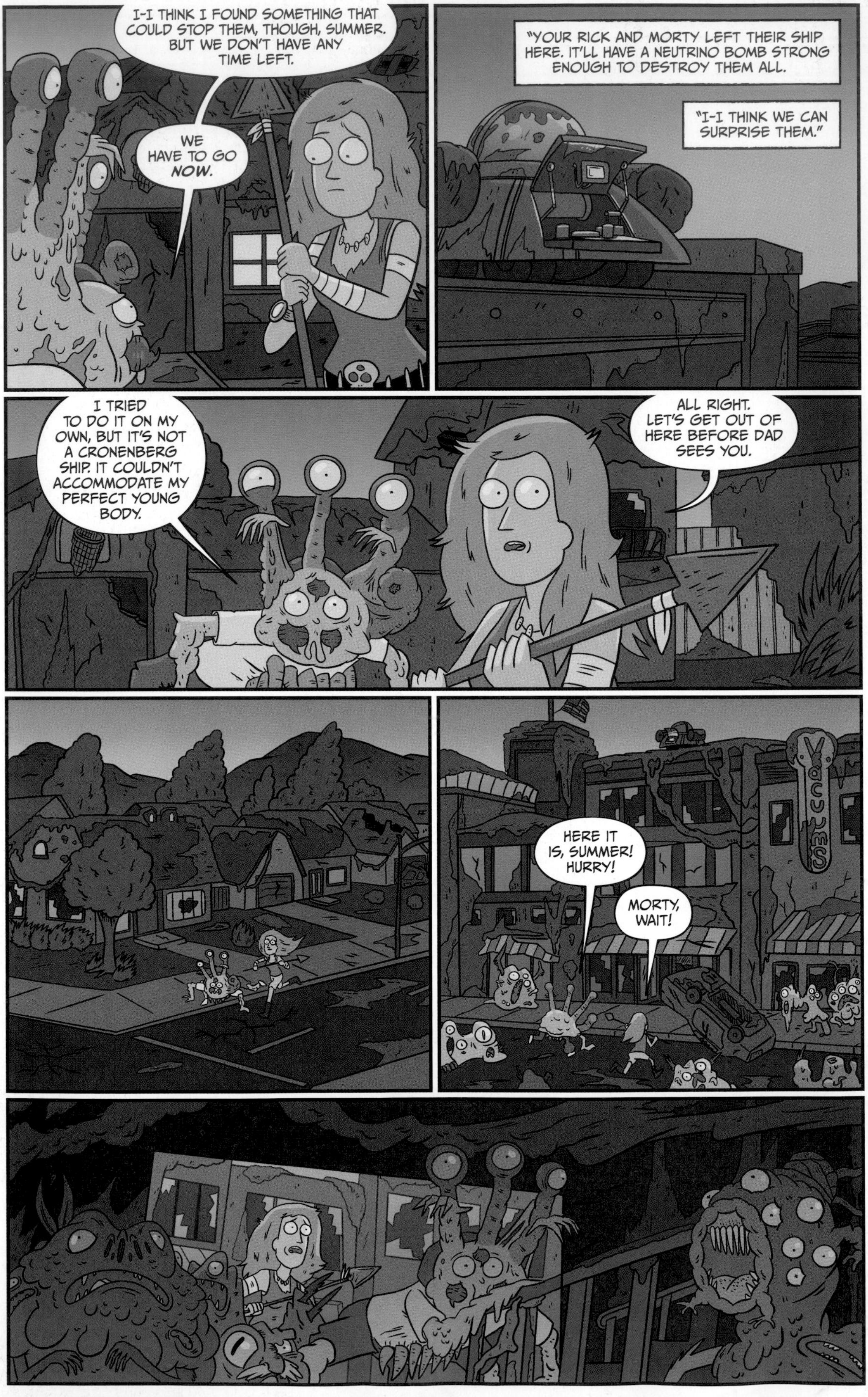
I-I THINK I FOUND SOMETHING THAT COULD STOP THEM, THOUGH, SUMMER. BUT WE DON'T HAVE ANY TIME LEFT.
WE HAVE TO GO *NOW*.
"YOUR RICK AND MORTY LEFT THEIR SHIP HERE. IT'LL HAVE A NEUTRINO BOMB STRONG ENOUGH TO DESTROY THEM ALL.
"I-I THINK WE CAN SURPRISE THEM."
I TRIED TO DO IT ON MY OWN, BUT IT'S NOT A CRONENBERG SHIP. IT COULDN'T ACCOMMODATE MY PERFECT YOUNG BODY.
ALL RIGHT. LET'S GET OUT OF HERE BEFORE DAD SEES YOU.
VACUUMS
HERE IT IS, SUMMER! HURRY!
MORTY, WAIT!

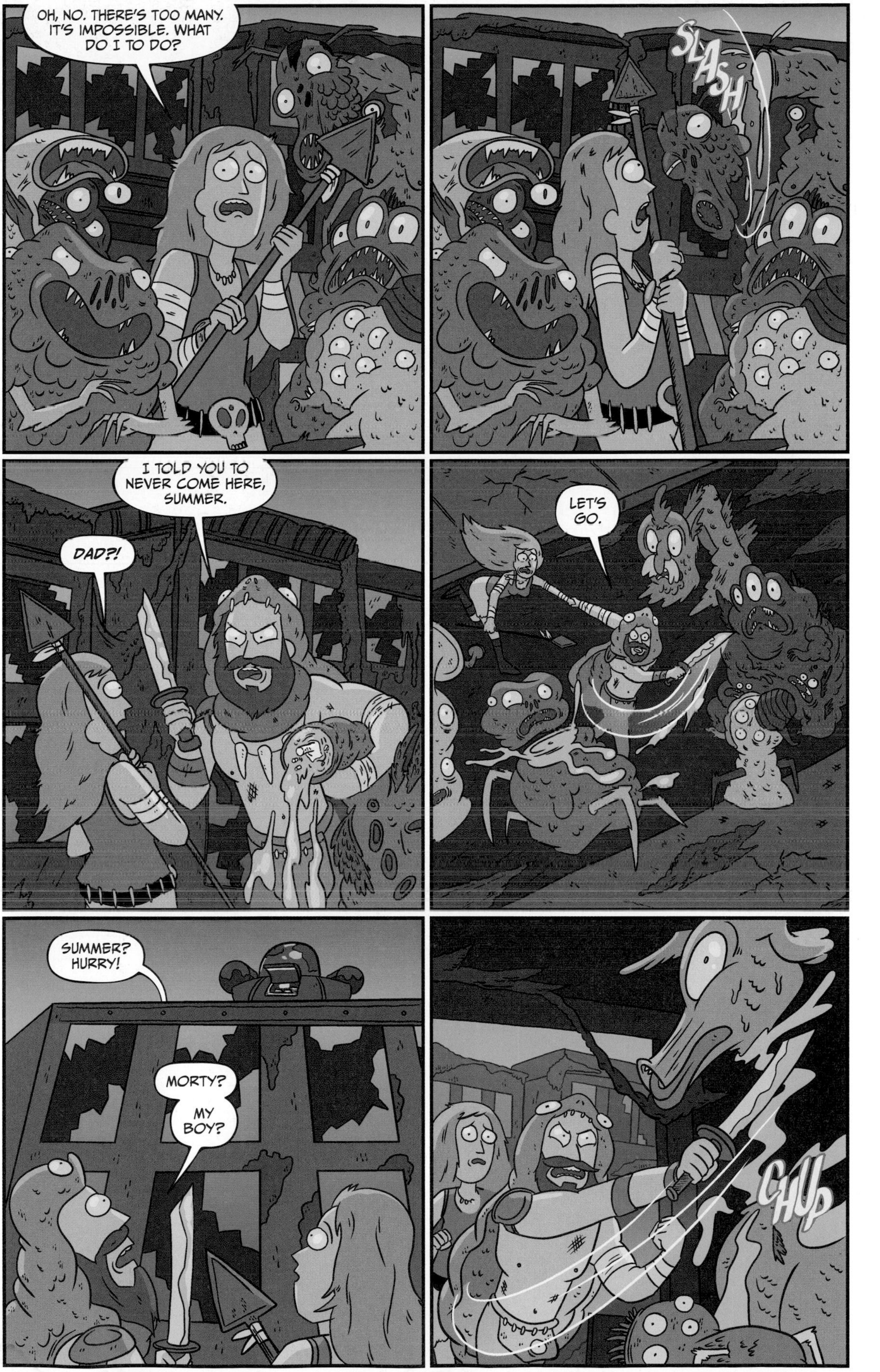
OH, NO. THERE'S TOO MANY. IT'S IMPOSSIBLE. WHAT DO I TO DO?
SLASH
DAD?!
I TOLD YOU TO NEVER COME HERE, SUMMER.
LET'S GO.
SUMMER? HURRY!
MORTY?
MY BOY?
CHUP

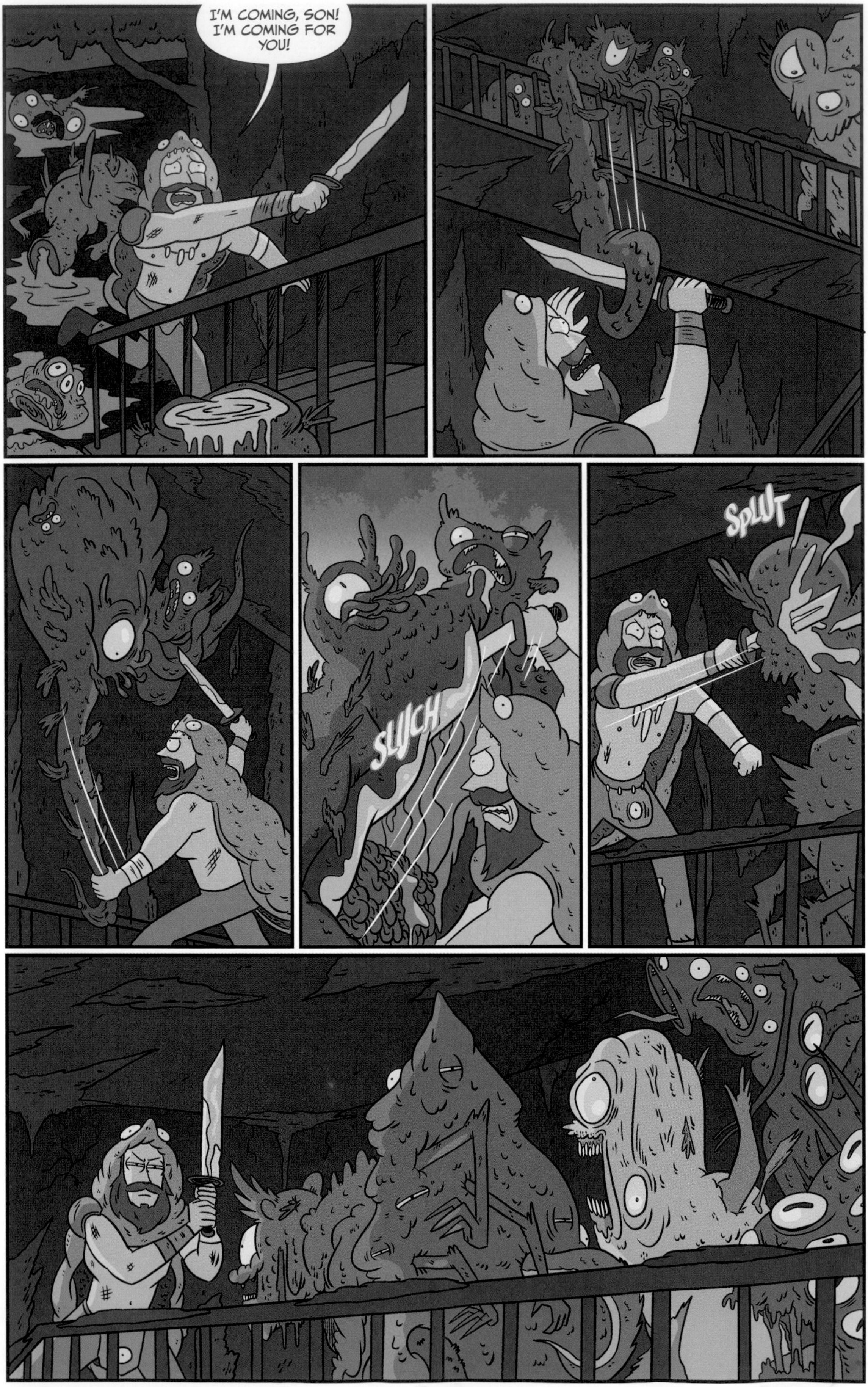
I'M COMING, SON! I'M COMING FOR YOU!
SLUCH
SPLUT

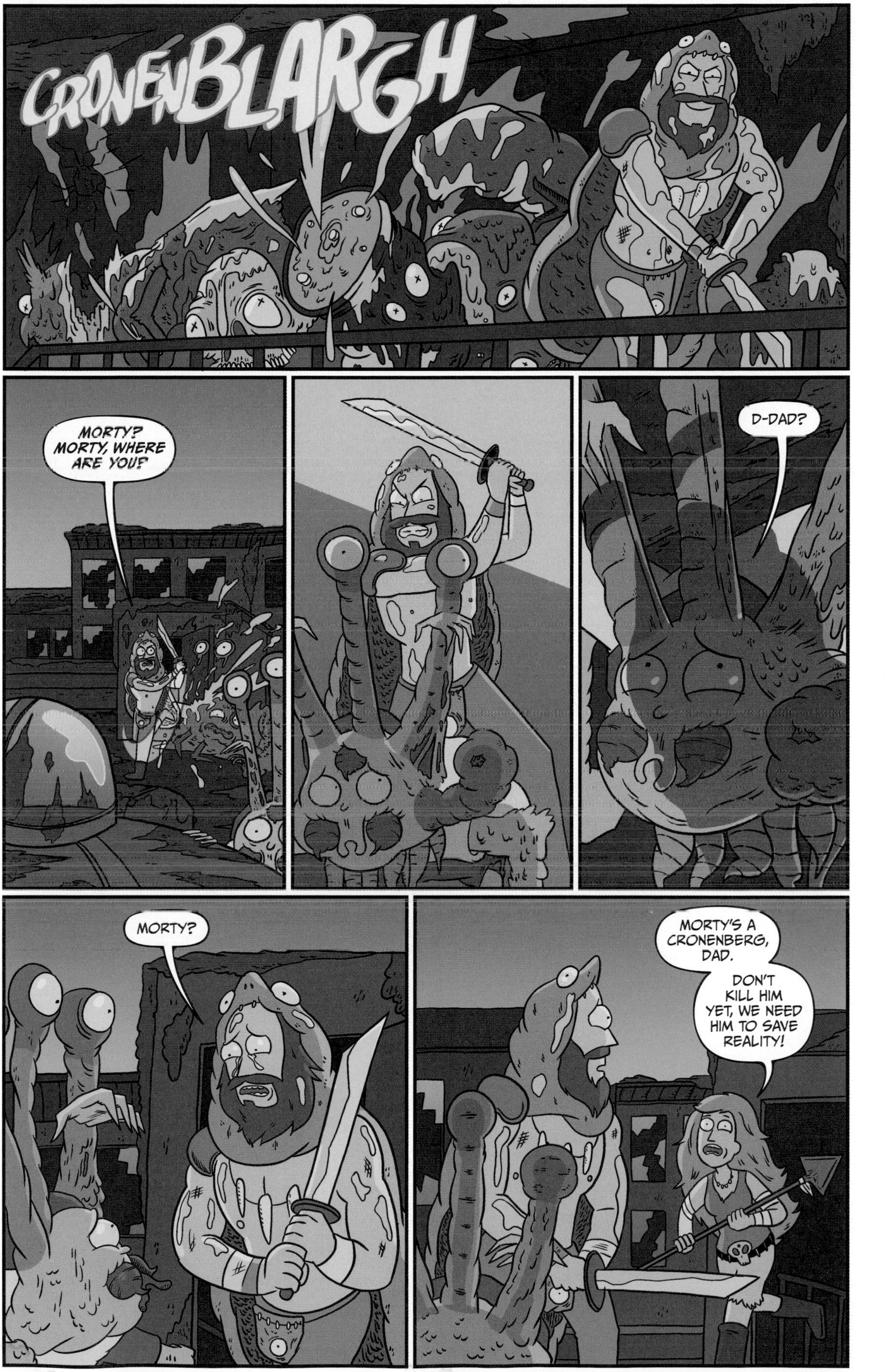
CRONENBLARGH
MORTY? MORTY, WHERE ARE YOU?
D-DAD?
MORTY?
MORTY'S A CRONENBERG, DAD.
DON'T KILL HIM YET, WE NEED HIM TO SAVE REALITY!

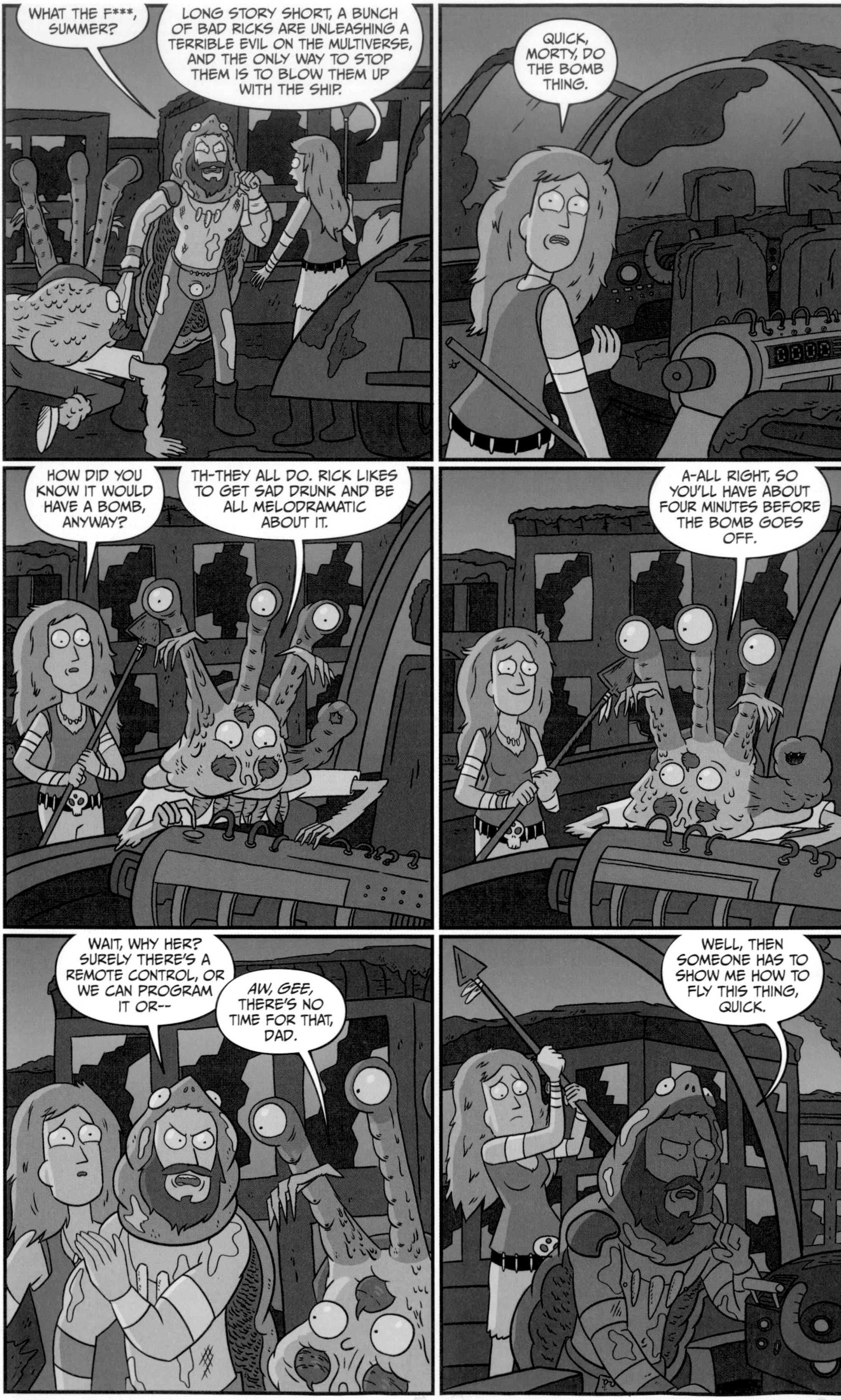
WHAT THE F***, SUMMER?
LONG STORY SHORT, A BUNCH OF BAD RICKS ARE UNLEASHING A TERRIBLE EVIL ON THE MULTIVERSE, AND THE ONLY WAY TO STOP THEM IS TO BLOW THEM UP WITH THE SHIP.
QUICK, MORTY, DO THE BOMB THING.
HOW DID YOU KNOW IT WOULD HAVE A BOMB, ANYWAY?
TH-THEY ALL DO. RICK LIKES TO GET SAD DRUNK AND BE ALL MELODRAMATIC ABOUT IT.
A-ALL RIGHT, SO YOU'LL HAVE ABOUT FOUR MINUTES BEFORE THE BOMB GOES OFF.
WAIT, WHY HER? SURELY THERE'S A REMOTE CONTROL, OR WE CAN PROGRAM IT OR--
AW, GEE, THERE'S NO TIME FOR THAT, DAD.
WELL, THEN SOMEONE HAS TO SHOW ME HOW TO FLY THIS THING, QUICK.

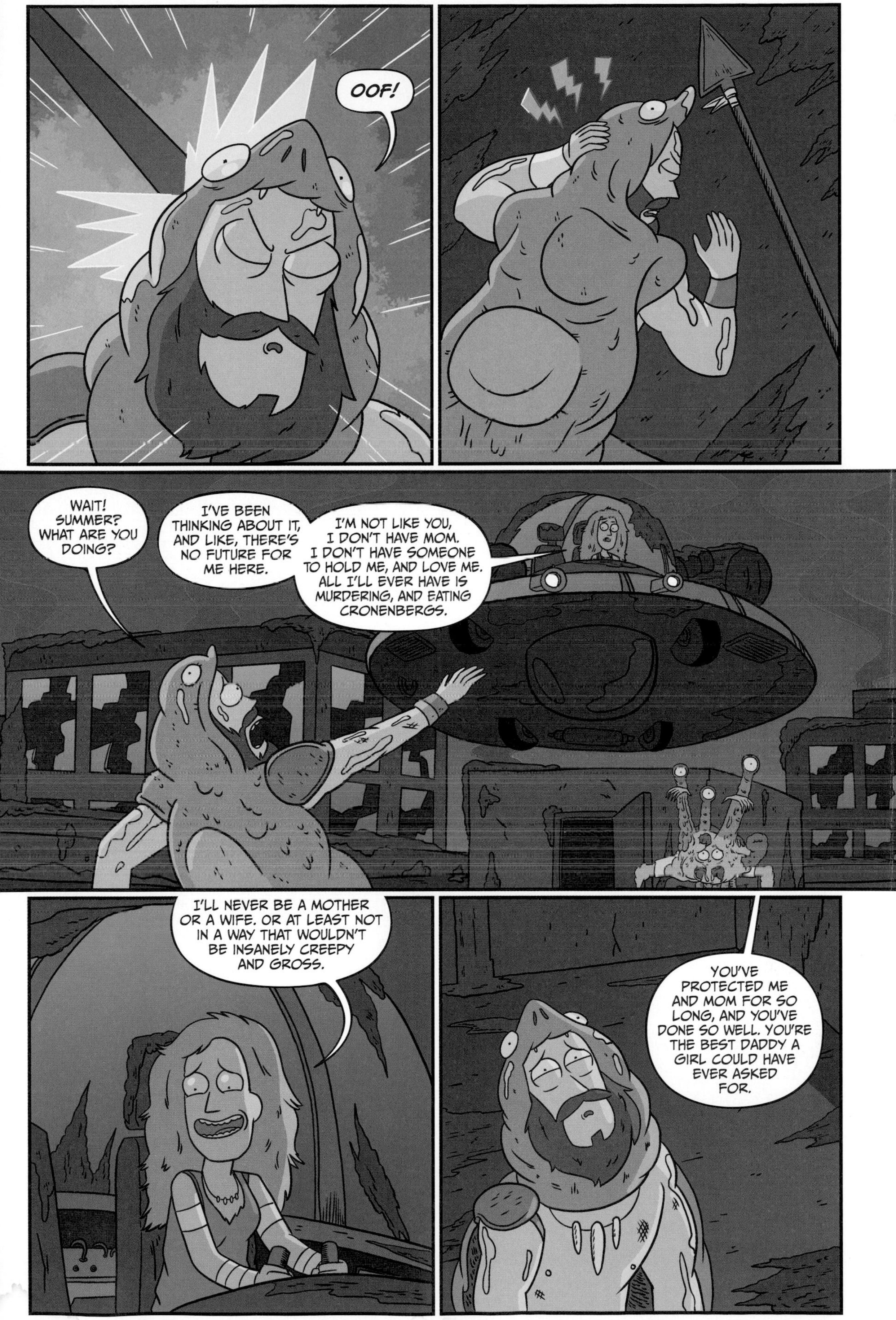
OOF!
WAIT! SUMMER? WHAT ARE YOU DOING?
I'VE BEEN THINKING ABOUT IT, AND LIKE, THERE'S NO FUTURE FOR ME HERE.
I'M NOT LIKE YOU, I DON'T HAVE MOM. I DON'T HAVE SOMEONE TO HOLD ME, AND LOVE ME. ALL I'LL EVER HAVE IS MURDERING, AND EATING CRONENBERGS.
I'LL NEVER BE A MOTHER OR A WIFE. OR AT LEAST NOT IN A WAY THAT WOULDN'T BE INSANELY CREEPY AND GROSS.
YOU'VE PROTECTED ME AND MOM FOR SO LONG, AND YOU'VE DONE SO WELL. YOU'RE THE BEST DADDY A GIRL COULD HAVE EVER ASKED FOR.

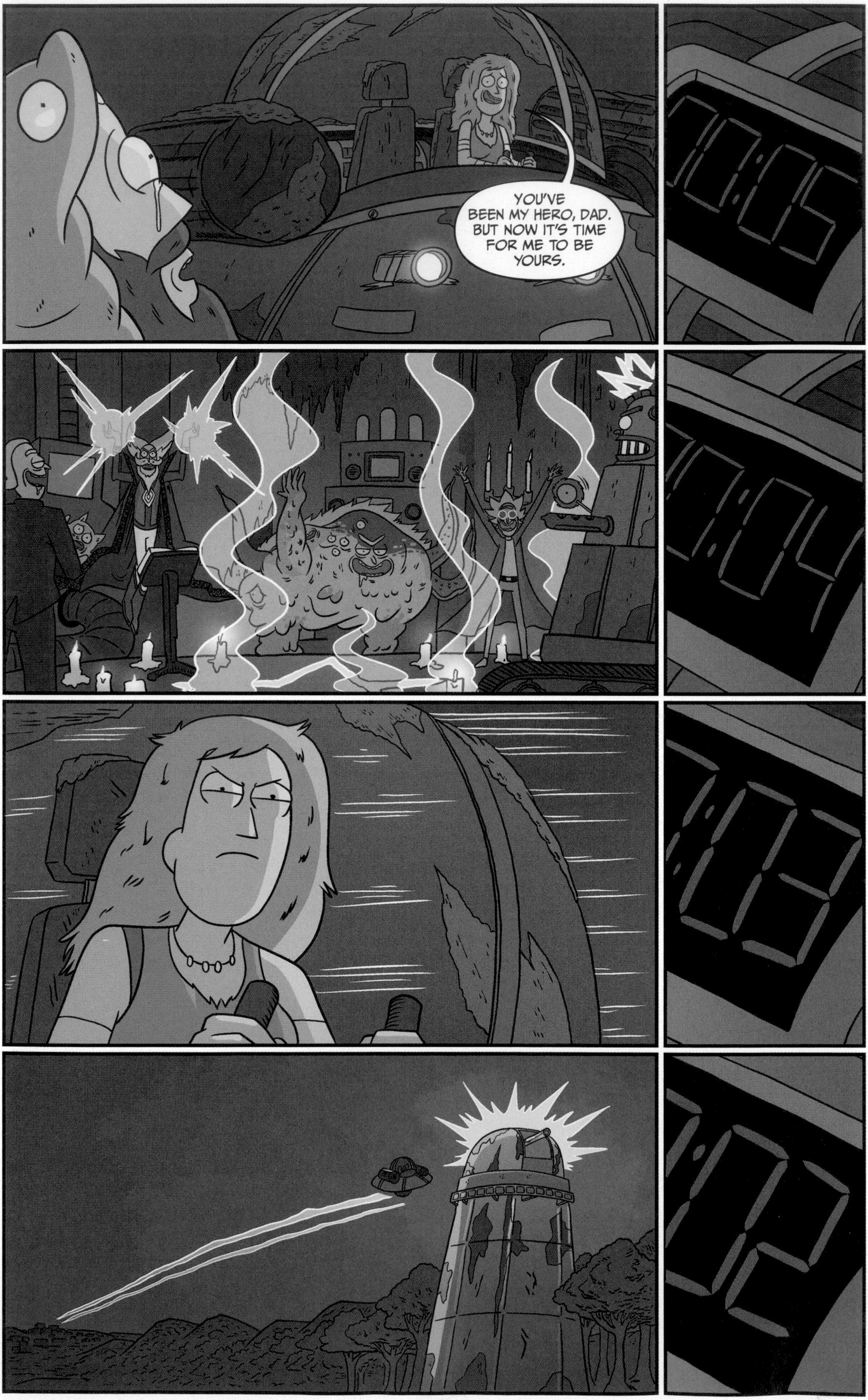
YOU'VE BEEN MY HERO, DAD. BUT NOW IT'S TIME FOR ME TO BE YOURS.

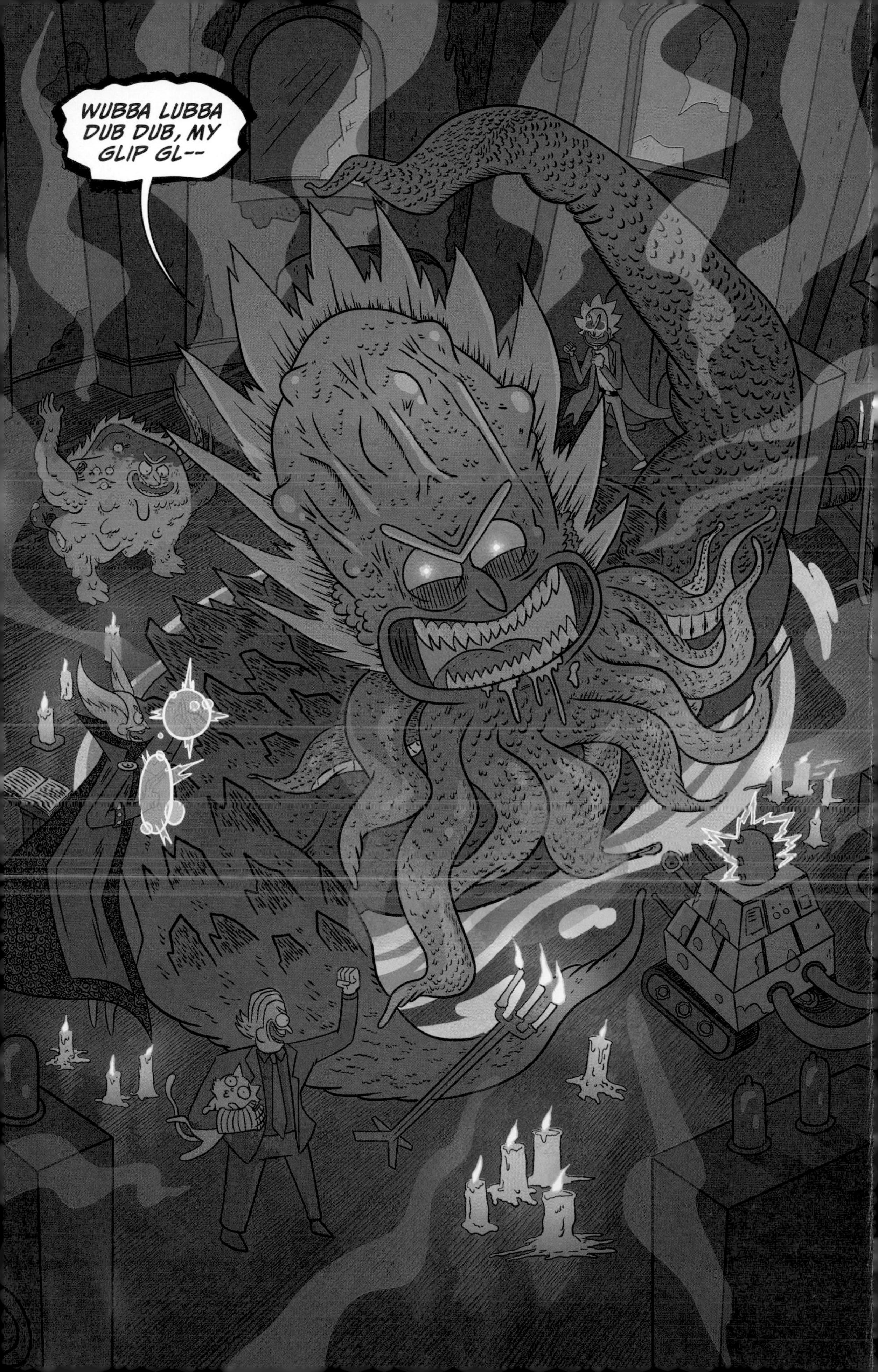
WUBBA LUBBA DUB DUB, MY GLIP GL--

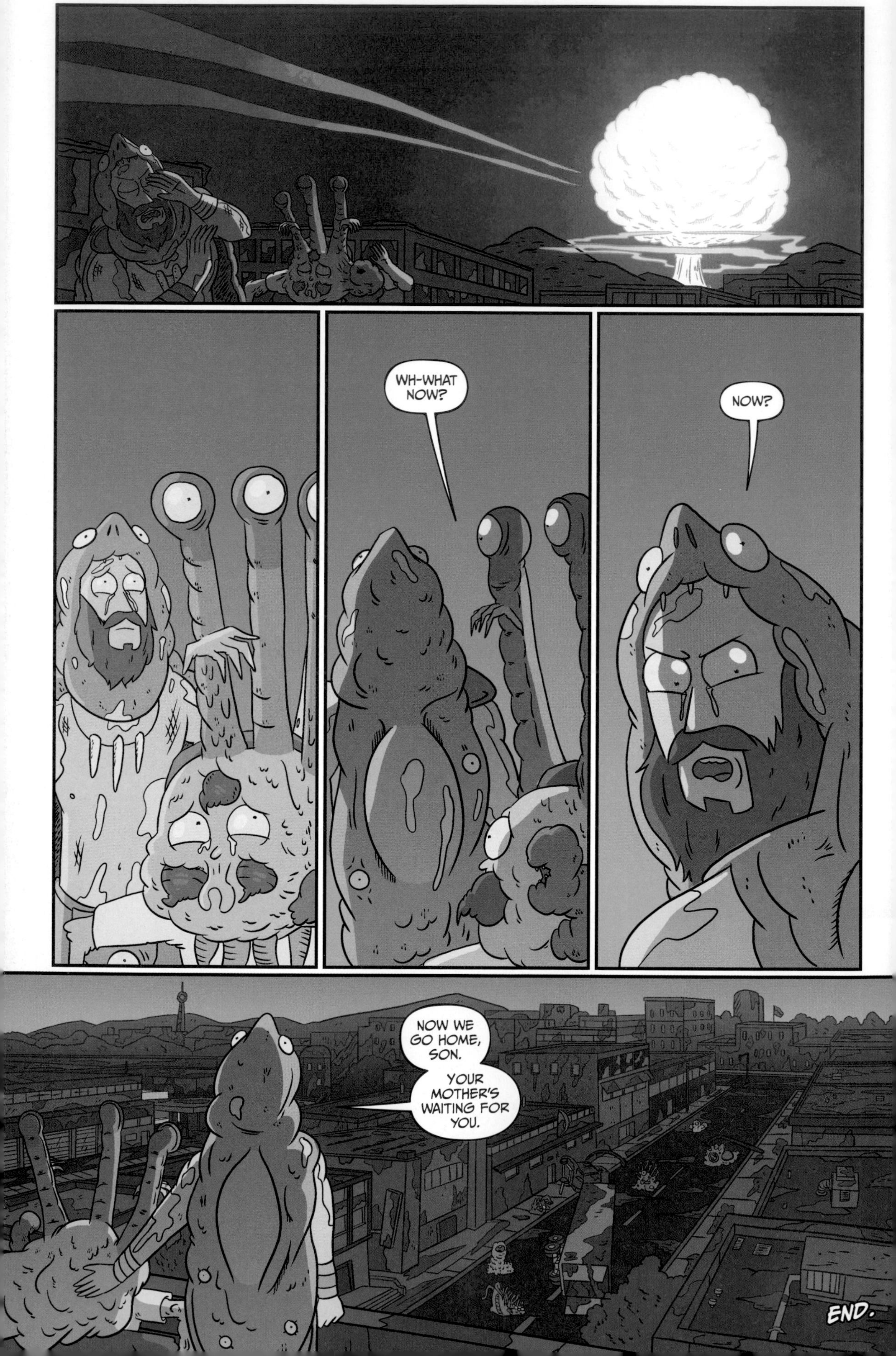
WH-WHAT NOW?
NOW?
NOW WE GO HOME, SON.
YOUR MOTHER'S WAITING FOR YOU.
END.

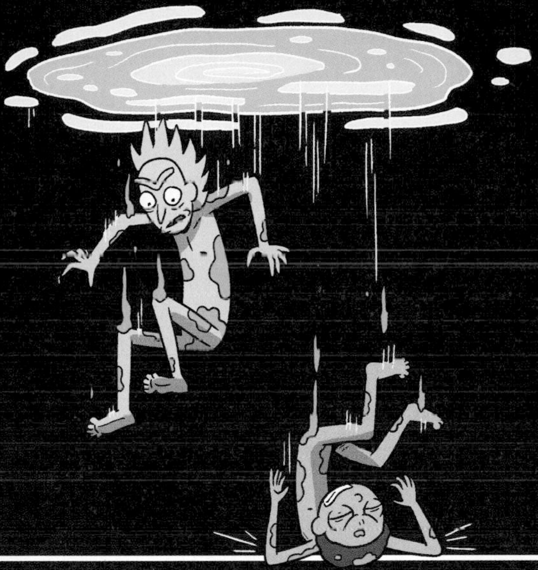

BONUS STORY

ADVENTURES IN THE PUBLIC DOMAIN

WRITTEN BY **TINI HOWARD** ILLUSTRATED BY **JARRETT WILLIAMS**
COLORED BY **SARAH STERN** LETTERED BY **CRANK!**

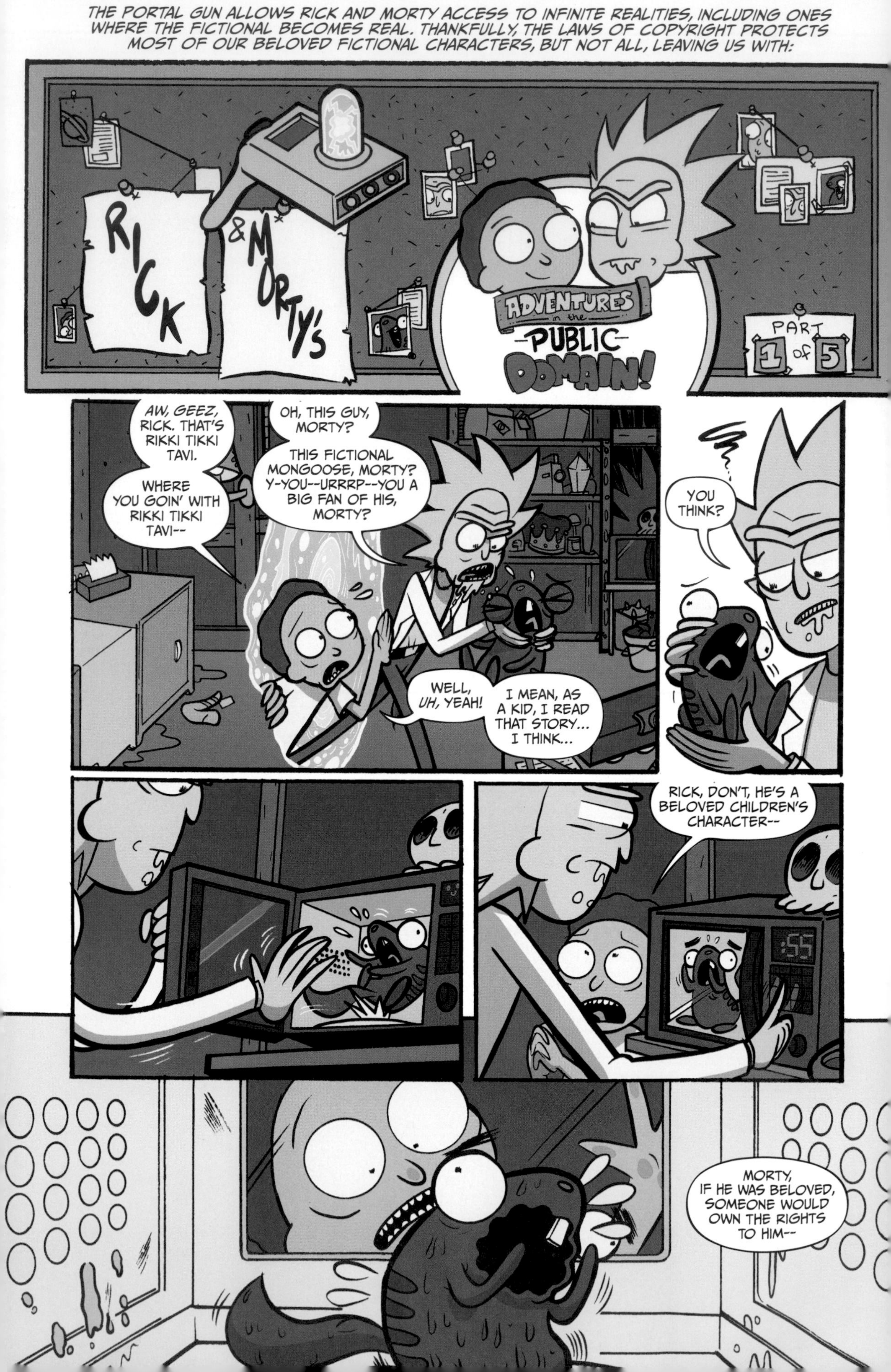
THE PORTAL GUN ALLOWS RICK AND MORTY ACCESS TO INFINITE REALITIES, INCLUDING ONES WHERE THE FICTIONAL BECOMES REAL. THANKFULLY, THE LAWS OF COPYRIGHT PROTECTS MOST OF OUR BELOVED FICTIONAL CHARACTERS, BUT NOT ALL, LEAVING US WITH:
RICK & MORTY'S
ADVENTURES in the PUBLIC DOMAIN!
PART 1 of 5
AW, GEEZ, RICK. THAT'S RIKKI TIKKI TAVI.
WHERE YOU GOIN' WITH RIKKI TIKKI TAVI--
OH, THIS GUY, MORTY?
THIS FICTIONAL MONGOOSE, MORTY? Y-YOU--URRRP--YOU A BIG FAN OF HIS, MORTY?
WELL, UH, YEAH!
I MEAN, AS A KID, I READ THAT STORY... I THINK...
YOU THINK?
RICK, DON'T, HE'S A BELOVED CHILDREN'S CHARACTER--
:55
MORTY, IF HE WAS BELOVED, SOMEONE WOULD OWN THE RIGHTS TO HIM--

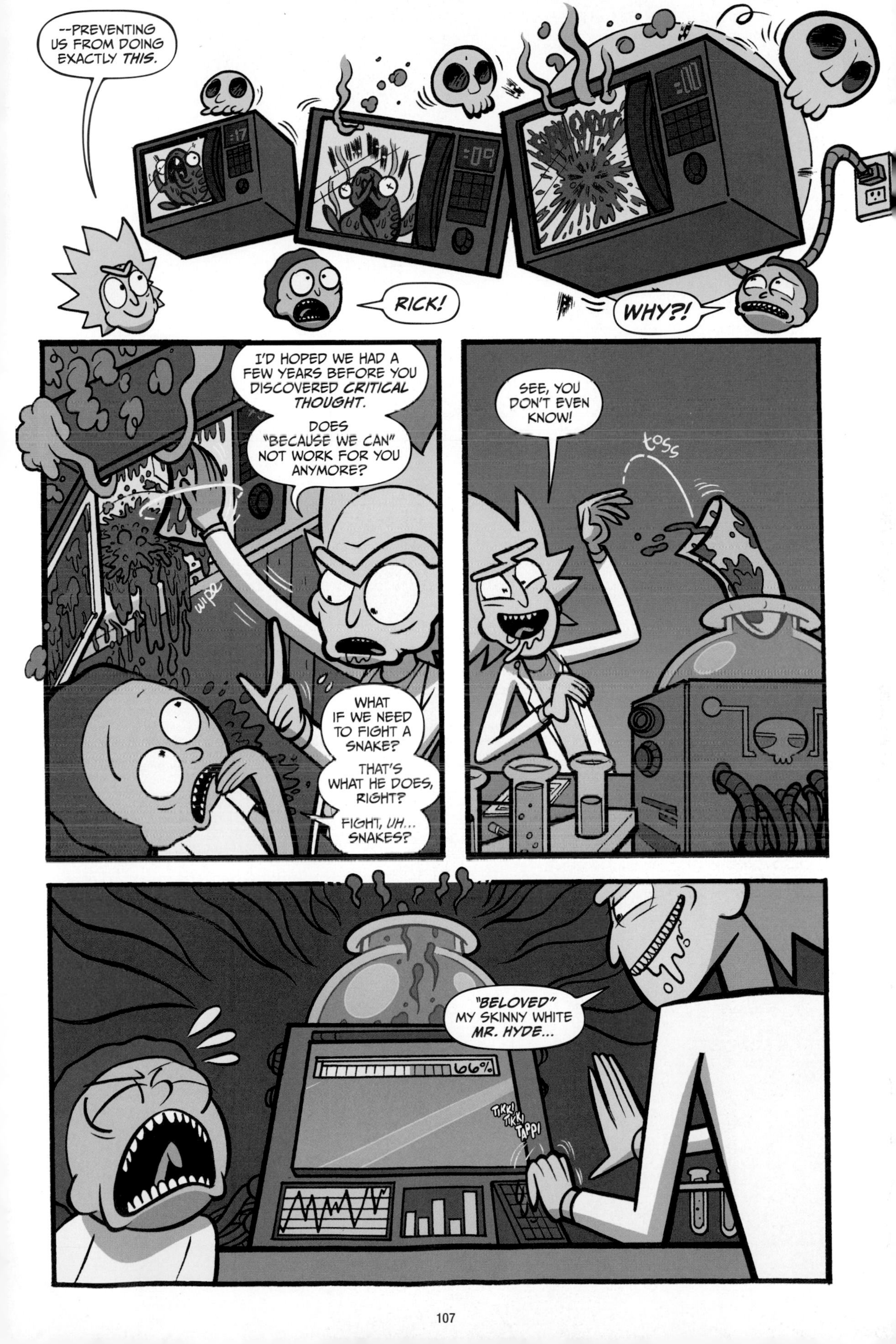
--PREVENTING US FROM DOING EXACTLY *THIS*.
:17
:09
:00
RICK!
WHY?!
I'D HOPED WE HAD A FEW YEARS BEFORE YOU DISCOVERED *CRITICAL THOUGHT*.
DOES "BECAUSE WE CAN" NOT WORK FOR YOU ANYMORE?
wipe
WHAT IF WE NEED TO FIGHT A SNAKE?
THAT'S WHAT HE DOES, RIGHT?
FIGHT, *UH*... SNAKES?
SEE, YOU DON'T EVEN KNOW!
toss
"BELOVED" MY SKINNY WHITE *MR. HYDE*...
66%
TIKKI TIKKI TAPP!

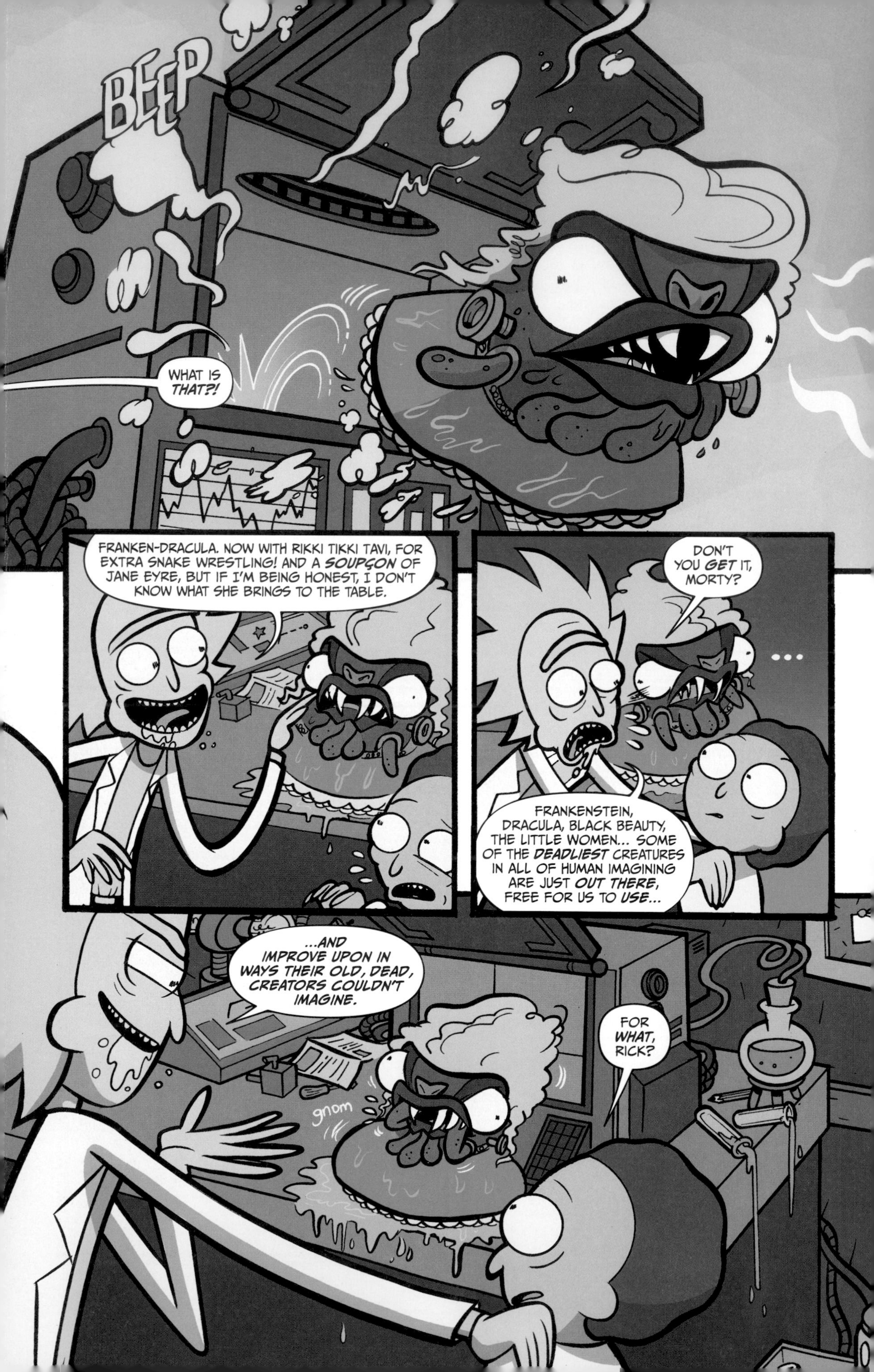

BEEP
WHAT IS THAT?!
FRANKEN-DRACULA. NOW WITH RIKKI TIKKI TAVI, FOR EXTRA SNAKE WRESTLING! AND A SOUPÇON OF JANE EYRE, BUT IF I'M BEING HONEST, I DON'T KNOW WHAT SHE BRINGS TO THE TABLE.
DON'T YOU GET IT, MORTY?
...
FRANKENSTEIN, DRACULA, BLACK BEAUTY, THE LITTLE WOMEN... SOME OF THE DEADLIEST CREATURES IN ALL OF HUMAN IMAGINING ARE JUST OUT THERE, FREE FOR US TO USE...
...AND IMPROVE UPON IN WAYS THEIR OLD, DEAD, CREATORS COULDN'T IMAGINE.
FOR WHAT, RICK?
gnom

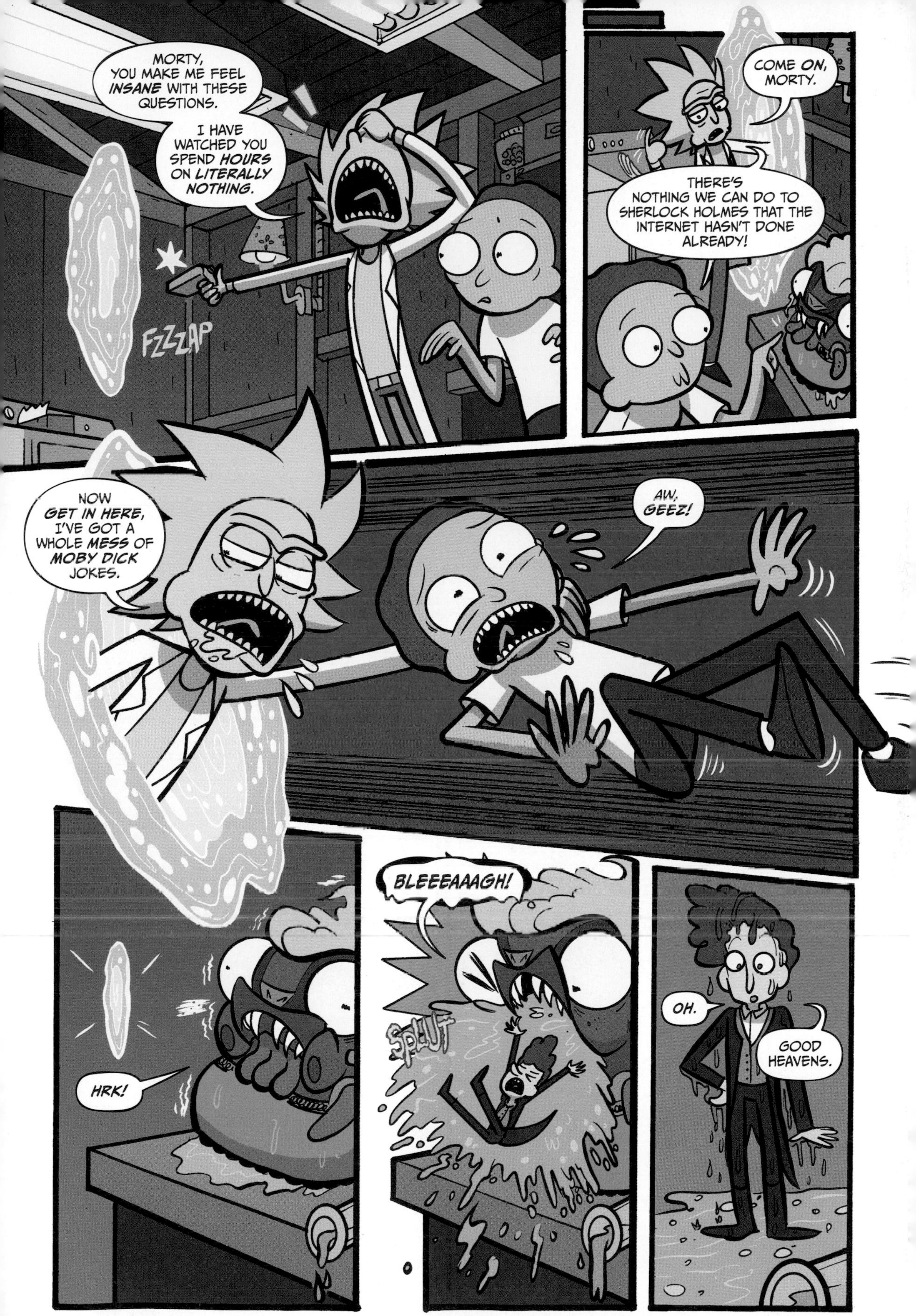
MORTY, YOU MAKE ME FEEL INSANE WITH THESE QUESTIONS.
I HAVE WATCHED YOU SPEND HOURS ON LITERALLY NOTHING.
FZZZAP
COME ON, MORTY.
THERE'S NOTHING WE CAN DO TO SHERLOCK HOLMES THAT THE INTERNET HASN'T DONE ALREADY!
NOW GET IN HERE, I'VE GOT A WHOLE MESS OF MOBY DICK JOKES.
AW, GEEZ!
HRK!
BLEEEAAAGH!
SPLUT
OH.
GOOD HEAVENS.

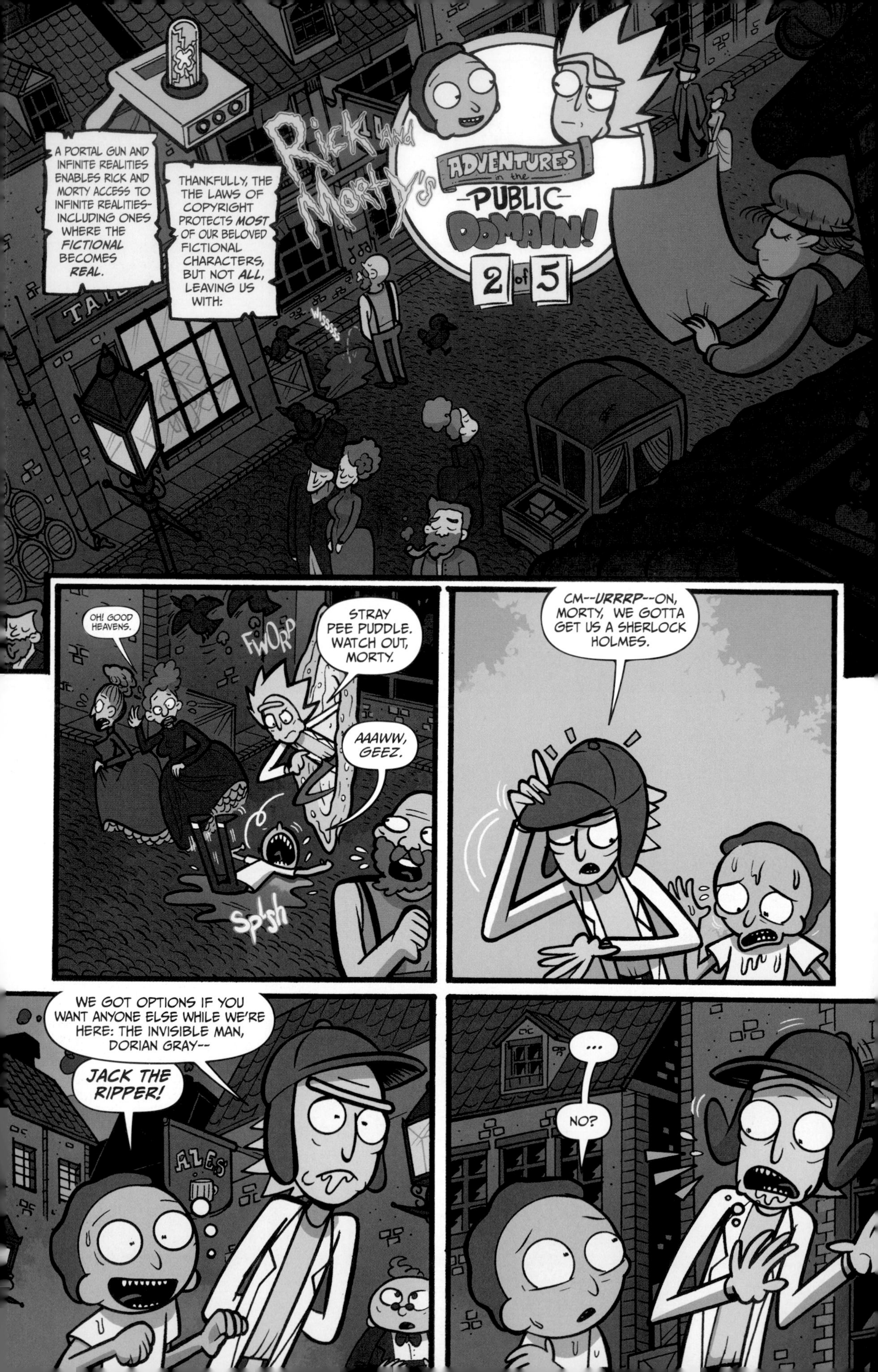
A PORTAL GUN AND INFINITE REALITIES ENABLES RICK AND MORTY ACCESS TO INFINITE REALITIES- INCLUDING ONES WHERE THE *FICTIONAL* BECOMES *REAL*.
THANKFULLY, THE THE LAWS OF COPYRIGHT PROTECTS *MOST* OF OUR BELOVED FICTIONAL CHARACTERS, BUT NOT *ALL*, LEAVING US WITH:
Rick and Morty's
ADVENTURES in the PUBLIC DOMAIN!
2 of 5
WISSSSS
OH! GOOD HEAVENS.
FWORP
STRAY PEE PUDDLE. WATCH OUT, MORTY.
AAAWW, GEEZ.
SPLSH
CM--*URRRP*--ON, MORTY, WE GOTTA GET US A SHERLOCK HOLMES.
WE GOT OPTIONS IF YOU WANT ANYONE ELSE WHILE WE'RE HERE: THE INVISIBLE MAN, DORIAN GRAY--
JACK THE RIPPER!
ALES
...
NO?

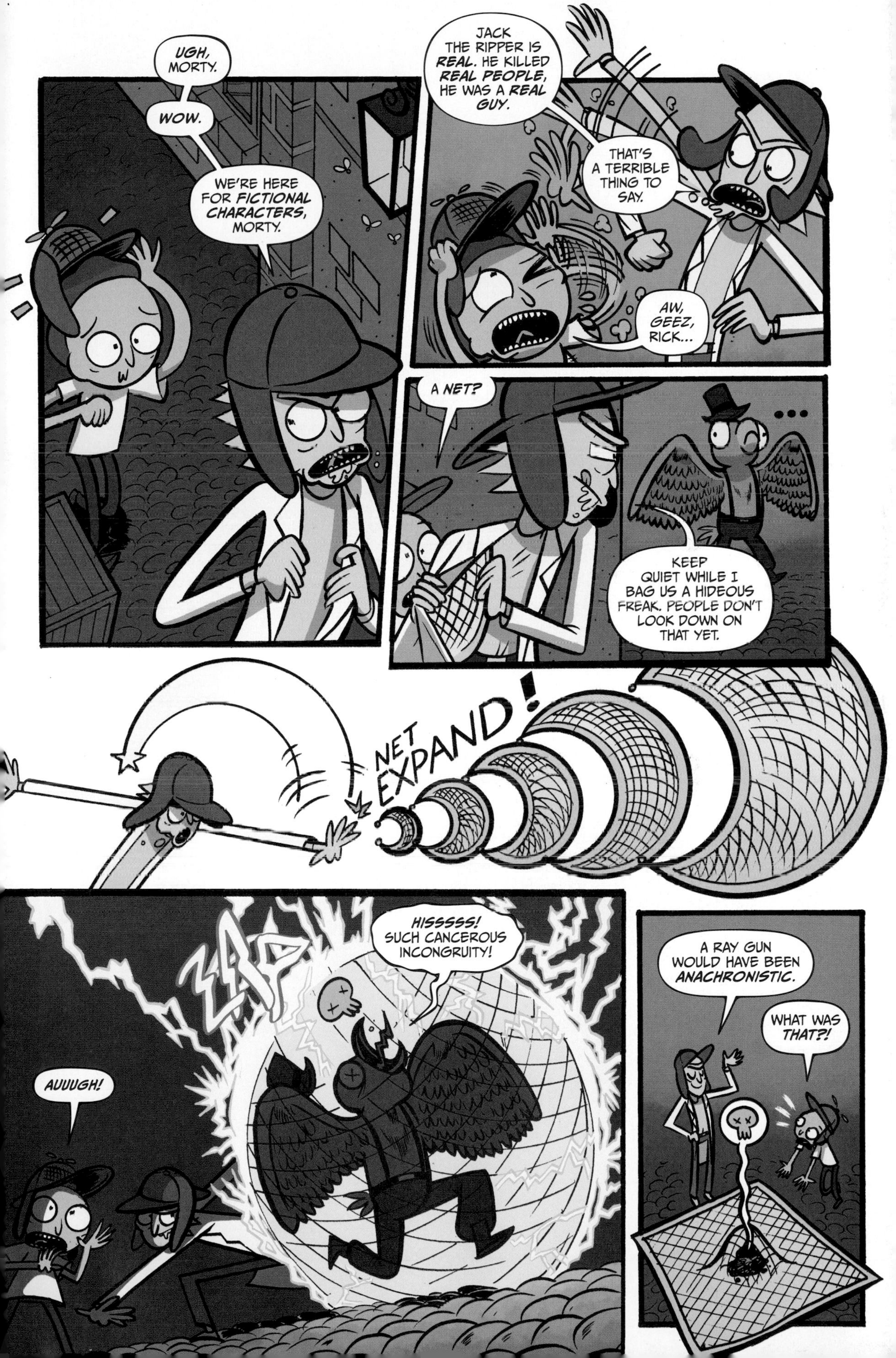
UGH, MORTY.
WOW.
WE'RE HERE FOR FICTIONAL CHARACTERS, MORTY.
JACK THE RIPPER IS REAL. HE KILLED REAL PEOPLE, HE WAS A REAL GUY.
THAT'S A TERRIBLE THING TO SAY.
AW, GEEZ, RICK...
A NET?
...
KEEP QUIET WHILE I BAG US A HIDEOUS FREAK. PEOPLE DON'T LOOK DOWN ON THAT YET.
NET EXPAND!
ZAP
HISSSSS! SUCH CANCEROUS INCONGRUITY!
AUUUGH!
A RAY GUN WOULD HAVE BEEN ANACHRONISTIC.
WHAT WAS THAT?!

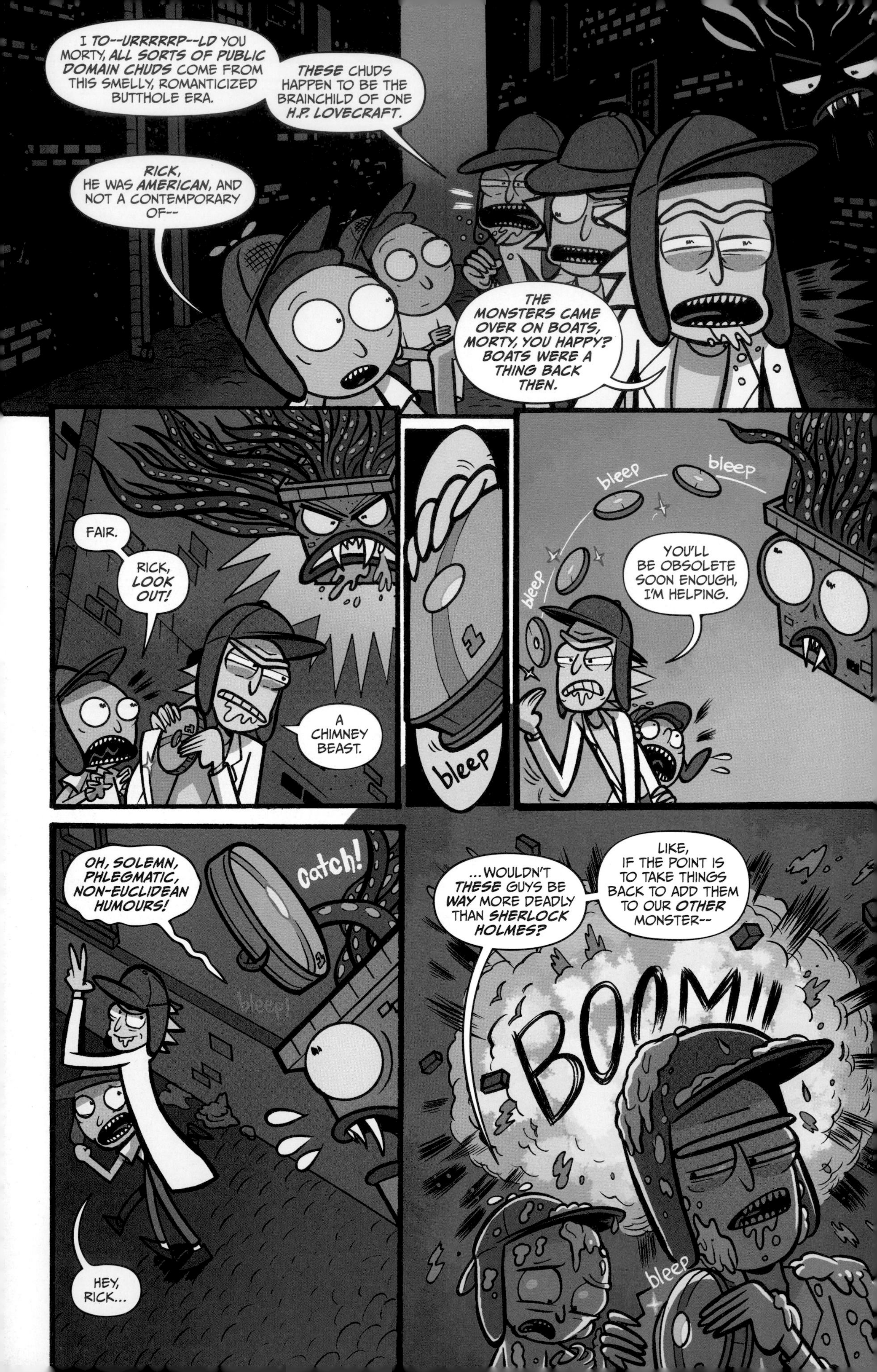
I TO--URRRRRP--LD YOU MORTY, ALL SORTS OF PUBLIC DOMAIN CHUDS COME FROM THIS SMELLY, ROMANTICIZED BUTTHOLE ERA.
THESE CHUDS HAPPEN TO BE THE BRAINCHILD OF ONE H.P. LOVECRAFT.
RICK, HE WAS AMERICAN, AND NOT A CONTEMPORARY OF--
THE MONSTERS CAME OVER ON BOATS, MORTY, YOU HAPPY? BOATS WERE A THING BACK THEN.
FAIR.
RICK, LOOK OUT!
A CHIMNEY BEAST.
bleep
bleep
bleep
bleep
YOU'LL BE OBSOLETE SOON ENOUGH, I'M HELPING.
OH, SOLEMN, PHLEGMATIC, NON-EUCLIDEAN HUMOURS!
catch!
bleep!
HEY, RICK...
...WOULDN'T THESE GUYS BE WAY MORE DEADLY THAN SHERLOCK HOLMES?
LIKE, IF THE POINT IS TO TAKE THINGS BACK TO ADD THEM TO OUR OTHER MONSTER--
BOOM!!
bleep

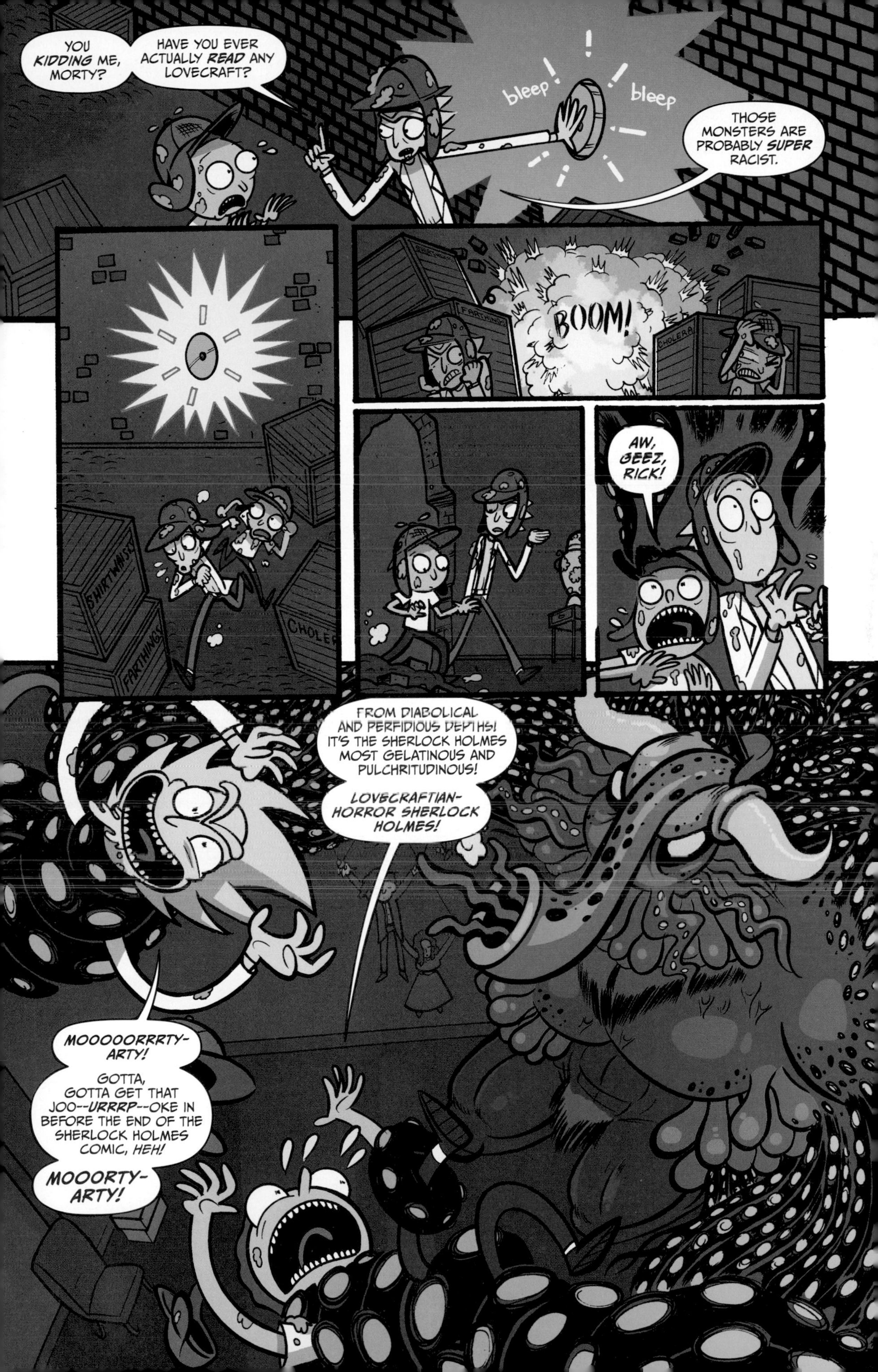
YOU KIDDING ME, MORTY?
HAVE YOU EVER ACTUALLY READ ANY LOVECRAFT?
bleep
bleep
THOSE MONSTERS ARE PROBABLY SUPER RACIST.
BOOM!
AW, GEEZ, RICK!
FROM DIABOLICAL AND PERFIDIOUS DEPTHS! IT'S THE SHERLOCK HOLMES MOST GELATINOUS AND PULCHRITUDINOUS!
LOVECRAFTIAN-HORROR SHERLOCK HOLMES!
MOOOOORRRTY-ARTY!
GOTTA, GOTTA GET THAT JOO--URRRP--OKE IN BEFORE THE END OF THE SHERLOCK HOLMES COMIC, HEH!
MOOORTY-ARTY!

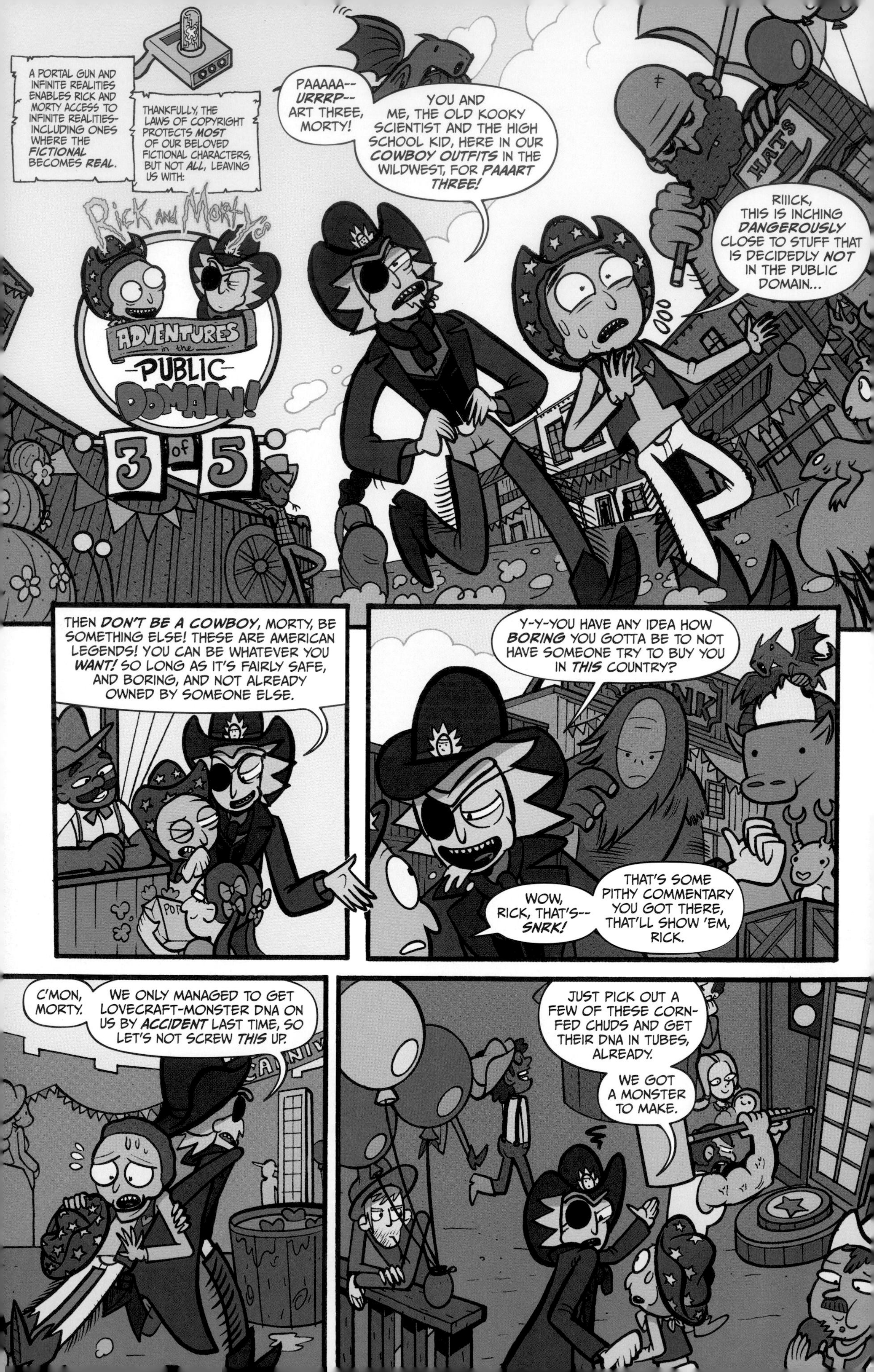
A PORTAL GUN AND INFINITE REALITIES ENABLES RICK AND MORTY ACCESS TO INFINITE REALITIES-INCLUDING ONES WHERE THE FICTIONAL BECOMES REAL.
THANKFULLY, THE LAWS OF COPYRIGHT PROTECTS MOST OF OUR BELOVED FICTIONAL CHARACTERS, BUT NOT ALL, LEAVING US WITH:
RICK AND MORTY'S
ADVENTURES in the PUBLIC DOMAIN!
3 of 5
PAAAAAA--URRRP--ART THREE, MORTY!
YOU AND ME, THE OLD KOOKY SCIENTIST AND THE HIGH SCHOOL KID, HERE IN OUR COWBOY OUTFITS IN THE WILDWEST, FOR PAAART THREE!
HATS
RIIICK, THIS IS INCHING DANGEROUSLY CLOSE TO STUFF THAT IS DECIDEDLY NOT IN THE PUBLIC DOMAIN...
THEN DON'T BE A COWBOY, MORTY, BE SOMETHING ELSE! THESE ARE AMERICAN LEGENDS! YOU CAN BE WHATEVER YOU WANT! SO LONG AS IT'S FAIRLY SAFE, AND BORING, AND NOT ALREADY OWNED BY SOMEONE ELSE.
Y-Y-YOU HAVE ANY IDEA HOW BORING YOU GOTTA BE TO NOT HAVE SOMEONE TRY TO BUY YOU IN THIS COUNTRY?
WOW, RICK, THAT'S--SNRK!
THAT'S SOME PITHY COMMENTARY YOU GOT THERE, THAT'LL SHOW 'EM, RICK.
C'MON, MORTY.
WE ONLY MANAGED TO GET LOVECRAFT-MONSTER DNA ON US BY ACCIDENT LAST TIME, SO LET'S NOT SCREW THIS UP.
JUST PICK OUT A FEW OF THESE CORN-FED CHUDS AND GET THEIR DNA IN TUBES, ALREADY.
WE GOT A MONSTER TO MAKE.

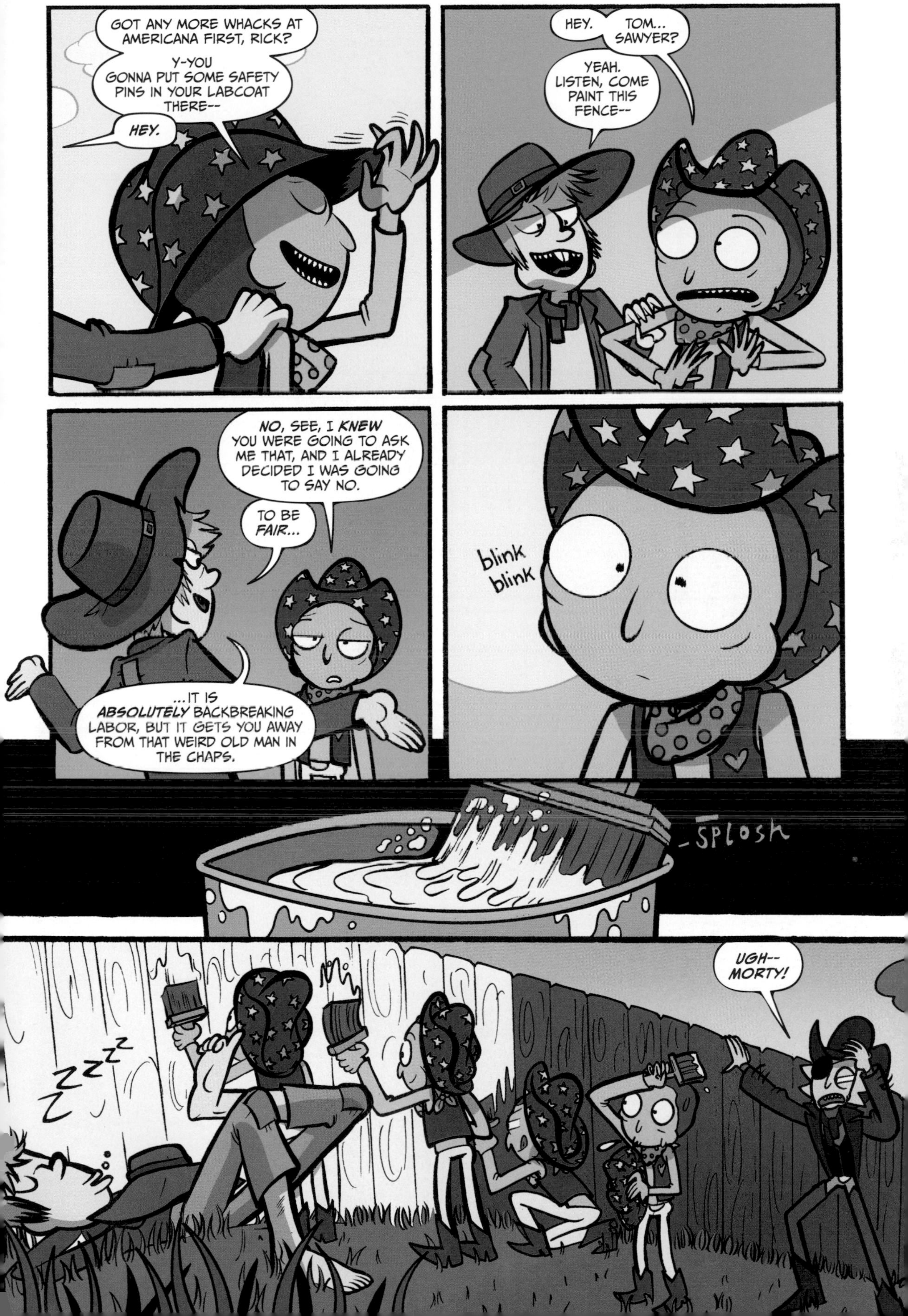

GOT ANY MORE WHACKS AT AMERICANA FIRST, RICK?
Y-YOU GONNA PUT SOME SAFETY PINS IN YOUR LABCOAT THERE--
HEY.
HEY.
TOM... SAWYER?
YEAH. LISTEN, COME PAINT THIS FENCE--
NO, SEE, I KNEW YOU WERE GOING TO ASK ME THAT, AND I ALREADY DECIDED I WAS GOING TO SAY NO.
TO BE FAIR...
...IT IS ABSOLUTELY BACKBREAKING LABOR, BUT IT GETS YOU AWAY FROM THAT WEIRD OLD MAN IN THE CHAPS.
blink blink
SPLOSH
ZZZZZ
UGH-- MORTY!

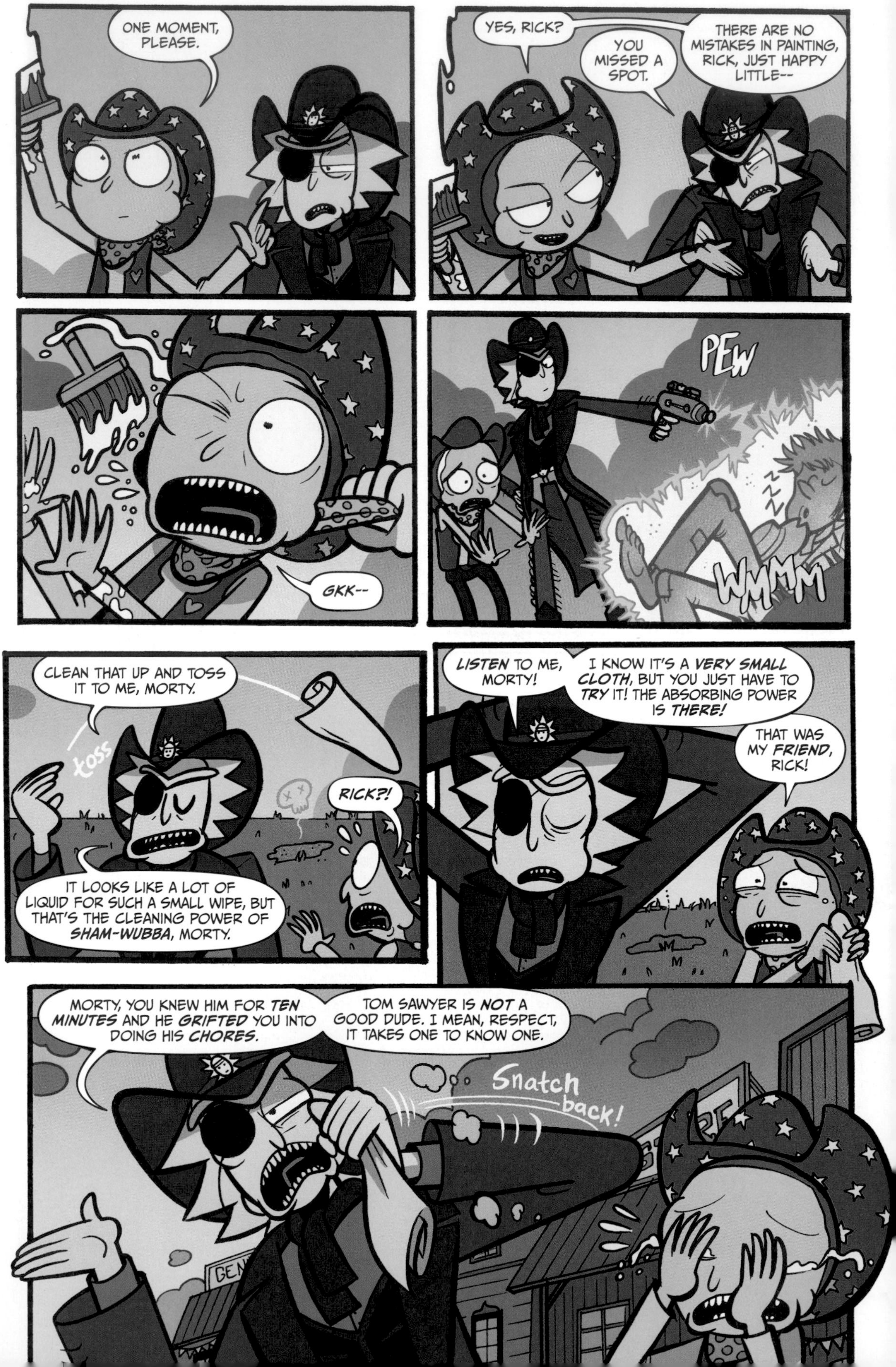
ONE MOMENT, PLEASE.
YES, RICK?
YOU MISSED A SPOT.
THERE ARE NO MISTAKES IN PAINTING, RICK, JUST HAPPY LITTLE--
GKK--
PEW
WMMM
CLEAN THAT UP AND TOSS IT TO ME, MORTY.
toss
RICK?!
IT LOOKS LIKE A LOT OF LIQUID FOR SUCH A SMALL WIPE, BUT THAT'S THE CLEANING POWER OF SHAM-WUBBA, MORTY.
LISTEN TO ME, MORTY!
I KNOW IT'S A VERY SMALL CLOTH, BUT YOU JUST HAVE TO TRY IT! THE ABSORBING POWER IS THERE!
THAT WAS MY FRIEND, RICK!
MORTY, YOU KNEW HIM FOR TEN MINUTES AND HE GRIFTED YOU INTO DOING HIS CHORES.
TOM SAWYER IS NOT A GOOD DUDE. I MEAN, RESPECT, IT TAKES ONE TO KNOW ONE.
Snatch back!

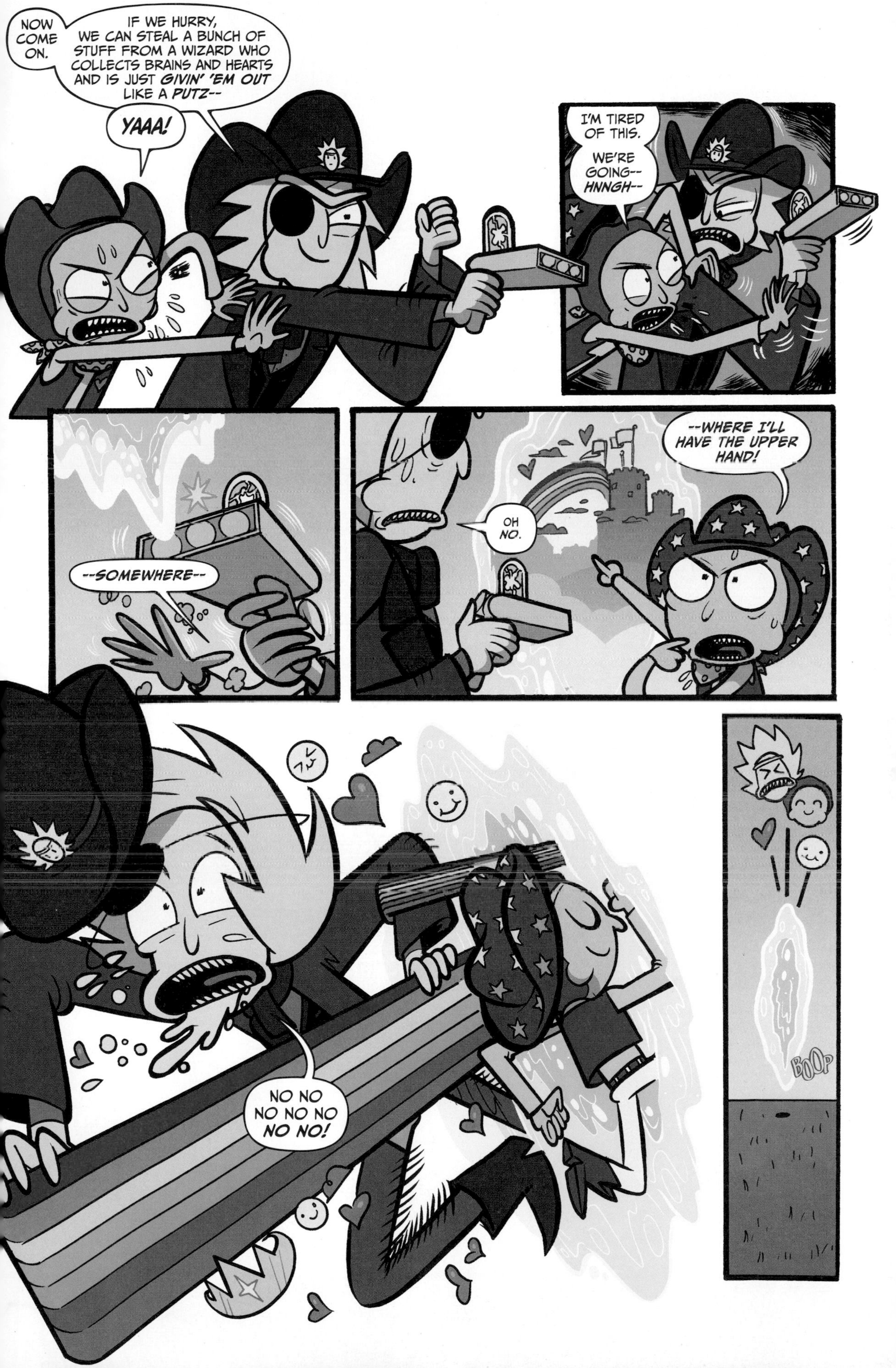
NOW COME ON.
IF WE HURRY, WE CAN STEAL A BUNCH OF STUFF FROM A WIZARD WHO COLLECTS BRAINS AND HEARTS AND IS JUST GIVIN' 'EM OUT LIKE A PUTZ--
YAAA!
I'M TIRED OF THIS.
WE'RE GOING-- HNNGH--
--SOMEWHERE--
OH NO.
--WHERE I'LL HAVE THE UPPER HAND!
NO NO NO NO NO NO NO!
BOOP

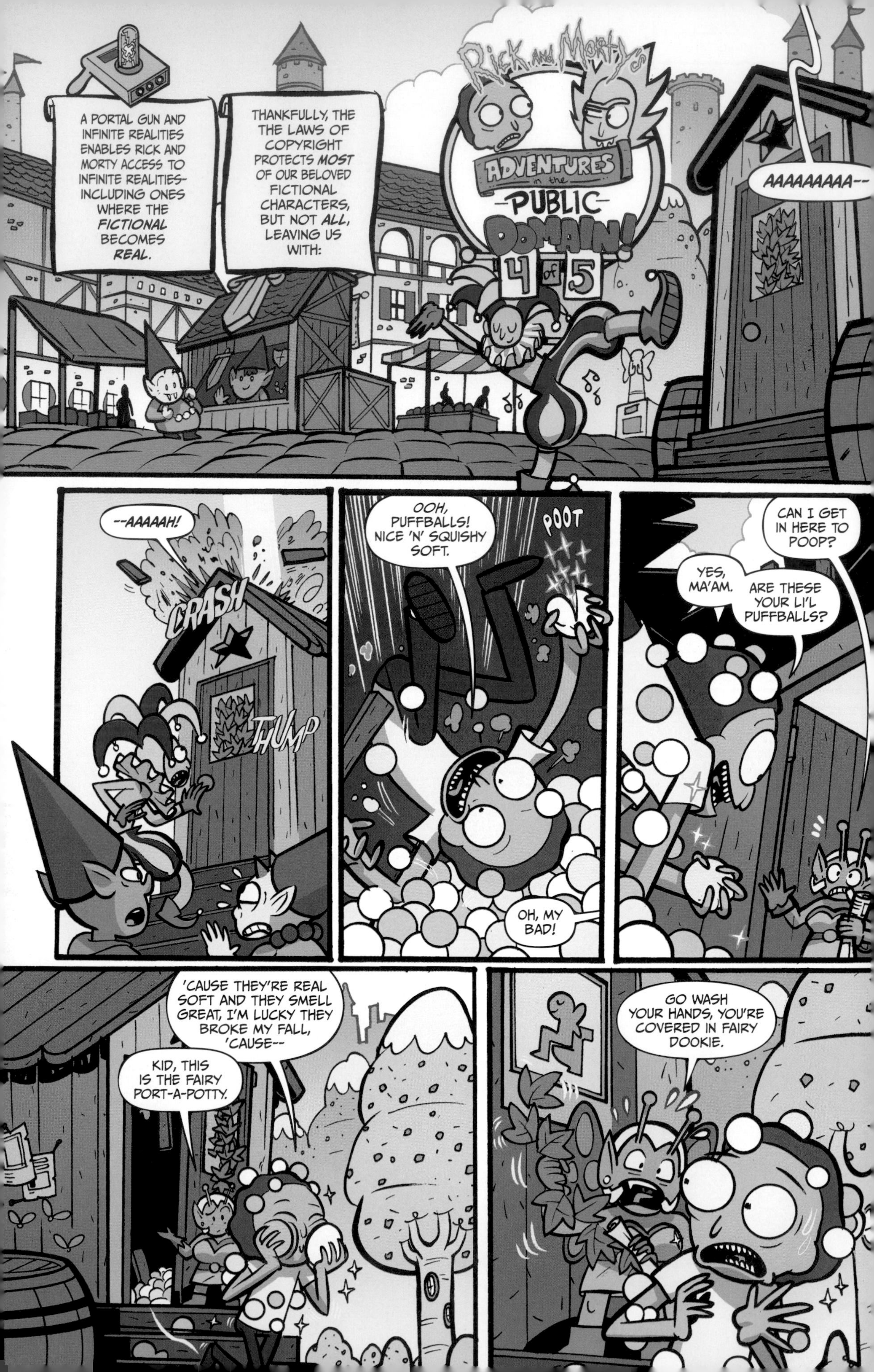
A PORTAL GUN AND INFINITE REALITIES ENABLES RICK AND MORTY ACCESS TO INFINITE REALITIES-INCLUDING ONES WHERE THE *FICTIONAL* BECOMES *REAL*.
THANKFULLY, THE THE LAWS OF COPYRIGHT PROTECTS *MOST* OF OUR BELOVED FICTIONAL CHARACTERS, BUT NOT *ALL*, LEAVING US WITH:
RICK AND MORTY'S
ADVENTURES in the PUBLIC DOMAIN!
4 of 5
AAAAAAAAA--
--AAAAAH!
CRASH
THUMP
OOH, PUFFBALLS! NICE 'N' SQUISHY SOFT.
POOT
OH, MY BAD!
CAN I GET IN HERE TO POOP?
YES, MA'AM.
ARE THESE YOUR LI'L PUFFBALLS?
'CAUSE THEY'RE REAL SOFT AND THEY SMELL GREAT, I'M LUCKY THEY BROKE MY FALL, 'CAUSE--
KID, THIS IS THE FAIRY PORT-A-POTTY.
GO WASH YOUR HANDS, YOU'RE COVERED IN FAIRY DOOKIE.

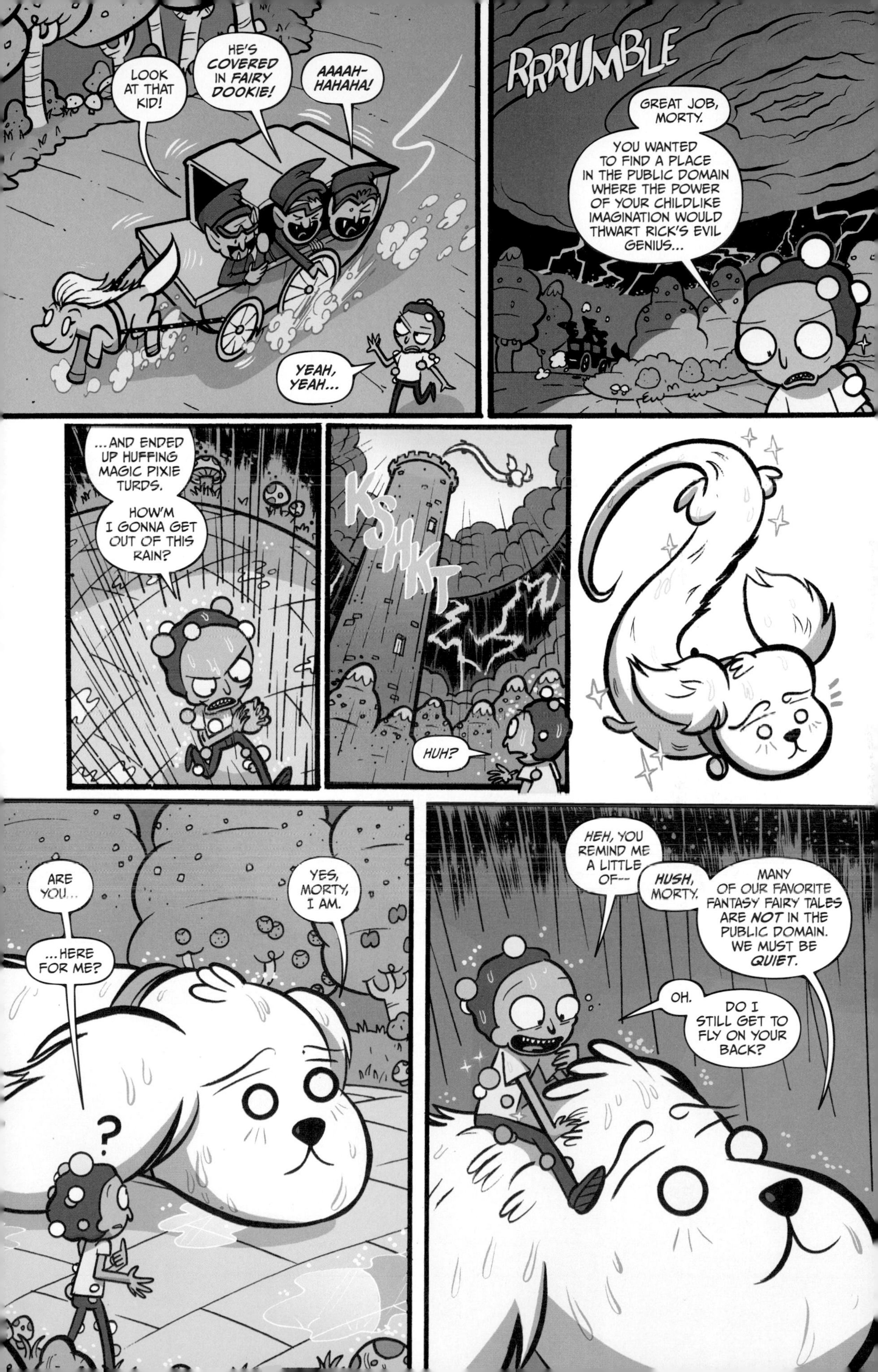
LOOK AT THAT KID!
HE'S COVERED IN FAIRY DOOKIE!
AAAAH-HAHAHA!
YEAH, YEAH...
RRRUMBLE
GREAT JOB, MORTY.
YOU WANTED TO FIND A PLACE IN THE PUBLIC DOMAIN WHERE THE POWER OF YOUR CHILDLIKE IMAGINATION WOULD THWART RICK'S EVIL GENIUS...
...AND ENDED UP HUFFING MAGIC PIXIE TURDS.
HOW'M I GONNA GET OUT OF THIS RAIN?
KSHKT
HUH?
ARE YOU...
...HERE FOR ME?
YES, MORTY, I AM.
?
HEH, YOU REMIND ME A LITTLE OF--
HUSH, MORTY.
MANY OF OUR FAVORITE FANTASY FAIRY TALES ARE NOT IN THE PUBLIC DOMAIN. WE MUST BE QUIET.
OH.
DO I STILL GET TO FLY ON YOUR BACK?

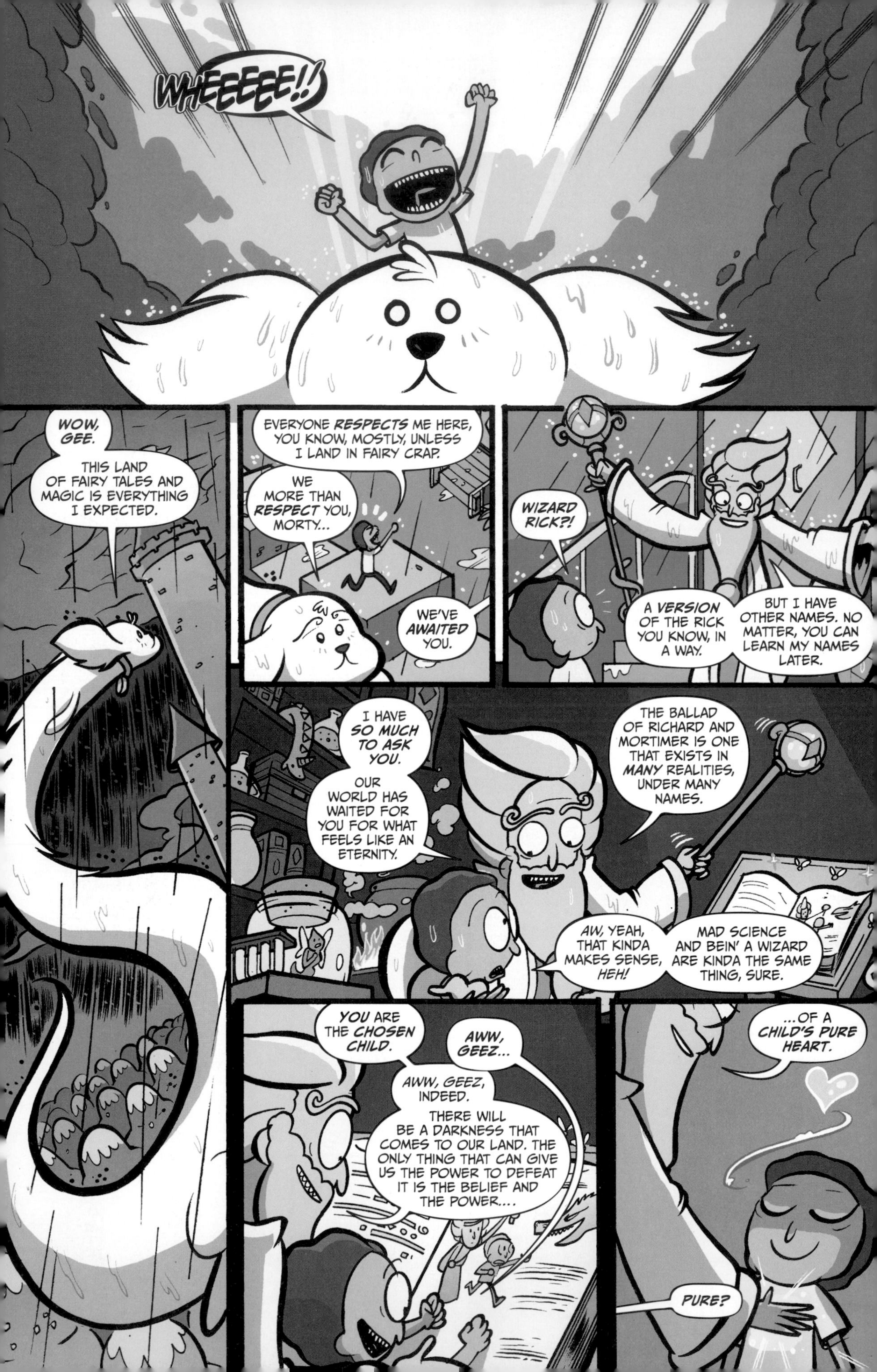
WHEEEEEE!!
WOW, GEE.
THIS LAND OF FAIRY TALES AND MAGIC IS EVERYTHING I EXPECTED.
EVERYONE RESPECTS ME HERE, YOU KNOW, MOSTLY, UNLESS I LAND IN FAIRY CRAP.
WE MORE THAN RESPECT YOU, MORTY...
WE'VE AWAITED YOU.
WIZARD RICK?!
A VERSION OF THE RICK YOU KNOW, IN A WAY.
BUT I HAVE OTHER NAMES. NO MATTER, YOU CAN LEARN MY NAMES LATER.
I HAVE SO MUCH TO ASK YOU.
OUR WORLD HAS WAITED FOR YOU FOR WHAT FEELS LIKE AN ETERNITY.
THE BALLAD OF RICHARD AND MORTIMER IS ONE THAT EXISTS IN MANY REALITIES, UNDER MANY NAMES.
AW, YEAH, THAT KINDA MAKES SENSE, HEH!
MAD SCIENCE AND BEIN' A WIZARD ARE KINDA THE SAME THING, SURE.
YOU ARE THE CHOSEN CHILD.
AWW, GEEZ...
AWW, GEEZ, INDEED.
THERE WILL BE A DARKNESS THAT COMES TO OUR LAND. THE ONLY THING THAT CAN GIVE US THE POWER TO DEFEAT IT IS THE BELIEF AND THE POWER....
...OF A CHILD'S PURE HEART.
PURE?

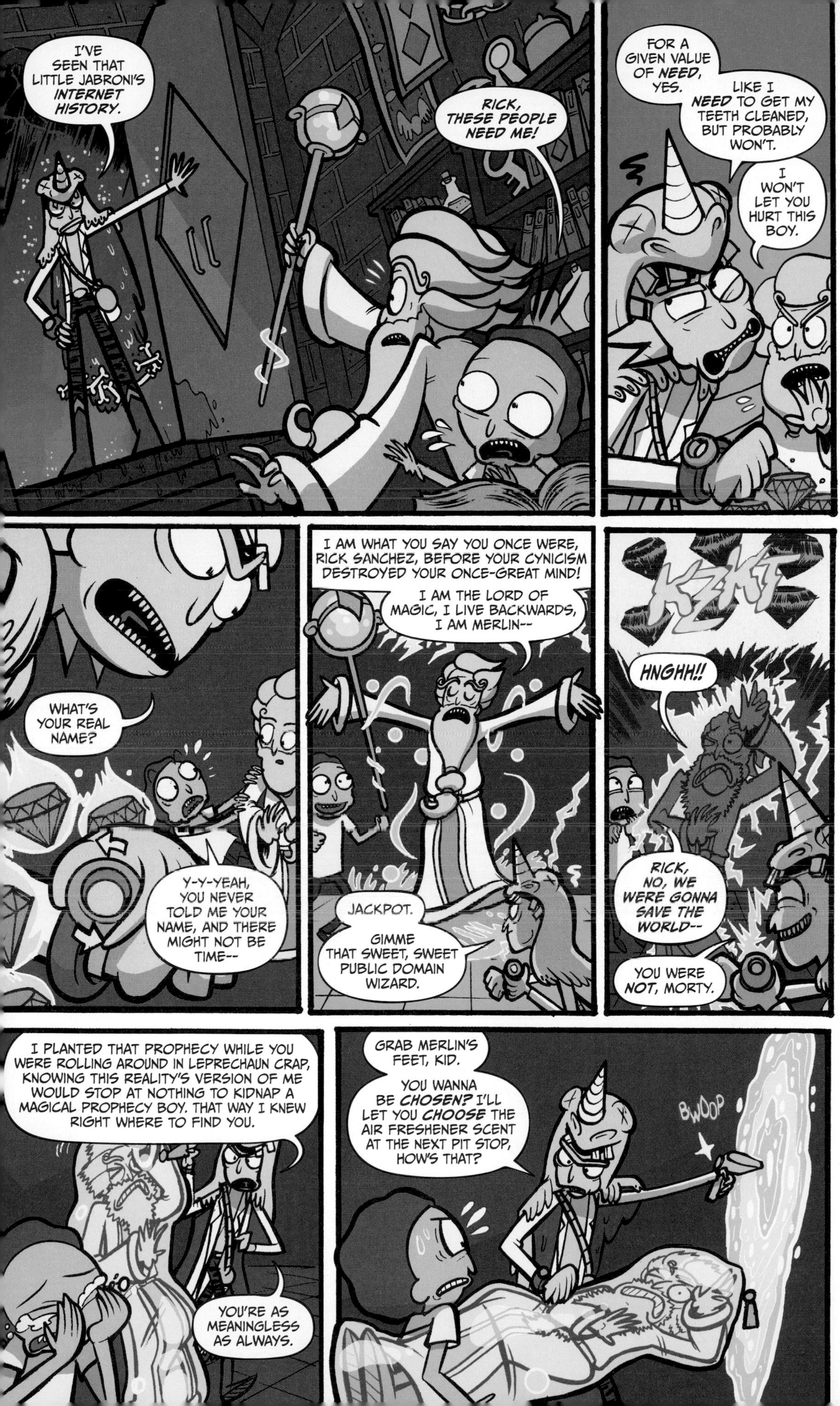
I'VE SEEN THAT LITTLE JABRONI'S INTERNET HISTORY.
RICK, THESE PEOPLE NEED ME!
FOR A GIVEN VALUE OF NEED, YES.
LIKE I NEED TO GET MY TEETH CLEANED, BUT PROBABLY WON'T.
I WON'T LET YOU HURT THIS BOY.
WHAT'S YOUR REAL NAME?
Y-Y-YEAH, YOU NEVER TOLD ME YOUR NAME, AND THERE MIGHT NOT BE TIME--
I AM WHAT YOU SAY YOU ONCE WERE, RICK SANCHEZ, BEFORE YOUR CYNICISM DESTROYED YOUR ONCE-GREAT MIND!
I AM THE LORD OF MAGIC, I LIVE BACKWARDS, I AM MERLIN--
JACKPOT.
GIMME THAT SWEET, SWEET PUBLIC DOMAIN WIZARD.
KZZKT
HNGHH!!
RICK, NO, WE WERE GONNA SAVE THE WORLD--
YOU WERE NOT, MORTY.
I PLANTED THAT PROPHECY WHILE YOU WERE ROLLING AROUND IN LEPRECHAUN CRAP, KNOWING THIS REALITY'S VERSION OF ME WOULD STOP AT NOTHING TO KIDNAP A MAGICAL PROPHECY BOY. THAT WAY I KNEW RIGHT WHERE TO FIND YOU.
YOU'RE AS MEANINGLESS AS ALWAYS.
GRAB MERLIN'S FEET, KID.
YOU WANNA BE CHOSEN? I'LL LET YOU CHOOSE THE AIR FRESHENER SCENT AT THE NEXT PIT STOP, HOW'S THAT?
BWOOP

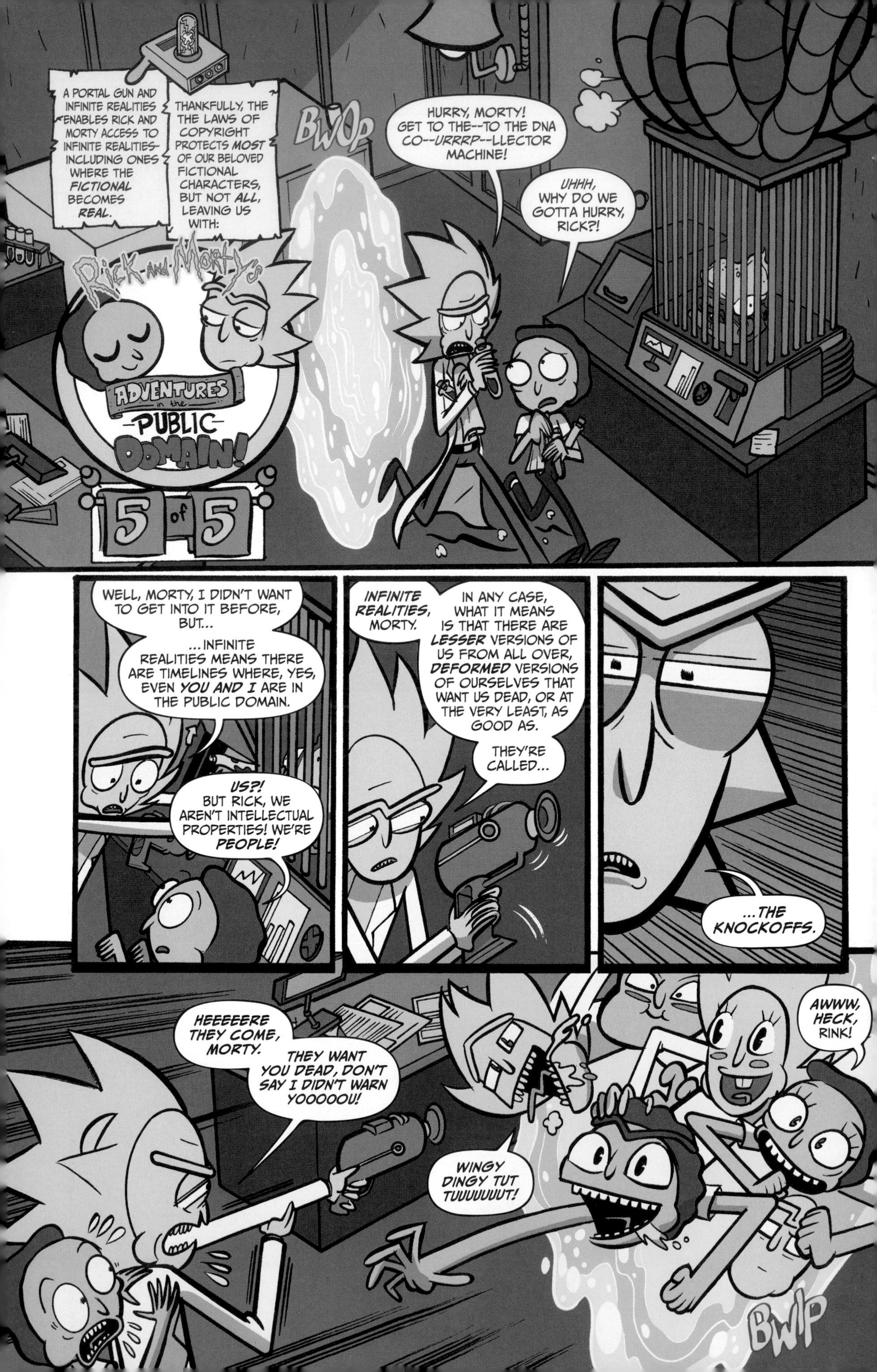
A PORTAL GUN AND INFINITE REALITIES ENABLES RICK AND MORTY ACCESS TO INFINITE REALITIES-INCLUDING ONES WHERE THE FICTIONAL BECOMES REAL.
THANKFULLY, THE THE LAWS OF COPYRIGHT PROTECTS MOST OF OUR BELOVED FICTIONAL CHARACTERS, BUT NOT ALL, LEAVING US WITH:
RICK AND MORTY'S
ADVENTURES in the PUBLIC DOMAIN!
5 of 5
BWOP
HURRY, MORTY! GET TO THE--TO THE DNA CO--URRRP--LLECTOR MACHINE!
UHHH, WHY DO WE GOTTA HURRY, RICK?!
WELL, MORTY, I DIDN'T WANT TO GET INTO IT BEFORE, BUT...
...INFINITE REALITIES MEANS THERE ARE TIMELINES WHERE, YES, EVEN YOU AND I ARE IN THE PUBLIC DOMAIN.
US?! BUT RICK, WE AREN'T INTELLECTUAL PROPERTIES! WE'RE PEOPLE!
INFINITE REALITIES, MORTY.
IN ANY CASE, WHAT IT MEANS IS THAT THERE ARE LESSER VERSIONS OF US FROM ALL OVER, DEFORMED VERSIONS OF OURSELVES THAT WANT US DEAD, OR AT THE VERY LEAST, AS GOOD AS.
THEY'RE CALLED...
...THE KNOCKOFFS.
HEEEEEERE THEY COME, MORTY.
THEY WANT YOU DEAD, DON'T SAY I DIDN'T WARN YOOOOOU!
AWWW, HECK, RINK!
WINGY DINGY TUT TUUUUUUUT!
BWIP

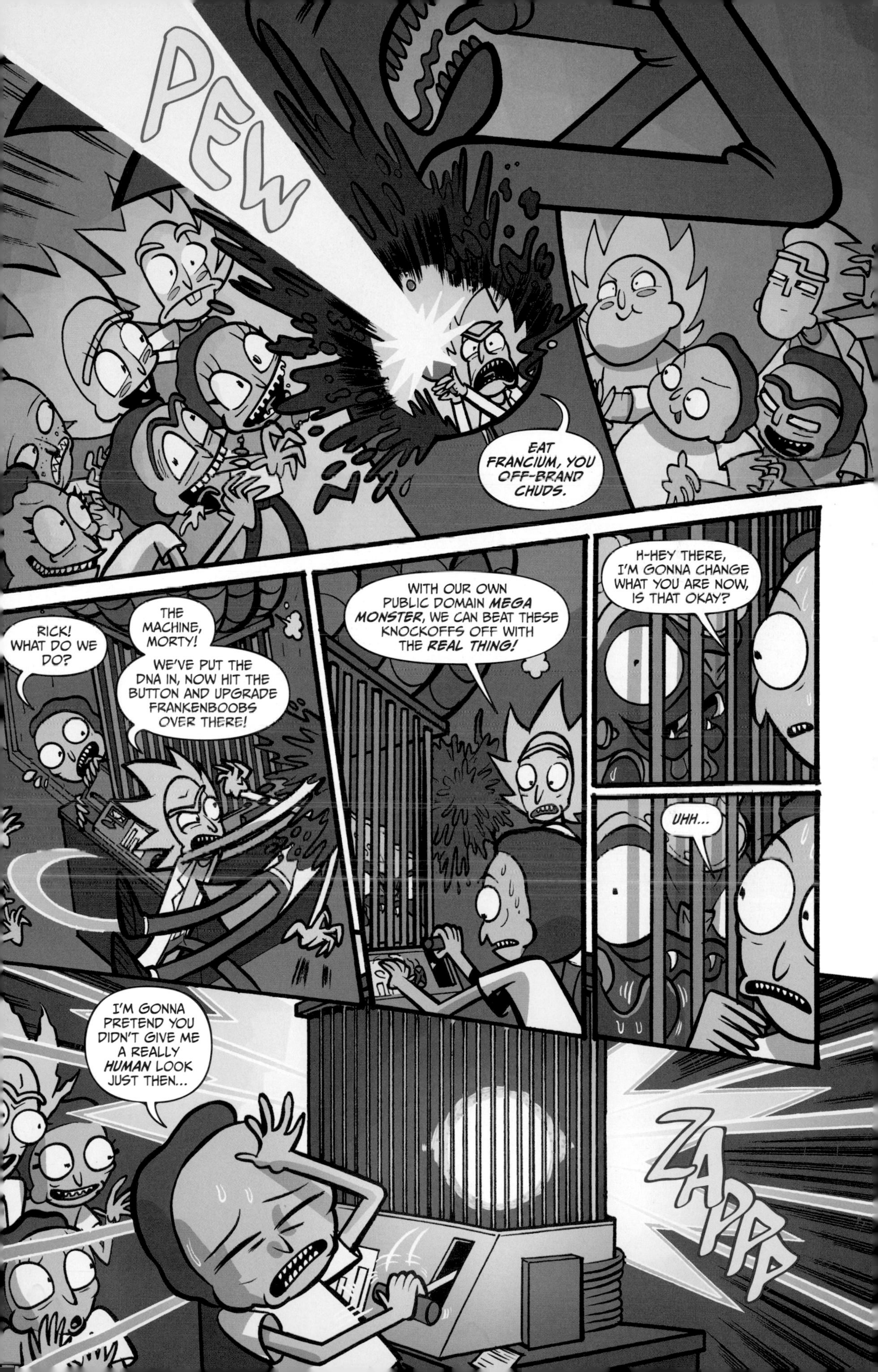
PEW
EAT FRANCIUM, YOU OFF-BRAND CHUDS.
RICK! WHAT DO WE DO?
THE MACHINE, MORTY!
WE'VE PUT THE DNA IN, NOW HIT THE BUTTON AND UPGRADE FRANKENBOOBS OVER THERE!
WITH OUR OWN PUBLIC DOMAIN MEGA MONSTER, WE CAN BEAT THESE KNOCKOFFS OFF WITH THE REAL THING!
H-HEY THERE, I'M GONNA CHANGE WHAT YOU ARE NOW, IS THAT OKAY?
UHH...
I'M GONNA PRETEND YOU DIDN'T GIVE ME A REALLY HUMAN LOOK JUST THEN...
ZAPPP

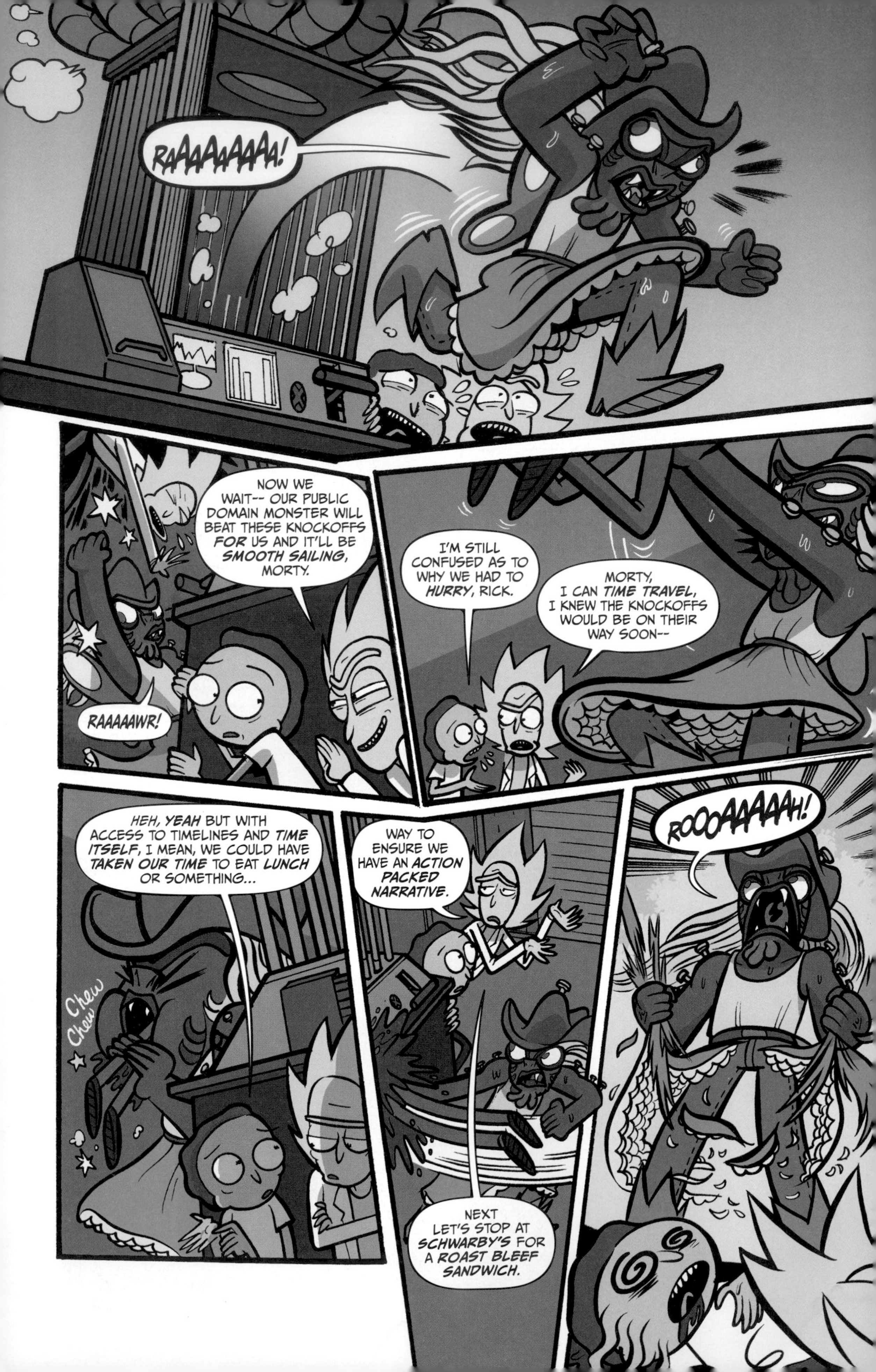
RAAAAAAAAA!
NOW WE WAIT-- OUR PUBLIC DOMAIN MONSTER WILL BEAT THESE KNOCKOFFS FOR US AND IT'LL BE SMOOTH SAILING, MORTY.
RAAAAAWR!
I'M STILL CONFUSED AS TO WHY WE HAD TO HURRY, RICK.
MORTY, I CAN TIME TRAVEL, I KNEW THE KNOCKOFFS WOULD BE ON THEIR WAY SOON--
HEH, YEAH BUT WITH ACCESS TO TIMELINES AND TIME ITSELF, I MEAN, WE COULD HAVE TAKEN OUR TIME TO EAT LUNCH OR SOMETHING...
Chew Chew
WAY TO ENSURE WE HAVE AN ACTION PACKED NARRATIVE.
NEXT LET'S STOP AT SCHWARBY'S FOR A ROAST BLEEF SANDWICH.
ROOOAAAAAH!

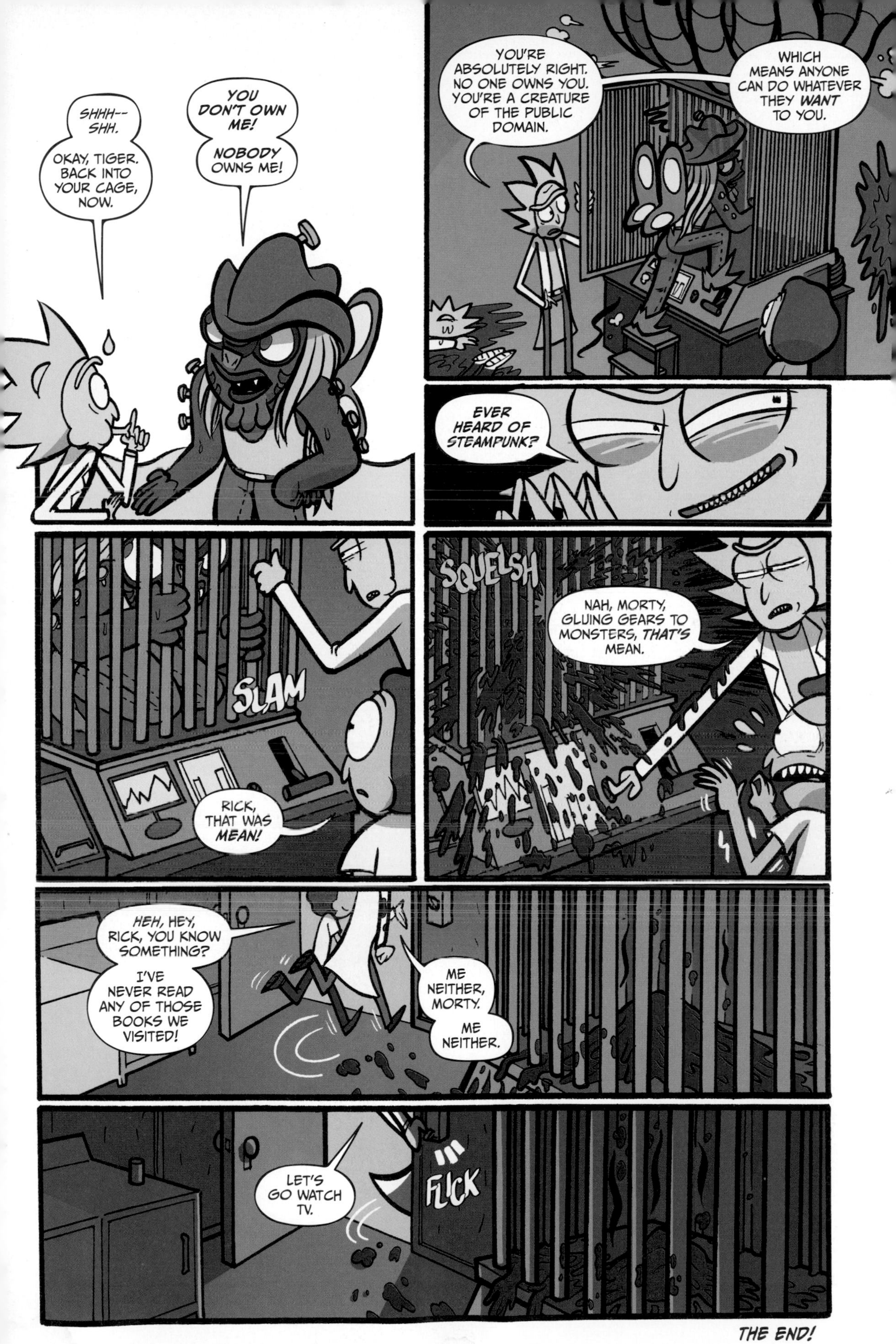
SHHH-- SHH.
OKAY, TIGER. BACK INTO YOUR CAGE, NOW.
YOU DON'T OWN ME!
NOBODY OWNS ME!
YOU'RE ABSOLUTELY RIGHT. NO ONE OWNS YOU. YOU'RE A CREATURE OF THE PUBLIC DOMAIN.
WHICH MEANS ANYONE CAN DO WHATEVER THEY WANT TO YOU.
EVER HEARD OF STEAMPUNK?
SLAM
RICK, THAT WAS MEAN!
SQUELSH
NAH, MORTY, GLUING GEARS TO MONSTERS, THAT'S MEAN.
HEH, HEY, RICK, YOU KNOW SOMETHING?
I'VE NEVER READ ANY OF THOSE BOOKS WE VISITED!
ME NEITHER, MORTY.
ME NEITHER.
LET'S GO WATCH TV.
FLICK
THE END!

DAN HARMON is the Emmy®-winning creator/executive producer of the comedy series *Community* as well as the co-creator/executive producer of Adult Swim's *Rick and Morty*™.

Harmon's pursuit of minimal work for maximum reward took him from stand-up to improv to sketch comedy, then finally to Los Angeles, where he began writing feature screenplays with fellow Milwaukeean Rob Schrab. As part of his deal with Robert Zemeckis at Imagemovers, Harmon co-wrote the feature film *Monster House*. Following this, Harmon co-wrote the Ben Stiller-directed pilot *Heat Vision and Jack*, starring Jack Black and Owen Wilson.

Disillusioned by the legitimate industry, Harmon began attending classes at nearby Glendale Community College. At the same time, Harmon and Schrab founded Channel 101, an untelevised non-profit audience-controlled network for undiscovered filmmakers, many of whom used it to launch mainstream careers, including the boys behind SNL's Digital Shorts. Harmon, along with Schrab, partnered with Sarah Silverman to create her Comedy Central series, *The Sarah Silverman Program*, where he served as head writer for the first season.

Harmon went on to create, write, and perform in the short-lived VH1 sketch series *Acceptable TV* before eventually creating the critically acclaimed and fan-favorite comedy *Community*. The show originally aired on NBC for five seasons before being acquired by Yahoo, which premiered season six of the show in March 2015. In 2009, he won an Emmy for Outstanding Music and Lyrics for the opening number of the 81st Annual Academy Awards.

Along with Justin Roiland, Harmon created the breakout Adult Swim animated series *Rick and Morty*™. The show premiered in December 2013 and quickly became a ratings hit. Harmon and Roiland have wrapped up season three, which premiered in 2017.

In 2014, Harmon was the star of the documentary *Harmontown*, which premiered at the SXSW Film Festival and chronicled his 20-city stand-up/podcast tour of the same name. The documentary was released theatrically in October 2014.

JUSTIN ROILAND grew up in Manteca, California, where he did the basic stuff children do. Later in life he traveled to Los Angeles. Once settled in, he created several popular online shorts for Channel 101. Justin is afraid of his mortality and hopes the things he creates will make lots of people happy. Then maybe when modern civilization collapses into chaos, people will remember him and they'll help him survive the bloodshed and violence. Global economic collapse is looming. It's going to be horrible, and honestly, a swift death might be preferable than living in the hell that awaits mankind.

Justin also really hates writing about himself in the third person. I hate this. That's right. It's me. I've been writing this whole thing. Hi. The cat's out of the bag. It's just you and me now. There never was a third person. If you want to know anything about me, just ask. Sorry this wasn't more informative.

KYLE STARKS is an Eisner-nominated comic creator from Southern Indiana, where he resides with his beautiful wife and two amazing daughters. Stealy values him at 32 and a half Grepples or 17-and-a-half Smeggles depending on market value at the current time. Check out his creator-owned work: *Kill Them All* and *Sexcastle*.

TINI HOWARD is a writer and swamp witch from the Carolina Wilds. Her work includes *Magdalena* from Image/Top Cow Comics, *Rick and Morty*™: *Pocket Like You Stole It* from Oni Press, and *Assassinistas* from IDW/Black Crown! Her previous work includes *Power Rangers: Pink* (BOOM! Studios), *The Skeptics* (Black Mask Studios), and a contribution to the hit *Secret Loves of Geek Girls*, from Dark Horse Comics. She lives with her husband, Blake, and her son, Orlando, who is a cat.

MARC ELLERBY is a comics illustrator living in Essex, UK. He has worked on such titles as *Doctor Who*, *Regular Show*, and *The Amazing World of Gumball*. His own comics (which you should totally check out!) are *Chloe Noonan: Monster Hunter* and *Ellerbisms*. You can read some comics if you like at marcellerby.com.

JARRETT WILLIAMS was born in New Orleans, LA and graduated from the Savannah College of Art & Design (MFA). He has three volumes of his pro-wrestling/adventure series *Super Pro K.O.!* for Oni Press. He has also completed *Hyper Force Neo* for Z2 Comics. He is currently working on a bunch of original comics but still finds time to play Overwatch. Check out his website at *superproko.squarespace.com* or you can find him on Instagram: @JarrettWilliams.

SABRINA MATI was born and raised in Chatsworth, California. Being passionate about drawing and cartoons for all her life, she pursued Media Arts and Animation over at the Art Institute of Hollywood and studied on weekends over at Concept Design Academy. While graduating year 2013, Sabrina landed her first gig in animation as an intern on *Adventure Time* and soon landed her first official job in production on Uncle Grandpa at Cartoon Network. She then worked on shows such as *Rick and Morty* S2 & 3, HBO's *Animals*, and *Harmon Quest* as a character designer. Sabrina just wrapped up on Matt Groening's new show: Disenchantment as a design cleanup artist. Her and a couple other colleagues currently have a podcast on YouTube called "Animation Success Stories" where they interview animation industry professionals on how they got to where they are today.

JUAN MEZA-LEON is a self-taught artist from the port town of Ensenada, Baja CA, Mexico. From a very early age he showed interest in art and storytelling. His passion for films, music and comic books; and the inspiration found within them, was the motivation behind pursuing a career in the industry. After working in several live action productions as a Set PA at the Fox Baja Studios in Rosarito, he got his first professional Storyboard job back in '99, on a small production (*The Expendables*, USA Networks) shot on location in Mexico. From there, his artistic journey took off. Doing the storyboards for shows like *Tremors: The Series*, several small productions and music videos. He eventually made his way to the U.S. where his trajectory in animation began when his portfolio got him signed with a talent agency in L.A. This allowed him the opportunity to work as a Story Artist in various animated projects for WB Animation, Nickelodeon, Bento Box, Disney and Hasbro to name a few. While at Nickelodeon he got promoted to Director where he got to work on the first season for *Kung-Fu Panda: Legends of Awesomeness* and *TMNT*. Juan went on to work for the show *Rick and Morty* as a Story Artist on the first season, then returned as Director for Season 2 & 3. While working as A.D. for Matt Groening's *Disenchantment* he also directed the Run the Jewels music video "Oh, Mama." He's currently back at WB Animation working on the upcoming *Harley Quinn* for DC Universe.

SARAH STERN is a comic artist and colorist from New York. Find her at sarahstern.com or follow her on Twitter at @worstwizard.

CHRIS CRANK letters a bunch of books put out by Image, Dark Horse and Oni Press. He also has a podcast with Mike Norton (crankcast.net) and makes music (sonomorti.bandcamp.com). Catch him on Twitter: @ccrank.

MORE BOOKS FROM ONI PRESS

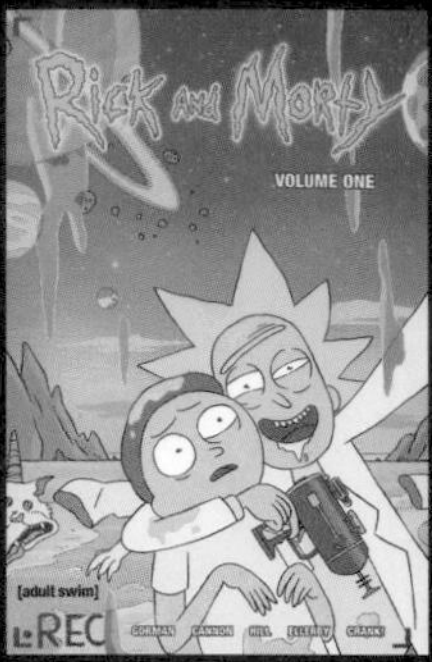
Rick and Morty
VOLUME ONE

RICK AND MORTY™, VOL. 1
By Zac Gorman, CJ Cannon, Marc Ellerby, and more
128 pages, softcover, color
ISBN 978-1-62010-281-7

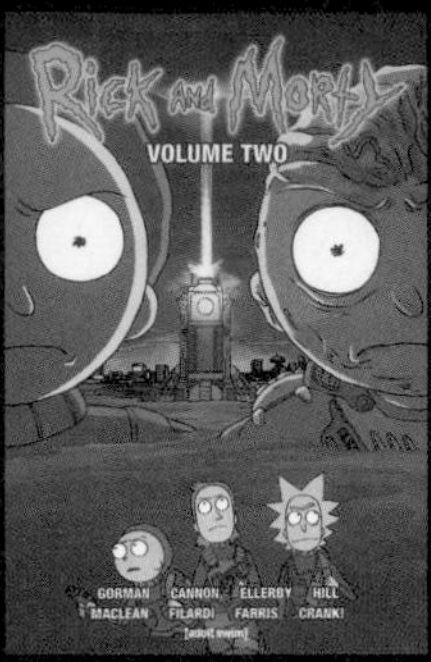
Rick and Morty
VOLUME TWO

RICK AND MORTY™, VOL. 2
By Zac Gorman, CJ Cannon, Marc Ellerby, and more
128 pages, softcover, color
ISBN 978-1-62010-319-7

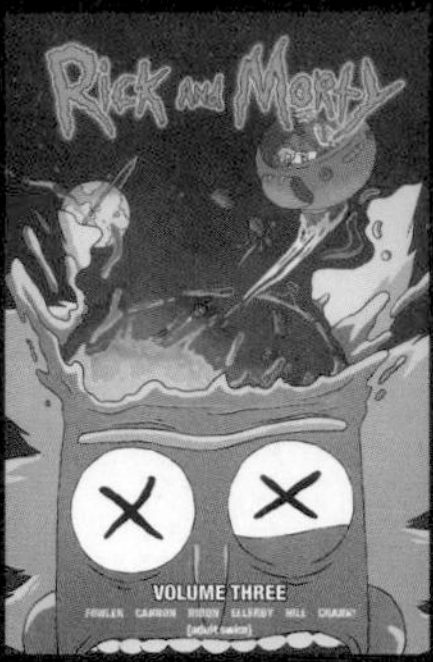
Rick and Morty
VOLUME THREE

RICK AND MORTY™, VOL. 3
By Tom Fowler, CJ Cannon, Marc Ellerby, and more
128 pages, softcover, color
ISBN 978-1-62010-343-2

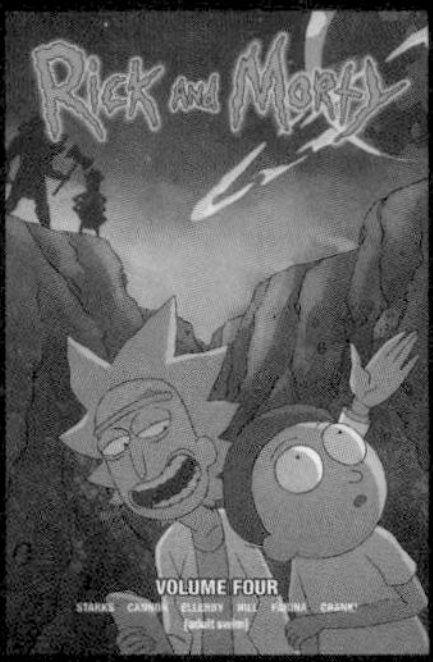
Rick and Morty
VOLUME FOUR

RICK AND MORTY™, VOL. 4
By Kyle Starks, CJ Cannon, Marc Ellerby, and more
128 pages, softcover, color
ISBN 978-1-62010-377-7

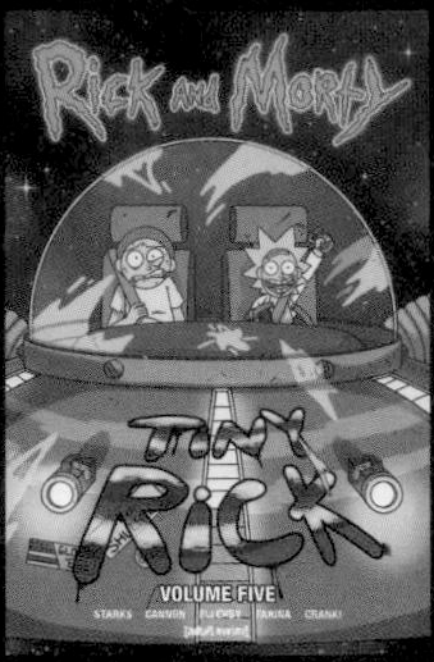
Rick and Morty
TINY RICK
VOLUME FIVE

RICK AND MORTY™, VOL. 5
By Kyle Starks, CJ Cannon, Marc Ellerby, and more!
128 pages, softcover, color
ISBN 978-1-62010-416-3

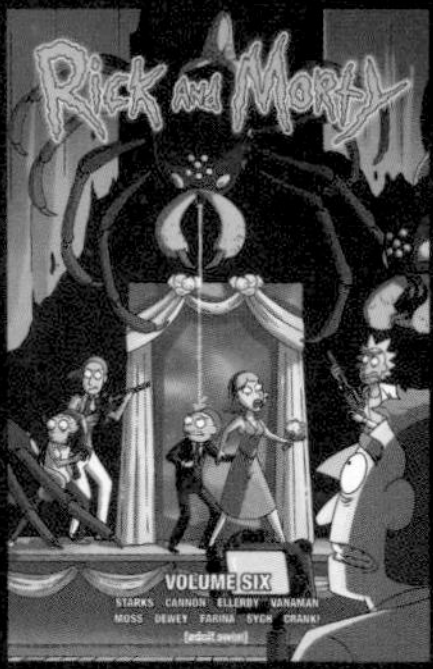
Rick and Morty
VOLUME SIX

RICK AND MORTY™, VOL. 6
By Kyle Starks, CJ Cannon, Marc Ellerby, and more
128 pages, softcover, color
ISBN 978-1-62010-452-1

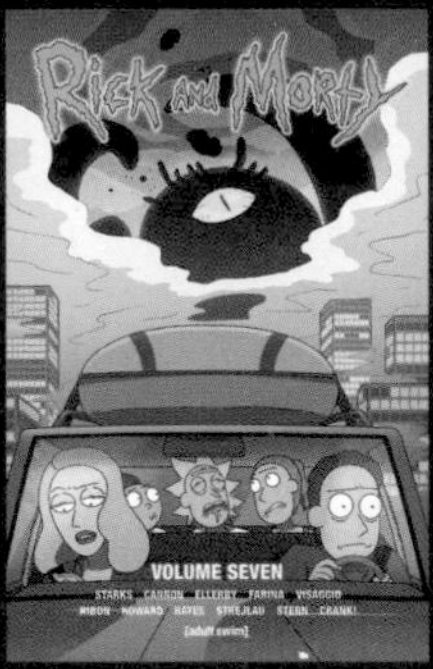
Rick and Morty
VOLUME SEVEN

RICK AND MORTY™, VOL. 7
By Kyle Starks, CJ Cannon, Marc Ellerby, and more
128 pages, softcover, color
ISBN 978-1-62010-509-2

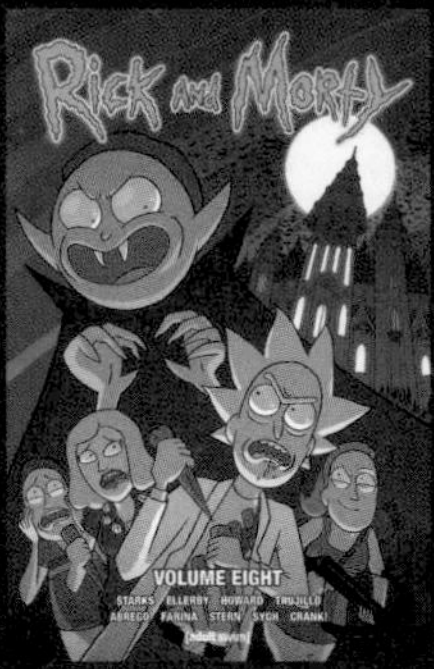
Rick and Morty
VOLUME EIGHT

RICK AND MORTY™, VOL. 8
By Kyle Starks, Tini Howard, Marc Ellerby, and more
128 pages, softcover, color
ISBN 978-1-62010-549-8

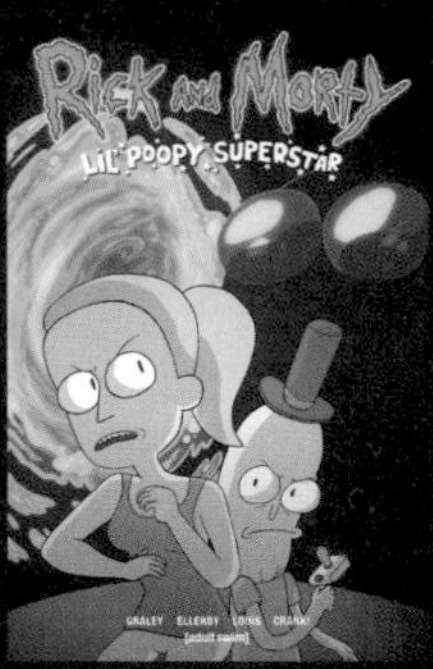
Rick and Morty
LIL' POOPY SUPERSTAR

RICK AND MORTY™: LIL' POOPY SUPERSTAR
By Sarah Graley, Marc Ellerby, and Mildred Louis
128 pages, softcover, color
ISBN 978-1-62010-374-6

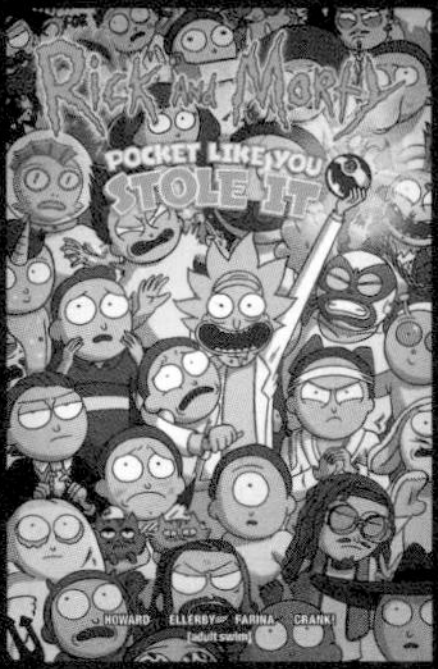
Rick and Morty
POCKET LIKE YOU STOLE IT

RICK AND MORTY™: POCKET LIKE YOU STOLE IT
By Tini Howard, Marc Ellerby, and Katy Farina
128 pages, softcover, color
ISBN 978-1-62010-474-3

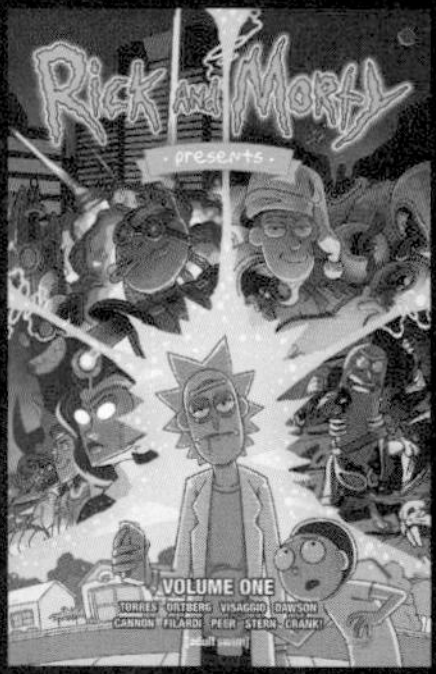
Rick and Morty
presents
VOLUME ONE

RICK AND MORTY™ PRESENTS, VOL. 1
By J. Torres, Daniel Ortberg, CJ Cannon, and more
136 pages, softcover, color
ISBN 978-1-62010-552-8

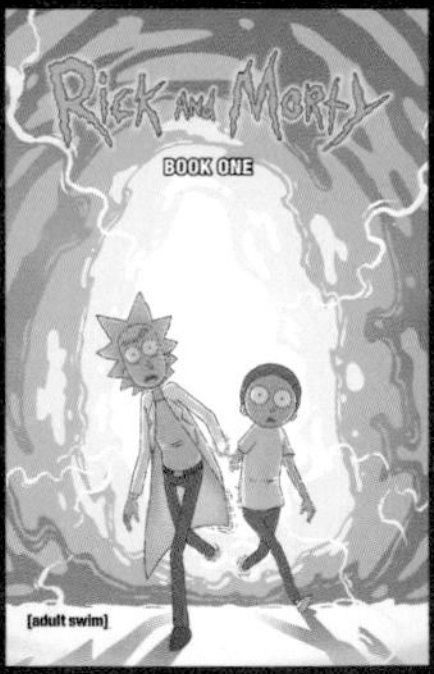
Rick and Morty
BOOK ONE
[adult swim]

RICK AND MORTY™ DELUXE EDITION, BOOK ONE
By Zac Gorman, CJ Cannon, Marc Ellerby, and more
296 pages, hardcover, color
ISBN 978-1-62010-360-9

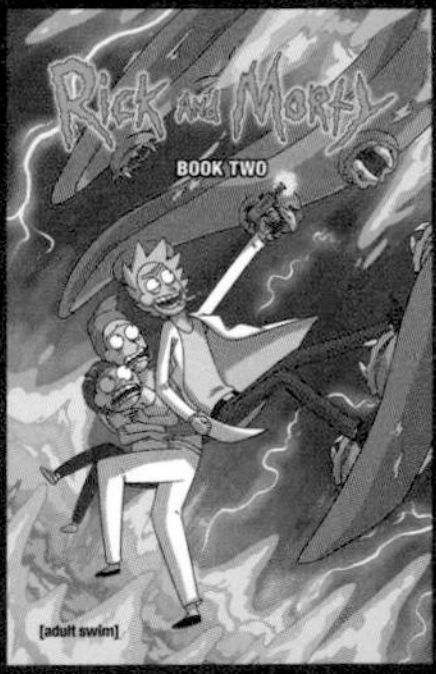
Rick and Morty
BOOK TWO
[adult swim]

RICK AND MORTY™ DELUXE EDITION, BOOK TWO
By Tom Fowler, Kyle Starks, CJ Cannon, Marc Ellerby, and more
288 pages, hardcover, color
ISBN 978-1-62010-439-2

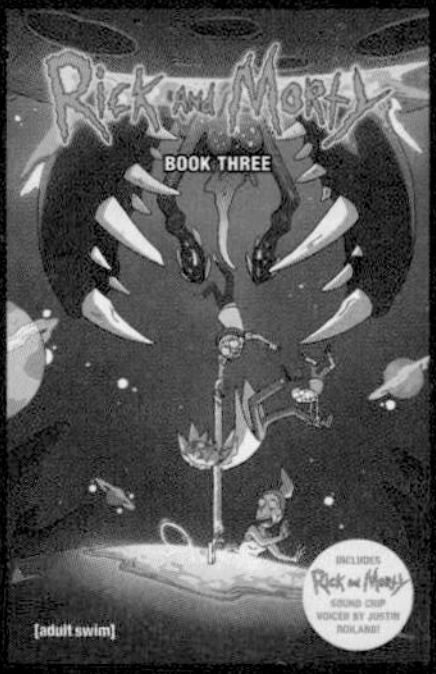
Rick and Morty
BOOK THREE
[adult swim]

RICK AND MORTY™ DELUXE EDITION, BOOK THREE
By Kyle Starks, CJ Cannon, Marc Ellerby, Sarah Graley, and more
288 pages, hardcover, color
ISBN 978-1-62010-535-1

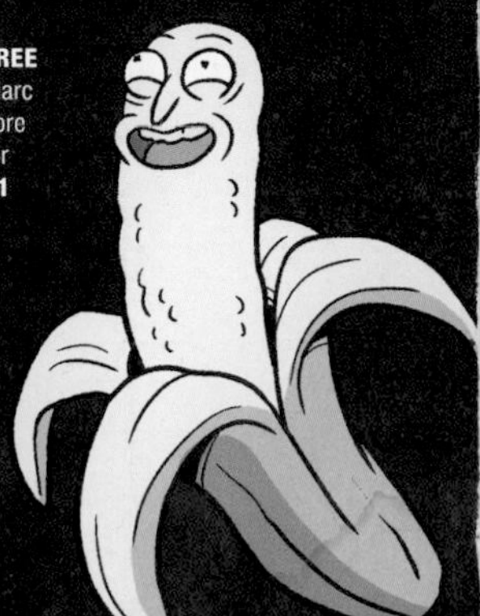

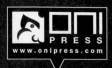

ONI PRESS
www.onipress.com

For more information on these and other fine Oni Press comic books and graphic novels visit **www.onipress.com.** To find a comic specialty store in your area visit **www.comicshops.us.**